THE LOST CAUSE

The Confederate Exodus to Mexico

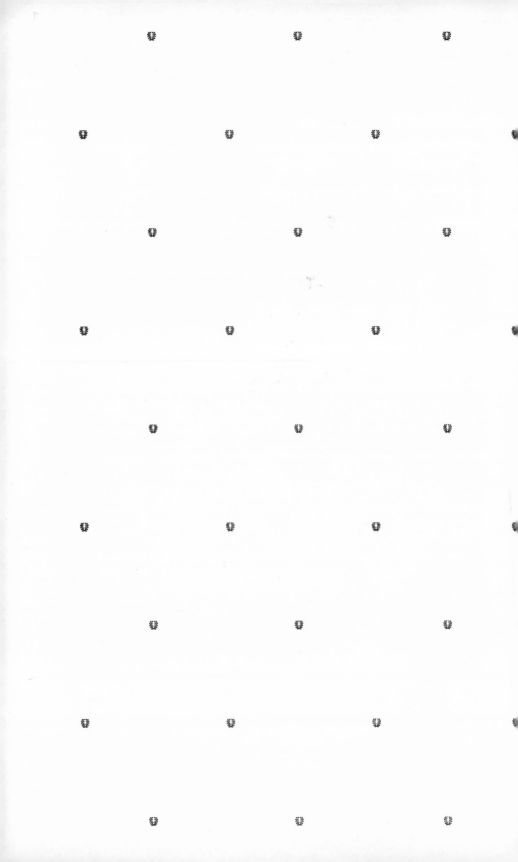

THE LOST CAUSE

The Confederate Exodus to Mexico

BY ANDREW F. ROLLE

with a Foreword by A. L. Rowse

University of Oklahoma Press

Norman

BY ANDREW F. ROLLE

Riviera Path (Verona, Italy, 1948)
An American in California: The Biography of William Heath Davis
(San Marino, 1956)
The Road to Virginia City: The Diary of James Knox Polk Miller
(editor) (Norman, 1960)
Occidental: The First Seventy-Five Years (Los Angeles, 1962)
California: A History (New York, 1963)
California: A Students' Guide to Localized History (New York, 1964)
The Lost Cause: The Confederate Exodus to Mexico (Norman, 1965)

THE PUBLICATION OF THIS VOLUME
HAS BEEN AIDED BY A GRANT FROM
THE FORD FOUNDATION.

Library of Congress Catalog Card Number: 65-11228

Copyright 1965 by the University of Oklahoma Press, Publishing Division of the
University. Composed and printed at Norman, Oklahoma, U.S.A.,
by the University of Oklahoma Press. First edition.

For Warren Jones
WHO ONCE INVESTIGATED
A SEEMINGLY LOST CAUSE
ON MY BEHALF

Foreword

BY A. L. ROWSE

Defeated causes in history are apt not to have justice done them in historiography. I dare say that this is true of the losing side in the American Revolution. It certainly seems to be the case with the Civil War.

As one uninstructed general reader among many, I am grateful to be told the story of the irreconcilables who, after the defeat of the South, left the United States and trekked into Mexico. It is a tale of hardship and discouragement, not the less sympathetic for that, starred by defeat and the collapse of many hopes, but illuminated by courage and a number of remarkable, sharply etched, idiosyncratic characters, such as General Shelby, the leading one, and others like Kirby-Smith, Governor Reynolds, and the scientific Commodore Maury, who became the confidant of the Emperor Maximilian.

The book adds a new chapter to our knowledge of the Civil War; it offers us one part, the most important one, of the whole story of the exodus from the South to various parts of the world. Here is an aspect of the struggle that is perhaps realized by few; a story that as a whole remains yet to be told.

We have reason to be grateful to Professor Rolle for the great deal of original research that has gone into this book, of travel in Mexico on the trails of these Southerners, and of work in the archives investigating the evidences that remain, when so many records of the defeated are lost.

vii

The book makes not only a contribution to Civil War history, or rather its consequences, but also to the history of Mexico—in particular the forlorn, imperial venture of Maximilian, backed by Napoleon III, but deserted by him (another consequence of the victory of the North) and left pitifully to face the firing squad at Querétaro. We are given a more sympathetic and informed account than usual of Maximilian's attempts to improve things in Mexico, his encouragement of the Southerners as colonists in the hope of making some progress in agriculture, and the symptomatic stories of the ill-fated colonies such as Carlota.

Defeat has its lessons no less than victory and, sometimes, offers a no less interesting story.

Preface

THIS BOOK deals with the flight abroad of those Confederates who refused to surrender after the American Civil War. These proud and defeated soldiers turned away from their native land only to be harassed by bandits and guerrillas, plagued by hardships of climate and poverty, and used as pawns in international politics. The story is about such Southerners, their struggles, and their adventures. It is enmeshed in the conflict between the consciences of the Confederate generals Jo Shelby and Robert E. Lee, between Mexico's competing rulers, Maximilian and Juárez, and between the French emperor, Napoleon III, and Lincoln's secretary of state, William H. Seward. It is the record of bitter and recalcitrant men who would not and could not surrender, men in the grip of Southern chivalry, men ruled by a code of ethics suited to a spirit of Manifest Destiny alive before the Civil War. Scorning defeat, the generals, governors, judges, and senators who left the South for exile were the irreconcilables of their era.

Historically we have scarcely ever allowed ourselves to believe that a better life could lie beyond the borders of our country. Although we are a people whose emigration to distant lands is almost nonexistent, during one moment of our history many believed their only salvation lay in flight from the United States. Thousands deserted a prostrate South to go to Mexico, to journey up the Orinoco, to live on the Venezuelan *llanos*, to cut hardwood at Belize in British Honduras, or to raise melons at Villa Americana in Brazil. After selling their Southern properties, they risked death by gunfire or smallpox, quite sure that was the proper course to follow. The Southern exiles did not know that flight below the border might mean death before a firing squad or the loss of all their worldly goods to brigands or defeat by pestilence and moral decay.

This book concerns primarily the exiles who went to Mexico, the country which received the largest migration of Confederates. But it also, necessarily, touches upon exiles who fled elsewhere and discusses their re-entry into the South. Because treatment of diplomacy, economics, and political life helps light up the landscape through which the exiles traveled, the reader will find here more than the record of individual Confederates. The book also treats the theme of expatriation as a whole.

In bringing this book to completion I have been aided by many persons and institutions. The late Professor J. G. Randall of the University of Illinois first suggested the subject; Professor Brainerd Dyer of the University of California at Los Angeles further encouraged interest in it and graciously commented upon an early draft of the manuscript. To Occidental College go my thanks for a Rockefeller Foundation grant-in-aid that allowed me to spend considerable time in Mexico. The basic research for this book was done in that country, where I used the facilities of the Universidad Nacional de México, the Biblioteca Nacional, the Archivo de la Nación, and the Hemeroteca Library in Mexico City. I wish particularly to acknowledge the services of the Instituto Nacional de Antropologia y Historia and of its director, Pablo Martínez del Río.

In the United States the Library of Congress, University of North Carolina Library, Missouri Historical Society, Bancroft Library, and the Henry E. Huntington Library made available basic English-language source materials on which that part of this work rests. Persons who took more than ordinary interest in the book's publication include Allan Nevins, Frances Squires Rolle, A. L. Rowse, Philip Van Doren Stern, Mary Elizabeth Massey, and Gloria Griffen Cline. My greatest debt, for advice in shaping the manuscript, is due Philip Winsor of New York City. None of these persons, however, should be held responsible for whatever shortcomings exist in the book.

Andrew F. Rolle
Occidental College

Los Angeles, California
January 21, 1965

Contents

Illustrations

THE LOST CAUSE

The Confederate Exodus to Mexico

❧

CHAPTER I

Scorning Defeat

ON A JULY DAY in 1865 a body of several hundred men slowly approached the northern banks of the Río Grande. Some moved on foot while others led horses and mules laden with saddlebags and camping gear. As an insistent wind whistled at their backs, they picked their way in clouds of dust through cacti and prickly pear. This was a motley group, clad in threadbare Confederate gray or in assorted civilian garb. They marched in a tired route step, and yet these men did not seem disunified or defeated. They retained that *esprit de corps* which military men can recognize immediately. They moved, not as rabble in retreat, but as a body of determined exiles.

The main body of these soldiers were from the Iron Cavalry Brigade of Missouri, commanded by General Jo Shelby, one of the few Confederate commanders who never surrendered to the Union forces pursuing him. As he and the remnants of his outfit had drawn close to the Río Grande, they had been joined by other escapees. The group stopped to rest awhile on the banks of the river; then two or three soldiers carefully wrapped a tattered flag around a boulder. One of the horsemen had carried the Stars and Bars—precious symbol of the past—on his guidon through many battles. With ceremony, the soldier threw the colors into the muddy waters of the river. Their heads bared, these troops stood stiffly at attention while a lone bugle sounded.

As they watched their flag sink slowly out of sight toward the

3

Río Grande's bottom, a transformation came over the men of the Iron Brigade. Shelby's troops knew that their battles were now ended. Never again would their lucky, daredevil commander (who had twenty-four horses killed under him during the war) lead them in battle against the North on one of his traditional sorrel stallions.[1] Their fine-blooded horses had given way to mules. Gone too were the waving ranks of parade spectators, the sound of drum and fife, and the cheers of the patriotic Confederate ladies who once lined the streets of Austin, Houston, and other Southern cities through which these troops had passed. Ended also was the cherished dream of invading the North and bringing the war to the homes of the hated Yankees. The Southern heartland was destroyed. The life that lay ahead was uncertain; the weather-beaten men who headed into exile were leaving behind homes, relatives, and loved ones under Yankee rule.

And now, after sinking their flag, Shelby's men filed down the sandy slopes of the river in columns of twos and threes. Using a makeshift bridge and various skiffs, the brigade got across the river at Eagle Pass.

The men of the Iron Brigade were not the first Southerners to flee into Mexico as the Civil War ended. Many others had crossed before them, and still others crossed in the following months, marching with haste through the Texas sagebrush to escape the Union forces relentlessly closing in on them. Shelby and his men were the largest single group to cross. Certainly no group had more spirit.

Long weeks of soul-searching lay behind these escapees about to descend upon the rugged barrancas, or canyons, of the Mexican province of Sonora. In wartime, Southern songsters had sung

[1] A quotation from the Sedalia (Missouri) *Democrat* in the Boonville (Missouri) *Weekly Advertiser*, February 22, 1878, states that Shelby "firmly believed and used often to say that he would never be killed in a fight while he rode a sorrel horse." On three occasions Shelby was wounded. "He had twenty-four horses killed under him in the various engagements where he was not hit, and in every single instance where the horse was killed and the rider escaped, the horse was a sorrel." Reference is reproduced in *Missouri Historical Review*, Vol. L (October, 1955), 217.

4

"When This Cruel War Is Over" in anticipation of a time when harmony would once more reign over the Cotton Kingdom. All Dixie had hoped that, somehow, Southern manhood might find its place again in a society that respected honor and valor. But many believed this an impossible hope.

Without question "the Southern rebellion" was legally classified under the statutory definition of treason. Federal law specified the penalty for treason as death. Yet, the punishment of treason on a mass scale by thousands of executions was recognizably impractical. The Federal Confiscation Act of July 17, 1862, indeed, made punishment by death only the most extreme sentence in a broad category of retribution. It also confirmed the President's power to pardon by proclaiming general amnesties. Lincoln proclaimed the first such mass amnesty on December 8, 1863.

In this and subsequent amnesty proclamations by President Andrew Johnson, full amnesty and pardon were, however, offered only to a part of the South's leaders. The North's treatment of Jefferson Davis, president of the Confederacy, symbolized the humiliation inflicted upon the South. From 1865 to 1867, Davis was first a fugitive, then a prisoner, shackled and chained at Fortress Monroe, Virginia. His experiences were a clear warning to soldiers and politicians who fled abroad that it was dangerous to return home.[2] Threats of trial for treason were ringing in the ears of former Confederacy leaders. Confederate Secretary of State Judah P. Benjamin, who fled to Cuba and then to England, wrote his sister that he had "preferred to risk death in attempting to escape than endure the 'savage cruelty' which he was convinced the Federals would inflict on any Confederate leader who might fall into their hands."[3]

At war's end such persons felt they no longer had a homeland. The burgeoning lands of the South were burned out, dead, and uninviting. Her cities, desolated by shellfire, did not seem places in which to start a new future.

Other Southerners, even after Lee's surrender at Appomattox,

[2] Myrta Lockett Avary, *Dixie After War*, 157.
[3] A. J. Hanna, *Flight into Oblivion*, viii.

thought the war was not yet lost. As late as February, 1865, before a deep gloom settled over the Confederacy, General Lee wrote to General Wise: "We have strength enough left to win our independence, and we are certain to win it, if the people will not give way to foolish despair."[4] Almost to the end, some Confederate leaders had goaded Southerners to fight on. Consequently, when Lee surrendered on April 9, 1865, Confederate troops farther west were not entirely prepared for it. Those military units operating on the fringes of the Confederacy were so remote from its capital at Richmond that they remained badly informed about the dire position of the South. It was inconceivable to some Confederate military commanders out west that the Confederacy would not fight on. Many officers had hoped that President Davis would carry the war to the Deep South, to Texas, and perhaps even into Mexico. General Richard B. Taylor, son of Zachary, still had part of an army intact in the Mississippi and Alabama areas. There "that devil," General Nathan Bedford Forrest, had scored notable last-ditch successes against invading Union forces. General Joseph E. Johnston's troops in North Carolina and General James S. Fagan's units in Arkansas also remained undefeated.

Admittedly, these generals thought victory a remote goal at best, especially after the fall of Atlanta in early September, 1864. Troops in Georgia even threatened, some months before that, to lay down their arms. But, despite the gloom of isolated units and of the Confederate high command, a number of officers and civilian officials—including President Davis himself—continued a spirit of personal defiance. Beyond the Mississippi River, far from Richmond, Atlanta, and Appomattox, a courageous undertone of confidence was never quite stamped out by defeats in the field. In the West especially, Generals Shelby, Magruder, Buckner, and Kirby-Smith commanded bodies of men which they thought could hold out longer. These commanders even mistakenly nursed the belief that France and England might yet intervene on behalf of the Southern cause.

Some Confederates who considered further battles for inde-

[4] *Richmond Dispatch*, February 17, 1865.

6

pendence hopeless felt that any surrender was bound to be ig-
nominious. They realized it meant subjugation of the South for
years to come and fought to stave off admitting this until the
last possible moment. Although the will to fight of many had van-
ished, the spirit of rebellion had not entirely flagged. On March
13, 1865, President Davis in an address to the Confederate Congress attempted to shore up sagging morale by reminding its
members of the alternatives to victory. Northern Senator James
G. Blaine charged later that "only a month before the time when
the Confederacy was in ruins and the members of its Congress
were fugitives from its Capital, they united in an inflammatory
address to the people of the South, urging them to continue the
contest." By the unanimous voice of the Confederate Senate and
House of Representatives, Blaine asserted, Southerners "were
told that if they failed in the war, the southern states would be
held as conquered provinces. . . . A still more terrible fate was
foretold. Not only would we [Southerners]be deprived of every
political franchise dear to freemen, but society would be degraded
to the level of slaves. . . . Not only would the property and estates
of vanquished rebels be confiscated, but they would be divided
and distributed among African bondsmen."[5]

Although the results of such severe admonishments by the Confederate Congress may not have been direct, these warnings undoubtedly influenced many apprehensive Southerners. By mid-
1865 many prominent persons and die-hards had already fled the
South. Some went abroad; still more departed for states in the
Middle and Far West. A man could travel out west and lose himself in the primitive vastnesses beyond the Rockies more easily
than he could endure a trip to the tropics of Central and South
America. Others thought it wiser to live inconspicuously in a
northern metropolis like New York than to seek anonymity
abroad. Many sensed the impracticality of sustaining their families in different and hostile cultures. Furthermore, the prominent

[5] James G. Blaine, *Twenty Years of Congress, 1861–1881*, II, 24–25. Blaine
believed that Davis spitefully prolonged the struggle because he could get no
recognition for himself or his government at Fortress Monroe in 1865.

Southern leaders Robert E. Lee and Lucius Q. Lamar condemned the idea of flight out of the South. Former Confederate General James E. Harrison, for example, co-operated fully with the Union armies in helping achieve peaceful demilitarization. When asked if he planned to flee from the South, he replied, "I have a horror of running from my country like a criminal." Harrison and most other officials believed they had "done nothing wrong, or unworthy of a high-toned gentleman."[6]

Within the United States itself, however, the exodus out of the Old South was great enough to affect the nation's population pattern. This movement helped make Texas, by 1880, the most populous state in the South. The population of other states farther west was also increased by fleeing Southerners.[7]

In opposition to the point of view of a Harrison were other Southerners who were too uncompromising to stay on in a South inundated by "Damnyankee" rulers. Typical of them was Judge John Perkins, a political leader in Louisiana and a member of the foreign affairs committee of the Confederate Congress. Before he fled to Mexico, in the certainty that he would be proscribed after the war, Perkins purposely set afire and burned to the ground his bayou plantation, containing irreplaceable art objects, vases, paintings, and statuary, not to speak of barns, trees, crops, and cotton presses.[8]

Other Southern leaders would surely have fled if they had possessed the money to make the expensive journey abroad. Newspapers everywhere gave wide play to the latest emigration schemes, both condemning and lauding such projects.[9] The Southern migration extended to Brazil, Cuba, Canada, Mexico,

[6] Quoted in William B. Hesseltine, *Confederate Leaders in the New South*, 99.

[7] E. Merton Coulter, *The South During Reconstruction, 1865–1877*, 186. Half a million inhabitants, many of them Southerners, arrived in Texas alone during the two years preceding 1876.

[8] Sarah A. Dorsey, *Recollections of Henry Watkins Allen*, 354.

[9] Opposition to the movement was voiced by such papers as the Charleston *Daily Courier*, the Raleigh *Standard*, the New Orleans *Times*, the Alabama *State Journal*, and *The New York Times*. See George D. Harmon, "Confederate Migration to Mexico," *Hispanic American Historical Review*, Vol. XVII (November, 1937), 458.

8

Venezuela, Jamaica, British Honduras, Egypt, Japan, indeed throughout the world. The story of those Confederate officers who joined the Egyptian Army or Brazil's new militia, or who became filibusters, coffee planters, and mining operators below the equator, remains neglected. From eight thousand to ten thousand Southerners ultimately emigrated to Latin America from the war-torn South. Of these, the most went to Mexico.[10]

The diary of one Southern woman, Mary Boykin Chesnut, reveals how the Confederate consciousness had long harbored the prospect of asylum in Mexico. As early as April 15, 1862, Mrs. Chesnut recorded the words of her husband: "What a bore this war is! I wish it was ended, one way or another." He had spoken to her of going across the border to take service in Mexico, and his wife replied: " 'Rubbish' I said. 'Not much Mexico for you! The enemy has flanked Beauregard at Nashville . . . we begin to see what we have lost.' " Yet on April 23, 1864, she recorded a soldier's comment: "We are not conquered! We are on our way to Maximilian in Mexico!"[11]

Several days after Lee's surrender, another Southern diarist, Miss Eliza Andrews, wrote: "There is complete revulsion in public feeling. No more talk about help from France and England, but all about emigration to Mexico and Brazil. We are irretrievably ruined."[12]

Most of those Southerners who impatiently fled to Mexico went as individuals or in small groups. These men came from no one place in the South; they were of no one social stratum. They had no single objective. Their leadership was haphazard, and they were unsure of what lay ahead. The men with Shelby represented talents and points of view of all descriptions. Former governors, generals, colonels, congressmen, judges, and the mayors of small and large towns all over the South joined carpenters, blacksmiths, coopers, farmers, and peddlers determined to live outside

[10] Statistics regarding numbers of persons entering Latin-American countries other than Mexico are in Lawrence F. Hill, "Confederate Exiles to Brazil," *Hispanic American Historical Review*, Vol. VII (May, 1927), 192–210.

[11] Mary Boykin Chesnut, *A Diary from Dixie*, 211, 523.

[12] Eliza F. Andrews, *Wartime Journal of a Georgia Girl*, 153–55.

9

the damnable Yankee dominion. They were alike only in that they scorned defeat together and that for each this journey was a flight into the unknown.

Almost a century has passed since Shelby's men crossed the Río Grande into Mexico, and their history has been fragmented by the passage of time. The inner feelings of those who left their homeland in its hour of greatest crisis are difficult to recapture today. We may call them extremists, yet none of them carried their bitterness and defeat so far as did Virginia's arch-Rebel Edmund Ruffin—the staunchest individual symbol of resistance to Northerners. On June 18, 1865, this pale, chilly little Yankee-hater, who, according to legend, had fired the first shot at Fort Sumter four years before, could think of no alternative to defeat other than to wrap himself in the Stars and Bars of Dixie, take gun in hand, and shoot himself. But those compatriots of the dis-illusioned Ruffin who headed into exile believed there was a more hopeful, a more reasonable solution to their plight than death.

❧

CHAPTER II

The General Who Never Surrendered

SHELBY OF MISSOURI was easily the most spectacular of the Confederate leaders who escaped into Mexico. A picture of this unusual leader and of his background, both before and after the war, is essential to an understanding of the Confederate exiles, for he was clearly their major hero. During the war this cavalry genius, a slight man with piercing, inquisitive eyes, was known as the Jeb Stuart of the West. Daring and direct, he was identified in battle by a streaming black ostrich plume curled above the wide brim of his soft Confederate cavalry hat. He eventually wore the wreath of a brigadier general on his collar. Called "Jo," because of his initials, just as Stuart was called "Jeb," he was then only in his early thirties and, despite his long and heavy black beard, almost boyish in appearance. Major General Alfred Pleasanton, who organized the Cavalry Corps of the Army of the Potomac and who fought Stuart in Virginia and Shelby in Missouri, once said, "Shelby was the best cavalry general of the South. Under other conditions he would have been one of the best in the world."[1]

Shelby had been one of the wealthiest slave and landowners in Lafayette County, Missouri. He came there from Lexington, Kentucky, where he was born December 12, 1830, and where he attended Transylvania University. By 1852 he operated a hemp-

---

[1] Quotation from Richmond *News Leader,* January, 1955, cited in *Missouri Historical Review,* Vol. XLIX (July, 1955), 411–12.

rope factory at Waverly, Missouri, and there married, in 1858, a distant cousin, Elizabeth Nancy Shelby. The bride came of a wealthy family and was sixteen years old at the time of her marriage. Shelby soon had to leave her behind.[2] During the Kansas border troubles from 1854–60, Shelby gratified his strong Southern sympathies by smuggling rifles across the Missouri line to young hotheads who sought to make a slave state out of that troubled frontier territory. He had no military education, but had enthusiasm and courage. In his own words, "I was in Kansas at the head of an armed force . . . I was there to kill Free-state men. I did kill them." Active and unafraid of danger, Shelby was frequently the center of controversy. In 1860 a French-born sawmill operator threw him through the pane of a front window in a saloon at Waverly, Missouri. Shelby, unharmed, apparently thrived on such activity.[3]

Shelby remained independent-minded, especially about his Southern sympathies. In 1861, when a cousin, the well-known Congressman Francis P. Blair (brother of Montgomery Blair, Lincoln's postmaster general and later a Union major general with General Sherman during the March to the Sea), offered to help Shelby obtain a Northern commission, he indignantly refused the favor. Shelby was one of the more than 100,000 Missourians to fight for the Confederacy in a crucially divided state. Personally wealthy, at the outbreak of war he organized and commanded a cavalry company at Newtonia, Missouri, at his own expense. In June, 1862, he and his unit formally joined the Confederate forces of General James E. Rains at Van Buren, Arkansas.

Shelby engaged in many of the Civil War battles of the West. He first made his name known by a series of raiding operations along the Mississippi. These were followed in 1862–63 by expeditions into southern Missouri and to Cape Girardeau in the

---

[2] United Daughters of the Confederacy, Missouri Division, *Reminiscences of the Women of Missouri During the Sixties*, 219–20.

[3] Quoted in William Elsey Connelley, *Quantrill and the Border Wars*, 288. Alexander Toponce, *Reminiscences of Alexander Toponce, Pioneer* (Salt Lake City, 1923), 42–44. Military events in Missouri are surveyed in Hans Christian Adamson, *Rebellion in Missouri, 1861.*

southeastern corner of that state with General John S. Marmaduke. Shelby and his Iron Brigade operated chiefly in Arkansas and Missouri throughout the war. He himself was wounded during an attack on Helena, Arkansas, coincidentally on July 4, 1863. At the battle of Prairie Grove, Shelby avoided capture only because Frank James and members of William C. Quantrill's guerrillas were in the area, an act for which Shelby remained eternally grateful.[4]

In Arkansas and Missouri, bands of brigands, known as "Jayhawkers," made frequent raids upon pioneer farmers, stealing horses and sometimes even robbing and murdering those against whom they held a private grudge. Jayhawkers often wore Confederate uniforms and sometimes claimed membership in Shelby's cavalry brigade. The brigade, well known for its appropriation of livestock and other movable property, became a humorous topic among jealous Confederate infantrymen attached to less spectacular military units. A song entitled "Shelby's Mule" was sung by lonely pickets by the light of campfires all over the West. For the first two lines of "Maryland, My Maryland" they would substitute the words:

> *Jo Shelby's at your stable door,*
> *Where's your mule? O where's your mule?*

Another stanza ran:

> *Ho boys! Make a Noise!*
> *The Yankees are afraid!*
> *The river's up, hell's to pay*
> *Shelby's on a Raid!*[5]

Shelby—like his close friends "Fighting Joe" Wheeler and John H. Morgan—became known as a highly energetic bushwhacker, a commander who staged sudden, daring raids and attacks upon Union-held towns along the frontiers of the Confederacy. For a

---

[4] Richard S. Brownlee, *Gray Ghosts of the Confederacy: Guerrilla Warfare in the West, 1861–1865,* 111.

[5] Samuel Chester, *Pioneer Days in Arkansas,* 52–53; Henry C. McDougal, *Recollections, 1844–1909,* 209.

time the murderous raiders of the guerrilla chieftain Quantrill were attached to Shelby's command and participated in his invasion of Missouri from Arkansas. Quantrill's band of guerrillas, on August 20, 1863, burned Lawrence, Kansas, and murdered 150 of her citizens in cold blood, an act from which Shelby later dissociated himself. This did not, however, prevent Union forces from hanging the General's aide when captured.[6]

In support of his superior, General Sterling Price, Shelby, with as many as two thousand troops, repeatedly attacked Missouri and Arkansas towns held by Federal forces. In 1863 he took the communities of Booneville, Bower Mills, Neosho, Stockton, Tipton, Humansville, and Warsaw. All these raids were carried out with a clear-eyed daring that firmly secured for Shelby the devotion of his troops. In the fall of 1863, about eight hundred troops of Shelby's division marched fifteen hundred miles to the Missouri River and back in thirty-four days through a state then filled with fifty thousand of the enemy. During that raid Shelby destroyed almost two million dollars in federal property and killed, captured, or wounded one thousand Union troops. On March 3, 1864, Shelby, ordered to garrison Princeton, on the Confederacy's Saline River defense line, with a force of only one thousand soldiers, impeded the Union Army division of General Frederick Steele, consisting of fifteen thousand men. On one occasion Steele wrote, "It seems Shelby is everywhere . . . with considerable force for the purpose of capturing steamers."[7]

In 1864, Shelby operated in close support of Sterling Price's "Army of the West" during the ill-fated Confederate raid of that year from Arkansas into Missouri. Together they attacked at Lexington and at the Little Blue River, then moved to Westport,

[6] Quantrill is described as having "supreme contempt" for Generals Shelby, Price, and all other uniformed military leaders. He was, indeed, forced out of his guerrilla command by these officers. Shelby later denounced Quantrill's role in the war. See Connelley, *Quantrill and the Border Wars*, 277-78, 228-89, 455. *The War of the Rebellion: Official Records of the Union and Confederate Navies* (hereafter *OR–Navies*) Series II, Vol. XXVI (Washington, 1917), 149.

[7] *Ibid.*, XXVI, 389. "This Missouri Confederate and His 'Iron Brigade' Never Surrendered," *Missouri Historical Review*, Vol. L (October, 1955), 67-69.

Missouri, where, in mid-October, they had to retreat under heavy Federal pressure. When Price moved toward Newtonia under withering fire, it was Shelby who covered his movements. Their campaign marked a general Confederate collapse along the border of Arkansas and Missouri. While Price's retreat was later the subject of great criticism in the South, he had little alternative; as for Shelby, if ever a general would have fought on, it was he. Had there been a chance to save his men, or to capture the state in which his wife and two little sons then lived, the dark-haired bushwhacker from Missouri would never have retreated.[8]

Pursued day and night by General E. B. Brown, Shelby

[8] Robert Underwood Johnson (ed.), *Battles and Leaders of the Civil War,* IV, 374–75.

marched southward for two hundred miles in an operation that has been called a masterpiece of retreat strategy. The Confederate's main object was to get out of Missouri in as good shape as possible. Sinking his wagons in the Missouri River on October 12, 1864, after destroying ten Federal forts, Shelby finally abandoned his own state. He spent the days of October 14, 15, and 16 in constant travel, halting only long enough to feed troops and horses and to snatch a few hours of rest. To get out of Missouri into Arkansas, he had to fight his way through the entire Union Army of the West, including side-stepping Major General J. M. Schofield's fifty thousand troops in Missouri. During his long, zigzagging retreat Shelby lost only two guns to the enemy, both of which he spiked.[9]

By late 1864 such scenes of retreat were becoming commonplace for Confederate forces almost everywhere. Farther to the east, relentless Northern military pressure would also force Lee's surrender to Grant at Appomattox, as Shelby's troops headed farther southward, temporarily beyond the din of battle. From Clarksville, Arkansas, Shelby, on October 26, pressed steadily by Union forces, crossed the Arkansas River for Texas and beyond.[10]

In those confusing days when the Confederacy was being shaken to pieces, no one was sure what the future would hold. Shelby was especially bitter about the overly rapid capitulation of Confederate commanders east of the Mississippi. He would surely have fought on had he possessed the supplies of eastern leaders who all outranked but seldom outfought him. A general who never surrendered, Shelby could think only in terms of regrouping and of battling onward.

[9] *The War of the Rebellion: Official Records of the Union and Confederate Armies* (hereafter *OR*), Series, I, Vol. XXII, Part I, 609–70.

[10] Shelby's wartime career is necessarily not fully treated in this book. Readers are referred to Bennett H. Young, *Confederate Wizards of the Saddle*, 195–221. The story of Shelby's Missouri Raid is strongly eulogized therein. His recruiting and morale-building operations are also stressed in *OR*, Series I, Vol. XLVIII, Part I, 1528. The Confederates west of the Mississippi are treated in Stephen B. Oates, *Confederate Cavalry West of the River*, 161ff.

Regardless of the outcome of the border fighting, Shelby cherished a secret, grand design for a last stand somewhere in the great Southwest. In Texas, or possibly even in Mexico, he planned to resist his Northern pursuers with whatever remaining troops he and other like-minded generals might be able to muster. Should Texas itself finally collapse, forcing their retreat into Mexico, Shelby hoped to throw his efforts behind whichever political faction in that country would promise him the most help. Mexico could be a new base from which reinvasion of the South might be launched, perhaps even with French or English help. Should resistance to the Union fail, there was always the chance for outright colonization in Mexico. Or so it seemed to a man who was desperate and ambitious and who has been called by one admirer the "brilliant, dashing, sagacious, and gloriously courageous Jo Shelby." His troops needed asylum, and their leader would accept it from any source.[11]

Much to the General's disgust, Shelby's Missouri Division, or Iron Brigade, disintegrated markedly during its protracted stay in Texas as scores of men deserted to return home; nonetheless some hundreds of the best remained. These were briefed by General Shelby on his plans, and they voted to give him power to determine the route of their march.

Some thousands of Confederates ultimately went to Mexico, but they did not accompany Shelby. Despite the boasts of contemporary commentators that he took several thousand men along, Shelby's group consisted of only a few hundred. Because of their restricted numbers it was easier to keep them under control.[12] As they marched through Texas, from Corsicana, Waco,

[11] McDougal, *Recollections,* 209; *Dictionary of American Biography* (hereafter *DAB*), XVII, 62–63; Daniel O'Flaherty, *General Jo Shelby, Undefeated Rebel,* 228–34.

[12] General Philip Sheridan of the United States Army concluded that 2,000 Confederate soldiers joined the Mexican imperialists, and Matías Romero, the Mexican minister to the United States, reported that there were some 3,000 American war veterans in the army of the Mexican Republic. See Richard O'Connor, *Sheridan the Inevitable,* 280. Theophilus Noel, *Autobiography and Reminiscences,* 320, makes a wild guess that 16,000 Confederate deserters went to Mexico; Charles G. Ramsdell, *Reconstruction in Texas,* 35, incorrectly estimates that as

Austin, and San Antonio, to Eagle Pass, these remaining troops presented a startling contrast to the looting, undisciplined bands of thieves, discharged Confederate veterans, and border drifters who in the lawless state sacked homes and robbed its citizens.

Shelby reminded his men that the Mexicans would undoubtedly look upon the brigade as invaders, foragers, or, indeed, almost filibusters. It was, therefore, especially important that they stir up as little enmity as possible. There was no difficulty with the civilian population on the Texas side of the border. The towns through which they passed provided whatever food or supplies the inhabitants could spare. Shelby's men received a particularly warm welcome at New Braunfels, a German community which toasted his force with "buckets of beer" in appreciation of their discipline while passing through town.[13]

The General's force had dwindled to only 132 men when it was joined in mid-June at San Antonio by various prominent generals, among them John B. Clark, Sr., of Missouri, Danville Leadbetter of Alabama, Thomas C. Hindman of Arkansas, and Sterling Price of Missouri. As he approached Eagle Pass, Shelby met former Governors Pendleton Murrah and Edward Clark of Texas and General William P. Hardeman of that state, as well as Governors Charles S. Morehead of Kentucky and Henry W. Allen of Louisiana. Generals John Bankhead Magruder, Trusten Polk, Monroe M. Parsons, George Flournoy, and Hamilton P. Bee, Colonels Thomas L. Snead, William M. Broadwell, William Conrow, J. H. R. Cundiff, Peter B. Wilks, William Standish, and many other officers also threw in their lot with Shelby.[14]

many as 3,000–12,000 men stayed with Shelby until he left for Mexico, but a private in Company C, Third Regiment, Missouri Cavalry (Shelby's brigade), gives the figure of 132 former soldiers. See Sam Box, "End of the War—Exiles in Mexico," Confederate Veteran, Vol. II (March, 1903), 122. George Creel, Rebel at Large, 27, states that 600 troops actually crossed the border with Shelby.

[13] John N. Edwards, Shelby and His Men, 543.

[14] Field and general grade officers accompanying Shelby were listed in the Mexican Times (hereafter MT) of September 16, 1865, a list reprinted in 39 Cong., 2 sess., House Exec. Doc. No. 76, p. 521. See ibid., House Exec. Doc. No. 1, Part III, 209–12, and Carl C. Rister, "Carlota, a Confederate Colony in Mexico," Journal of Southern History, Vol. XI (February, 1945), 36.

On June 17, 1865, after resting several days at the Menger Hotel in San Antonio to reorganize, Shelby moved slowly toward the Mexican border. On July 4, 1865, a symbolic day, he and his men engaged in the ceremony of lowering the Dixie banner into the water of the Río Grande, which, as we have seen, was the division's last act on United States soil. This occasion inspired Colonel Alonzo Slayback's poem, "The Burial of Shelby's Flag," which became well known in the South. The ode begins:

A July sun, in torrid clime, gleamed on an exile band,
   Who, in suits of gray,
   Stood in mute array
On the banks of the Río Grande.
They were dusty and faint with their long, drear ride,
And they paused when they came to the river side,
   For its wavelets divide,
   With their flowing tide
Their own dear land, of youth, hope, pride,
And comrades' graves who in vain had died,
From the stranger's home in a land untried . . . .

This ballad of no poetic merit goes on much too long; nevertheless it kindled a satisfying glow among Confederates.

Shelby's group did not suffer for want of supplies as they marched off into what one of them called "a land untried." They possessed several thousand British Enfield muskets, ten new French artillery pieces with ammunition, 40,000 rounds of small arms ammunition, and whole "bushels of gun caps."[15] Each man was equipped with a Sharps's breech-loading carbine and four navy revolvers with 120 rounds for each type. They also carted along derringers, horse pistols, and unwieldly family blunderbusses.

Shelby was determined to take with him every item of any conceivable use. His men loaded their commissary train, consisting of nine twelve-mule wagons, with whisky, salt pork, bacon,

[15] Edwards, *Shelby and His Men*, 543. This and the author's *Shelby's Expedition to Mexico,* although firsthand accounts, are so laudatory as to be of limited objective value.

molasses, rice, dried fruit, pickles, preserves, and other delicacies. Each pack mule carried large and heavy saddlebags covered by canvas tarpaulins to keep out the rain. Placed on top of this load were cooking utensils and individual pieces of mess gear covered with gray blankets and tied down with strong ropes.

Certain commodities were especially appreciated by the men. As the party camped at night among the organ cacti and prickly pear of northern Mexico, the cases of Kentucky sour mash which they had hoarded helped them forget the uncertainties ahead.

Thus began Shelby's march across an almost endless wilderness of inhospitable plains, dotted only periodically by a few settlements. Near these a handful of Mexicans tended scrawny upland sheep pastures and narrow fields. The very cultivation of these isolated plots seemed in defiance of nature. This was a terrain to test severely the endurance of all who ventured upon it.

✿

CHAPTER III

North Versus South in Mexico

UNKNOWINGLY, Shelby was leading his men into a buzz saw, whose jagged teeth included Mexico's tremendously confused political climate, her irreconcilable military factionalism, and the debased status of life below the border. Poverty was even more pronounced there than in the South, and the rewards for common labor were meager in a society where hordes of *peones* competed for work. The Confederate hopefuls were, furthermore, heading into a country which, like their own, was torn asunder by warfare.

A year before the arrival of Shelby's men, Napoleon III of France had placed a puppet emperor, the sandy-bearded, pink-cheeked Austrian Archduke Maximilian, and his attractive consort, Princess Carlotta of Belgium, on a phantom throne in Mexico. An understanding of Maximilian's role is vital to comprehension of the struggle that took place between the North and the South below the border. The arrival in Mexico of a seemingly boyish ruler—imposed upon the Mexicans from without—was bound to affect the outcome of the Confederate exodus. In December, 1861, France, England, and Spain had landed troops at Vera Cruz to force the government of Benito Juárez, Mexico's Indian leader, to meet its debts to these powers. On April 9, 1862, the English and Spaniards withdrew after they recognized Napoleon's far-reaching ambitions. Among these was his dream to destroy the Anglo-Saxon hegemony in the New World and to revive the old French empire and with it that Latin glory which his uncle, Napoleon I, had once proclaimed throughout the world. Now Napoleon III, in support of disgruntled anti-Juárist clericalists and his empress, Eugénie, sent long lines of troops heading into the heart of Mexico. Unexpected Mexican resistance at Puebla by the troops of General Zaragosa held the French in check until the summer of 1863. However, in June the capital capitulated. French legions next drove the republican forces out of central Mexico, captured Guanajuato, Querétaro, and Guadalajara, and moved toward Durango, Monterrey, and Chihuahua, still farther north.

The next year Mexico's new emperor arrived in the land of the serpent and the eagle. Following a staged popular demonstration and welcome at Vera Cruz by obsequious officials on May 28, 1864, Maximilian entered Mexico City on June 12 under a canopy of triumphal arches decorated with flowers. Immediately he found himself locked in combat with the great mass of the adherents of Juárez. That Mexican leader had fled from the capital and was directing his struggle against the French from northern Mexico. At first Maximilian was grateful for the backing of Napoleon's troops; eventually he would realize that this support was at best a tragic blessing.

Napoleon III did not anticipate opposition to his Mexican operations from the United States, then involved in its exhausting Civil War. For a time he believed that the South would win that war, and his relatively friendly attitude toward Southerners was based on this premise. He authorized French shipyards to sell armed vessels for use by the Confederacy against the government of Abraham Lincoln and spoke sympathetically about the Southern cause. Napoleon overlooked the underlying power of the Union. Nor did he take the full measure of Juárez, whose *peones* soon raided Maximilian's troops, stole supplies furnished him by the French, blew up imperial communications, and disrupted Napoleon III's delicate power position in Mexico. By 1865 the French situation in Mexico had become precarious. *Juarista* bands were arrayed in strength across the remote windblown deserts of the border country through which most Confederates were then escaping out of the South.

The Southerners who flocked into Mexico during 1865 were hardly aware of these complex events. Even Shelby did not comprehend the passionate resistance to Maximilian posed by the creole and mestizo population of Mexico.

For most of Shelby's men Juárez was just another of many Mexican chieftains whose role they did not quite understand. They scarcely sensed that the Mexican people regarded this bronze-colored, stony-faced Zapotecan as the leader of a social movement to which they were devoted. Furthermore, most Confederates did not dream that many Mexicans hated foreigners and that invaders like Shelby reminded them of the humiliating American assault on Chapultepec Castle twenty years before during the Mexican War. Patriotic Mexicans still felt dishonored by that surrender of their capital to invading gringos and by the cession of large portions of their territory to the *Yanquis*. Mexicans remembered that two hated foreign emblems had flown over their national palace—the Stars and Stripes of the United States and the tricolor of France. Mexico clamored for independence from foreign invaders. And its watchdog was Juárez.

Although Maximilian would cautiously welcome Shelby's men, the Emperor was not master of his own house. Operating out of the hills and canyons of numerous northern hideouts, Juárez still acted as though his were the true government of Mexico. The Indian's decrees demonstrated increasing hostility toward foreigners. Juárez refused to guarantee the safety of those Confederates who showed friendship for Maximilian and decreed a punishment of from four years' imprisonment to death for any foreigner serving in the forces of Maximilian. In time this would bring harassment to a number of Confederates.[1]

[1] A Juárez decree guaranteeing safety to foreigners was issued on March 3, 1861, and suspended by Decree No. 5860 of May 8, 1863. See *Legislación Mexicana. Colección completa de las disposiciones legislativas* . . . , IX, 613–14. Decree No. 6144 of October 31, 1867, punishing foreigners in Maximilian's army, was published in *ibid.*, X, 109–10.

Despite Juárez' warnings, as early as January 12, 1865, Maximilian's official publication, the *Diario del Imperio*, invited large-scale immigration to Mexico. Even earlier, in 1863, *L'Estafette*, Mexico City's French newspaper, had prophesied that thousands of Confederate refugees would seek new homes in Mexico. In November of that year the paper reproduced a brochure entitled *France, Mexico, and the Confederacy* that purportedly represented the Emperor's mind regarding colonization. Before Shelby's men began to arrive, Maximilian had made extensive land concessions to German, French, and Austrian immigrants.[2] His government, however, realized that any substantial migration must be an overland one from the United States. Mexico, it reasoned, especially needed American agriculturalists to introduce new methods of farming to its war-torn land. What was more natural than that these migrants should be *rurales* from the American South, a predominantly agricultural region? That South had been befriended during the War by Napoleon's France —a French-Mexican-Confederate entente therefore seemed especially appropriate. All this activity was in the background of the later Confederate exodus to Mexico.

These sentiments were not to prove popular with Mr. Lincoln's government. Throughout the war Lincoln's secretary of state, William H. Seward, feared the possibility of an open French alliance with the Confederacy, and he exercised extreme caution with regard to the French occupation of Mexico. He was careful to offend neither Napoleon's France nor Maximilian's Mexico, but, during the last two years of the Civil War, he made clear his government's firm disapproval of their violation of the Monroe Doctrine. Seward hoped to find some means of removing French troops from the Western Hemisphere without armed conflict.[3]

As time passed and the French stayed on interminably in Mexico, Union military leaders, including Generals Ulysses S. Grant

[2] Alfred J. and Kathryn Abbey Hanna, "The Immigration Movement of the Intervention and Empire as Seen Through the Mexican Press," *Hispanic American Historical Review*, Vol. XXVIII (May, 1947), 226, 232, 237.

[3] Samuel Flagg Bemis (ed.), *American Secretaries of State and Their Diplomacy*, VII, 106–10.

and Philip Sheridan, grew impatient over Seward's caution. These army chieftains wanted a tougher policy, one that would diminish the aid which the Confederates were receiving from the French imperialists in Mexico and their deluded puppet, Maximilian.

During the war the Union military command was particularly concerned over the large-scale traffic in goods destined for the Confederacy which entered the South via Mexico. The Union blockade could not include the mouth of the Río Grande. The middle of that stream formed the boundary between the United States and Mexico, and its free navigation was guaranteed by existing treaties. Trade between foreign neutral ports could not be molested under international law. The diplomatic doctrine of "continuous voyage" clearly protected ships sailing between such ports as London and Matamoros. Thus law and geography presented the Confederates with a means of breaking the Union blockade.

When the South on April 25, 1862, lost her greatest harbor—New Orleans—following its capture by Commodore David Farragut, the Mexican town of Matamoros became her best port of entry. Matamoros was a dusty and wild place, filthy and diseased, especially in the summer, and situated about thirty miles from the mouth of the Río Grande on the mud flats across from Brownsville, Texas. Cargoes destined for the Confederacy arrived at Matamoros not only from foreign ports but even (almost unbelievably) from Union harbors on the East Coast of the United States. According to a report of the Federal government, shipmasters requested clearances of ships from New York to Matamoros only about once a year before the Civil War. In the next three crucial years, however, 152 vessels were cleared out of New York for Matamoros with cargoes, in large measure not destined for Maximilian but for Juárez' forces or for the Confederacy. The traffic destined for Mexico was, of course, legal. But it was the Confederate trade that was responsible for the greatest growth of Matamoros. Toward the end of the Civil War the population of the place had increased from eight thousand to fifty thousand persons.

Despite Yankee pride in their blockade, British skippers in large numbers slipped through the Union net, hiding along inlets located miles from major ports, steaming elusively up the maze of small channels, sounds, canals, and rivers of the sandy Texas delta country. Loading Rebel cotton along the lagoons that dotted the Texas-Mexican coastal confines was, in fact, rare sport. Only light-draught vessels could cross the Río Grande's sandbar and sail up the shallow and sluggish river to Matamoros. Ships with a draught of more than six feet of water had to ride at anchor on the open sea and discharge their cargoes into lighters that carried merchandise ashore across the shoals. Little centerboard sailing schooners could, however, pass over the bar on a dark night and slip upriver, if the captain knew his way about or had a good pilot aboard. To the Confederate high command the success of this traffic was vitally important; such craft were entrusted with the job of getting the cotton and bringing back everything else needed by both the army and civilians.[4]

During the war as many as eighty ships at one time awaited discharge of their cargoes off the sand spit at Brazos de Santiago, below Matamoros. By 1863 a steamship service between the mouth of the river and London had been established, which helped increase the size not only of Matamoros but of Monterrey, the provincial capital of Nuevo León, by two thirds in three years.[5] Fast English vessels like the *Celt*, the *Dashing Wave*, and the *Sea Queen* intermittently sailed up the river with goods for the Confederacy. Foreign suppliers were paid in cotton, much of it from the famous King Ranch in Texas, which shipped thousands of bales across the river. Tom Lea's history of the ranch relates how Captain Richard King's homesite became a great depot for cotton moving south. Hundreds of passing wagons helped whiten the surrounding chaparral and other brush with flying lint that

---

[4] Hamilton Cochran, *Blockade Runners of the Confederacy*, 202–208, 217; Nannie May Tilley (ed.), *Federals on the Frontier*, 247 n. ff.

[5] Hanna and Hanna, "The Immigration Movement," *Hispanic American Historical Review*, Vol. XXVIII (May, 1947), 233.

blew off the bales on their way to Matamoros. At that port King had his own fleet of steamboats to haul cotton down the muddy river to the salt-water ships waiting off Brazos de Santiago. He eventually placed his "Cottonclads" behind a front of Mexican ownership, and, flying the "Turkey Buzzard," or Mexican flag, at their mastheads, they ran up and down the Río Grande at will, even entering the Gulf of Mexico under the nose of Farragut's Union blockaders.

Furthermore, nothing could prevent these blockade runners and English ships of shallow draught from hauling strategic cargoes to Matamoros. Throughout the war such vessels, carrying thousands of Enfield rifles, cases of pistols, cartridges, boots and shoes, bales of blankets, liquors, and even bicarbonate of soda, unloaded their goods without much interference.

This supply operation was a great boon for Confederate troops in the remote Southwest, far from the supply centers of the East. In fact, some of the men who later fled out of the Confederacy into Mexico first learned about that country because of these wartime activities. Cargoes from Mexico were used largely within the Trans-Mississippi Department as there were no railroads leading out of Texas. This in turn contributed to the independence of western commanders and altered the circumstances under which they later surrendered. Many of Shelby's supplies and those of fellow commandants in Arkansas and Texas had come from Matamoros, and the Confederates had learned to depend upon that port for material aid and sustenance. It is no wonder that they also looked sympathetically toward Mexico as an escape hatch.

During the war United States authority at Matamoros had been represented by Consul E. Dorsey Etchison. He had repeatedly sent frantic dispatches to Washington out of his white adobe consulate about the mountains of supplies pouring into Confederate Texas. He found it embarrassing when Mexicans asked him to lunch with Rebel agents and English sea captains then smuggling cargoes into the South. The United States Consul suffered from steadily worsening spirits; Matamoros was located in no man's land, and Secretary of State Seward in Washington seemed indifferent to the need of policing the border thoroughly.[6]

Maximilian's imperialists continued to send goods to the withering but still menacing Confederate forces in the West during the last days of the Civil War. In 1864, Santiago Vidaurri, once Juárist governor of Coahuila and Nuevo León and later an imperialist, had come to a confidential understanding with General John Bankhead Magruder, commanding in Texas, and a Confederate agent at Monterrey, Juan A. Quintero, to pass into the Confederacy increased quantities of contraband, particularly lead and saltpeter. This arrangement had become especially vital toward the end of the war when lead was virtually unobtainable west of the Mississippi. Vidaurri's control over the state of Tamaulipas, with its port of Matamoros, made this Mexican chieftain, like General Tomás Mejía, Maximilian's Yankee-hating political and military chieftain in the Mexican north, an important Southern ally. The French and Maximilian's troops were scattered throughout vital areas of northern Mexico, and similar arrangements were negotiated by the Confederates with the imperialist governors of Chihuahua and Sonora, both of whom helped funnel goods into the South.

On March 7, 1864, Vidaurri—before he was forced to flee into Texas by Juárez—facilitated the entry into Mexico of twelve thousand bales of cotton, assuring a gross return of $2,400,000

[6] James Russell Soley, *The Blockade and the Cruisers*, 37–38; Abraham Zvenigrad, "The Matamoros Trade During the Civil War" (M.A. thesis), 19–30; Kathryn Abbey Hanna, "Incidents of the Confederate Blockade," *Journal of Southern History*, Vol. XI (May, 1945), 222–29. About the American consul at Matamoros, Union General Lew Wallace wrote Grant: "Our consul, Mr. Etchison, whom Mejía is said to have outraged, is a humbug, a drunkard, and a fool. His official conduct was unworthy of our government. He has mutilated the books of his consulate. He charged our own citizens unwarrantable fees, and I am assured on excellent authority that it can be established that he has in his pockets several thousand dollars in gold not his own. Even his washerwoman was left unpaid." See Lew Wallace, *An Autobiography* (2 vols., New York, 1906), II, 827. Documents concerning the Union blockade and Matamoros are in *OR–Navies*, Series I, Vol. II, 97–104, 112, 158, 349.

to the financially hard-pressed South—on one transaction alone.[7]

Considerable correspondence passed between General Edmund Kirby-Smith, commander of the Confederacy's Trans-Mississippi Department, and General Magruder, his representative in Texas, concerning supplies coming into the Confederacy through Texas. From his headquarters at Shreveport, Louisiana, Kirby-Smith wrote Magruder on June 27, 1863, a letter that reveals much about the importance of this trading:

> You will impress, or cause to be impressed, through General Bee, commanding the West Mil. Sub-district of Texas, the cotton and transportation necessary for meeting the immediate wants of the Department and for keeping up the credit of the Government.

With an eye on local politics in Texas, Kirby-Smith continued:

> Good policy would dictate that these impressments, until after the election for Governor, should be made in the vicinity of the Rio Grande and Nueces, and where the election will be least influenced.

Because Magruder was worried about his unpopularity in impressing cotton from merchants, shippers, and growers, his superior continued in a reassuring mood, stating that he knew "the peculiar temperament of the Texas people, the importance of your maintaining your popularity," and that he was "perfectly willing that the odium of the measure, if any, should fall on myself and that your usefulness in that District should remain unimpaired." On August 1, 1863, Kirby-Smith further indicated the extent of cooperation he expected from Magruder in the operation of the vital Mexican traffic:

> I have the honor to send you by Lt. Sampson of the Ordnance Dept.

[7] The Mexican tariff imposed on cotton imports amounted to $8.00 a bale, and this *jefe* pocketed $96,000 in coin on the shipment. After selling this cotton for $200 a bale, Vidaurri fled from the Juárists to join Confederate friends on a stock ranch purchased in Texas. He later became Maximilian's minister of Hacienda and president of his ministry. See United States Congress, *Papers Relative to Mexican Affairs Communicated to the Senate, June 16, 1864, by the President of the United States*, 392–93, and Samuel B. Thompson, *Confederate Purchasing Operations Abroad*, 108–27.

a copy of a proposal to furnish a large amount of ammunition at Matamoros Exchange for cotton. . . . You will do all in your power to ensure the prompt delivery of cotton in exchange for the ammunition so that there will be no miscarriage on our part.[8]

Matamoros was not the only depot for Confederate trading in Mexico. Also participating in this traffic across the Río Grande was the squalid Mexican border port of Bagdad, some twenty-five miles southeast of Brownsville, Texas, near the Gulf of Mexico. Like Matamoros this once sleepy village, peopled by ne'er-do-wells and border drifters, provided a sanctuary which could not be touched by Union forces. Bagdad's traffic, clandestine and open, was estimated as even larger than that of Baltimore or New Orleans. General Lew Wallace, who quietly visited the Río Grande for Grant, wrote his chief in 1865 that he could stand on his launch "and count at least a hundred vessels of all kind lying at Bagdad."[9]

These Mexican ports were visited by both Union and Confederate officials. Among them was the South's Commander Raphael Semmes who, after completion of his daring Atlantic raids aboard the cruiser *Alabama*, slipped back into the Confederacy via Bagdad and Matamoros. He counted sixty ships at Bagdad, some laden with goods for the South, others with Northern supplies for Juárez. He also observed innumerable shanty warehouses of unplaned boards situated on its river beach as well as billiard saloons and grog shops. The dusty, rutted lanes of this makeshift town were crowded with wagons hauling cotton and mysterious unmarked cases. "Teamsters cracked their whips in

---

[8] E. Kirby-Smith to J. B. Magruder, June 27, August 1, 1863, Eldridge Manuscripts, Box No. 47, Huntington Library. Other letters passed between Kirby-Smith and Magruder that are also in this collection.

[9] Quoted from Carl Coke Rister, *Border Command*, 14, and *OR*, Series I, Vol. XLVIII, Part I, 937, cited in William Diamond, "Imports of the Confederate Government from Europe and Mexico," *Journal of Southern History*, Vol. VI (November, 1940), 502. Diamond (p. 499) cites a source to the effect that the Confederate-Mexican trade was large enough for one firm alone to keep sixty wagons running from Monterrey to San Antonio, Texas. See the perceptive article by Robert W. Delaney, "Matamoros, Port for Texas During the Civil War," *Southwestern Historical Quarterly*, Vol. LVIII (April, 1955), 473–87.

the streets, and horsemen, booted and spurred, galloped hither and thither," the sea dog wrote in his memoirs. Below the Río Grande whites, blacks, mulattos, Indians, Rebels, and Yankees had all learned to work and profit together, money being the binding ingredient which Semmes noted when he described the Yankees there: "The shanties were his, and the goods were his. He kept the hotels, marked the billiards, and sold the grog."[10]

Sir Arthur Fremantle, a British traveler who entered the South via Matamoros and Bagdad, also reported seeing many Confederates and Yankees along the border at war's end. After noting seventy ships lying off Bagdad, he ran into some "rough and dirty" members of Duff's Confederate Cavalry on the streets of Bagdad whose dress "consisted simply of flannel shirts, very ancient trousers, jack-boots with enormous spurs and black felt hats, ornamented with the lone star of Texas."[11] Not a few former Southern supply sergeants ended up on Bagdad's streets, their pockets lined with money earned by selling stolen Confederate goods. The extent of desertion and sale of Confederate goods is revealed by a typical entry (of May 25, 1864) in the diary of one Confederate soldier: "A. Morris and S. J. Mooney are detailed to follow a Mr. George and arrest him. He is on his way to Mexico with a load of cotton."[12]

As Mexican-Confederate co-operation remained close, Secretary of State Seward steadfastly withheld diplomatic recognition from Napoleon's Austrian puppet. Although Seward's policies toward Maximilian seemed weak to Grant and Sheridan, the Secretary relied upon diplomatic rather than military pressure in

[10] Raphael Semmes, *Memoirs of Service Afloat, During the War Between the States,* 790–93. See also Edward Boykin, *Ghost Ship of the Confederacy,* 385. See also *OR—Navies,* Series I, Vol. II, Series II, Vols. II and III.

[11] Sir Arthur James Fremantle, *Three Months in the Southern States,* 2–4. This particular edition, printed in the wartime South, is bound in wallpaper. Another edition was printed in Edinburgh and London.

[12] W. W. Heartsill, *Fourteen Hundred and 91 Days in the Confederate Army* (ed. by Bell Irvin Wiley), 206. In another entry (p. 201) this diarist noted: "Jno W. McDonald and S. O. Moodie are detailed arrest Yankee deserters, who have taken the oath at Marshall and are now trying to make their way into Mexico on forged passports."

order to weaken Napoleon's power in Mexico. Seward hoped Maximilian would discourage the shipment of contraband goods from Mexican ports into the South. The Emperor desperately wanted Union diplomatic recognition—as much as the various Confederate envoys sent to visit him were eager to be recognized by his regime. Maximilian, therefore, was forced to hide his sympathy for the South. Napoleon, too, was forced increasingly to mask his desire for a Southern victory; the North was winning the war. Caught in a diplomatic squeeze, Maximilian dared not give overt assistance to the Confederacy. Only in subtle ways could he help the South—one of these was to invite Confederate immigrants below the border during and after the war.[13]

Maximilian's General Mejía personally discussed immigration with Confederates in Texas during the last days of the war. On one occasion he tried to get Maximilian himself to visit Confederate officers on the United States frontier, reputedly to forestall a rumored invasion of Mexico by impatient Confederates in Arizona and New Mexico, who were concerned about Union supplies getting to Juárez from Mexican ports on the Pacific.[14] They,

[13] James Morton Callahan, *Evolution of Seward's Mexican Policy*, 62; James Morton Callahan, *American Foreign Policy in Mexican Relations*, 306. A good short account of Confederate-Mexican diplomacy is Frank L. Owsley, *King Cotton Diplomacy*, 88–145. About the Confederate envoys sent to Maximilian, see Clement Eaton, *A History of the Southern Confederacy*, 80.

[14] Unfortunately, little documentation for this exists. Concerning the situation in New Mexico see "Gov. Connolly's Proclamation Organizing the Militia of New Mexico" and other documents in Frank Moore (ed.), *The Rebellion Record*, 170. In the same work see also "Rebel Operations in New Mexico," a report by Brigadier General Henry H. Sibley, 465–68, and "Secession in New Mexico," 212–13. President Jefferson Davis commissioned Sibley, a brigadier general, with authority to raise three regiments of cavalry in West Texas for the occupation of New Mexico. The Confederate invasion of New Mexico was based on the erroneous notion that once they equipped themselves in Texas, they could weather the wilds of the West. With captured supplies from friendly Mexicans, they could march first from San Antonio to Fort Bliss, Texas, and on to the New Mexican border. Eventually the Confederates were forced to evacuate New Mexico, when the Colorado volunteers and California column started out to rescue other Union troops in the Southwest. The immensity of the Confederate pretensions in the West actually made their venture impractical from the start. See Robert Lee Kerby, *The Confederate Invasion of New Mexico and Arizona, 1861–1862*, 48–50.

indeed, coveted such ports for their own supply operations. Union and Confederate threats to Mexican territory gave both Juárez and Maximilian cause for worry. Although they were enemies, neither wanted an invasion of Mexico from the north.[15]

How supplies got to Juárez and who would control the land and sea routes in and out of Mexico had become crucial during the war. Union officers wanted to use the port of Guaymas on the west coast of Mexico as a supply center for Juárez. A Texas-Confederate legion had, in 1861–62, overrun Arizona and New Mexico, intent upon placing the Southwest under the Stars and Bars. Late in 1864 (the exact date is unclear) Washington authorities went so far as to consider sending a Federal expedition from San Francisco to land at Guaymas and march through Sonora to attack these troops and Confederate forces in Texas. Diplomatic sanction for this plan had been obtained from Juárez. The turmoil in Mexico, and the Civil War as well, had made these enormous, untamed lands virtually independent. Throughout the war, western Rebels were on the verge of using Arizona and New Mexico as a springboard to attack California, which remained loyal to the Union.[16]

Back in Washington toward the end of the war, a small but determined knot of Union politicians close to the White House favored stronger action against the Confederates in the Far West and against Maximilian. Important Union military leaders also

[15] Rister, *Border Command*, 9–10, 13; Charles S. Walker, "Causes of the Confederate Invasion of New Mexico," *New Mexico Historical Review*, Vol. VIII (January, 1933), 76–97. *OR*, Series I, Vol. L, Part I, 825–26, discusses treatment accorded representatives of the Confederate commander in New Mexico, General Sibley; see also W. H. Watford, "Confederate Western Ambitions," *Southwestern Historical Quarterly*, Vol. XLIV (October, 1940), 175.

[16] See Appendix A below on Confederates in New Mexico and Arizona. Avery C. Moore's *Destiny's Soldier* is a biography of General Albert Sidney Johnston, who commanded the Union Army's Department of the Pacific before making his way overland to join the Confederacy. See also Martin H. Hall, *Sibley's New Mexico Campaign*, 32, 50–51, 122, 226, and Ray C. Colton, *The Civil War in the Western Territories*, 98; *OR*, Series I, Part IV, 167–74; and Series I, Part IX, 70B. The rumored Union occupation of Guaymas by troops under command of General Edwin V. Sumner is described in Hall, 42.

questioned Seward's "slow and poky caution" toward the Emperor. During Lincoln's presidency and later in President Johnson's administration, Seward was put on the defensive whenever Mexican affairs were discussed at the White House. His critics included the vocal Secretary of the Interior, James Harlan, and Shelby's cousin, Postmaster General Montgomery Blair, as well as Blair's brother, General Francis P. Blair. Along with General Lew Wallace, the Blairs and Harlan advocated shipping Juárez more munitions—instead of simply "goods"—and also spoke out for a military attack upon Maximilian's French-sponsored regime. This clique tried hard to get the ear of the entire War Department.[17]

So long as a war within their own country was on, however, General Grant had to be more realistic than the Harlan-Blair-Wallace faction. Not until after Appomattox could Grant encourage so wild a dream as going after Maximilian and the fleeing Confederates. Yet Mexico remained an important base from which a reinvasion of the United States might be mounted should Confederate generals like Jo Shelby or Sterling Price or Kirby-Smith ever reorganize their forces below the border. In late 1864, one must remember, the possibility of Confederate President Jefferson Davis' fleeing southward to attempt a possible comeback was still given wide credence by Union military men.

In the press and among Washington officialdom, sentiment grew for sending a countervailing force into Mexico. President Lincoln and later his successor felt the pressure. General Grant officially warned both presidents of the Mexican threat to peace. Throughout 1864-65 the Juárez government's minister to Washington, Matías Romero, further agitated for a strong Union stand along the border. The danger had been and was still two-fold: Mexico was definitely a supply point for the Confederacy *during*

[17] During July, 1865, after the war was over, Secretary of the Navy Gideon Welles recorded in his diary that Seward felt called upon, at a cabinet meeting of July 14, to defend his cautious policies toward Maximilian and Napoleon III in order "to counteract a speech of Montgomery Blair . . . in which he makes an onslaught on Seward and Stanton, as well as France." Grant and Sheridan joined in serious criticism of Seward. See *Diary of Gideon Wells*, II, 333.

the war, and she was a potential staging area for reinvasion of the South *after* the war. Juárez especially feared impairment of his operations by Southern invaders, especially if these sided with Maximilian.

The Confederate contacts with Mexico were a threat to everyone but the South. Union forces would have to slam shut the Mexican border to fleeing or defending Confederates. After Appomattox more Union troops were freed for patroling operations out west. So were some of Grant's key commanders, among them Sheridan and Sherman.

An advocate of much stronger aid to Juárez was the impatient General Wallace—a tall volunteer Federal officer from Indiana. Fearing a coalition of Confederate and imperialist forces, Wallace patriotically raised money from friends, back in Indiana and elsewhere, to supply Juárez. While Juárez was grateful enough for the help he received, the Mexican leader was wary of too much intervention and once stated: "We don't want Americans. It is true they may help to drive the French out, but who the devil will drive the Americans out?"[18]

The Union, to help Juárez, quietly stepped up shipments of gunpowder, lead, and other military supplies by a number of routes. This material was kept flowing to Juárez' capital at Paso del Norte (today's Ciudad Juárez) opposite El Paso.[19]

Both the Union and Confederacy, thus, kept an eagle eye on

[18] See Irving McKee, *"Ben-Hur" Wallace*, 90–112, and A. W. Barber (comp.), *The Benevolent Raid of General Lew Wallace. MT*, September 24, October 1, 1866, January 22, 1867, issues, told how the "shoddy shoulder-strapped phantom . . . wheezy ramshackled" Wallace, after the war ended, arrived at Matamoros with one thousand "filibusterers." See also *DAB*, XIX, 375–76. Wallace, a sometimes brilliant but erratic misfit in the military service, eventually ended his Mexican misadventures a lonely, bankrupt, and disappointed officer. He only found the success he craved at a much later date as governor of New Mexico territory and as the author of the popular novel *Ben Hur*. See Appendix B below on Wallace.

[19] The aid to Juárez is described in W. W. Mills, *Forty Years at El Paso*, 85–93. For the operations of the brilliant Matías Romero, see J. Fred Rippy, "Mexican Projects of the Confederates," *Southwestern Historical Quarterly*, Vol. XXII (April, 1919), 291–317. See also Bemis, *American Secretaries of State*, 107–109. In a pamphlet entitled *Correspondencia entre la Legación de la Re-*

their respective Mexican and Far Western operations. Both sides dreamed of conquering the American Southwest, with all its spiny cactus, vast spaces, deserters, and mineral wealth.[20]

As Confederate defeat drew close, the nearness of Mexico and the well-known sympathy of Maximilian for the South reminded many Southerners that escape was the only obvious alternative to surrender. Like Shelby, they knew that the life-giving outlet of the war years was also a ready-built escape hatch. With every week during the spring of 1865, wholesale Confederate escape became increasingly likely.

Despite General Grant's warnings, this was not a possibility that disturbed Abraham Lincoln. In his memoirs, Grant stated that he had "often spoken of the matter to Mr. Lincoln and the Secretary of War but had never heard any special views from them to enable me to judge how they felt about it. I inferred," wrote Grant, "that they felt a good deal as I did, but were unwilling to commit themselves while we had our own troubles upon our hands."[21]

When, on Good Friday, April 14, 1865, the very last day of his life, the President, his cabinet, and General Grant talked over the momentous news of Lee's surrender and the impending collapse of the South, Lincoln remarked that there were men in Congress who nurtured feelings of hate and vindictiveness which he did not share. He ardently wished that there should be no bloody persecutions of the secessionists, even the worst of them. "I suppose, Mr. President," said his new postmaster general, William Dennison, "you would not be sorry to have them escape out of the

---

pública Mexicana en Washington, el Departamento de Estado de los Estados Unidos de América, y el gobierno de México, Romero complains about arms and equipment going to Maximilian from New York to Vera Cruz. Union forces countered this by sending supplies to Juárez via Ben Holladay's West Coast steamship line at Guaymas, Mexico, as well as by using the port of Matamoros.

[20] Kerby, *Confederate Invasion of New Mexico and Arizona,* 79–80; Noel, *Autobiography and Reminiscences,* 60; W. H. Watford, "The Far-Western Wing of the Rebellion, 1861–1865," *California Historical Society Quarterly,* Vol. XXXIV (June, 1955), 125–248.

[21] *Personal Memoirs of U. S. Grant,* II, 546.

country?" "Well," said Mr. Lincoln slowly, and with a tinge of wit, "I should not be sorry to have them out of the country; but I should be for following them up pretty close, to make sure of their going." Warming to his subject, he then shouted, "Frighten them out of the country, open the gates, let down the bars, scare them off!"[22]

One Mexican historian states that twenty-five thousand Confederate soldiers were seen by Maximilian as potential settlers along a barrier zone in northern Mexico. His government, in fact, was even interested in employing the Confederate forces of General James E. Slaughter, at Brownsville, Texas, to prevent northern volunteers from joining the armies of Juárez.[23]

In such an atmosphere it is no wonder that General Grant, especially after Appomattox, felt oppressed by the thought of a wholesale Confederate escape to strengthen permanent military control of Mexico by a foreign power. The more he contemplated the situation, the more he determined that, somehow, the military must stem the Confederate tide below the border.

[22] Benjamin P. Thomas, *Abraham Lincoln: A Biography,* 517; Frederick W. Seward, *Reminiscences of a War-Time Statesman and Diplomat, 1830–1915,* 255.

[23] Vicente Riva Palacio (ed.), *México a través de los siglos,* V, 714.

❧

CHAPTER IV

Waiting for Mr. Davis

BEFORE SHELBY crossed the Río Grande, Confederate military activities out west centered about an almost mystical figure. This was General Edmund Kirby-Smith, who, since March 7, 1863, had commanded the Trans-Mississippi Department with headquarters at Shreveport, Louisiana. Kirby-Smith was, therefore, Shelby's superior officer. One of eight full generals in the Confederate Army, this pious Episcopalian was a curious combination of hardened soldier and devout churchgoer whose "highest ambition," according to intimates, was to take holy orders once the war ended. Although only forty-one years of age in 1865, he looked something like a biblical patriarch. Like Shelby, most of the Confederate commanders wore beards which made them appear older, wiser, and more sober than they sometimes were. The preoccupied Kirby-Smith, his sunken cheeks reflecting years of tense responsibility, with his piercing blue eyes and great full beard hanging down his chest, seemed almost Mosaic in appearance. But this external appearance bore little relationship to the position which this general held.

Up to the end of the war Grant showed great respect for the potential threat of Kirby-Smith's command. When General William Tecumseh Sherman, about to cut a wide swath through Georgia, asked Grant's assurance that no eastern Confederate armies could successfully move against him, Grant told him "that his real danger was from Kirby-Smith who commanded the

Trans-Mississippi Department." Grant believed that if Kirby-
Smith should escape General Frederick Steels's Arkansas troops
and get across the Mississippi River, he might move dangerously
toward the Union's eastern flank and Sherman himself.[1]

Kirby-Smith never did break out of the defense perimeter held
by the Trans-Mississippi command along the Big River. He had
plenty of problems within that command. No general commanded a larger area. The Trans-Mississippi area included Texas, Louisiana, Arkansas, and the Indian Territory farther to the west
and north of Texas. After the fall of Vicksburg, on July 4, 1863,
the General's area of jurisdiction was severed from what the Confederate military called the Cis-Mississippi East—as distinguished
from the Trans-Mississippi West. Consequent isolation of his
command led it to be called "Kirby-Smithdom." The department
was therefore left to defend and supply itself during the remaining two years of the war.

Running his barony left Kirby-Smith little time for metaphysi-
cal pursuits. Not all of his problems derived from Union action.
His command was also the terminus for numerous opinionated
and quarrelsome general officers. Richmond developed a ten-
dency to use the department "as a place to send disgruntled or
unsuccessful high-ranking officers."[2]

Kirby-Smith also supervised running of the Union blockade
along the western Gulf of Mexico, the sale of cotton abroad, and
the smuggling of goods into Texas and Louisiana from Matamoros and Bagdad. He automatically encouraged close relations
between his forces and the Mexican imperialists. It is clear that his
purpose was to open a natural gateway into Mexico through
which his men might one day pass. But he did not want it to
become an escape route for deserters as long as the war lasted.
In fact, co-operation with the Mexicans actually helped prevent
this. Once in 1865, for example, when the "C.S. Depository," or

---

1 Grant, *Memoirs, II*, 323.

2 John Q. Anderson, *A Texan Surgeon in the C.S.A.*, i–ii. Among the unsuccessful eastern Commanders to be sent to the Trans-Mississippi area was General John B. Magruder, who engaged in a quarrel with Lee on the subject.

paymaster, at San Antonio deserted "Kirby-Smithdom" for Mexico, laden with large sums of Confederate currency, General Majía's Mexican imperialists courteously helped track him down. Such desertions to Mexico, were not, incidentally, limited to enlisted men but also included well-placed officers, including, on one occasion, a Confederate general, D. M. Frost.[3]

To deal more harshly with such matters of loyalty and to get increased efficiency out of his command, President Davis after the fall of Vicksburg delegated extraordinary powers to Kirby-Smith. Ultimately the General acknowledged subservience to no one. His Trans-Mississippi Department was by far the most independent of all the Confederate commands. It operated factories, ran mines, made powder and gun-castings, and in short, was as self-supporting as possible. On paper at least, Kirby-Smith assumed the powers of the Confederate presidency in the West. Eventually all orders to his command were issued by its commander, instead of from inaccessible Richmond, capital of the Confederacy.[4]

Some believed all this power was given to one general so that he and Jefferson Davis might lead die-hard hotspur remnants across the Río Grande into Mexico should the North win the war. There is an almost persistent ambiguity regarding just what Davis' plans were. We do know that others made various plans

[3] See Ella Lonn, *Desertion During the Civil War,* 64–65. On Frost, see Appendix D below and his published *Letter to Gen. Sterling Price, Accompanied by Official Documents,* and Frost to Confederate War Dept., November 30, 1864, Graham Papers, Missouri Historical Society (St. Louis). Among these papers see also T. C. Reynolds to E. Kirby-Smith, November 15, 1881; John S. Marmaduke to E. Kirby-Smith, November 15, 1881; W. P. Johnson to E. Kirby-Smith, November 30, 1881. The "C.S. Depository" was Judge G. W. Palmer, who was accompanied by Major John F. Bryant of the C.S.A. and Adolfo Mennet and D. L. Wilson, both Texans. See General James E. Slaughter's correspondence with Mejía in *OR,* Series I, Vol. XLVIII, Part I, 1398–1401.

[4] See Florence E. Holladay, "The Powers of the Commander of the Confederate Trans-Mississippi Department," *Southwestern Historical Quarterly,* Vol. XXI (1918), 279–98, 333–59; Diamond, "Imports of the Confederate Government from Europe and Mexico," *Journal of Southern History,* Vol. VI (November, 1940), 498; see also Kirby-Smith's own article, "The Defense of the Red River," in *Battles and Leaders,* IV, 369–74.

for him. The Confederate president evidently hoped to retreat toward "Kirby-Smithdom," where he could make a stand. If this failed, Mexico was the next best place to try a last-ditch stand. Such plans were obviously much more than talk. A close associate of President Davis, Brigadier General Basil W. Duke, wrote of his last days with the chief Confederate leader, and of the hopes for his future:

> It was the general opinion that Mr. Davis could escape if he would, but that was largely induced by the knowledge that extraordinary efforts would be made to prevent his falling into the hands of the enemy. . . . We were all convinced that the best we could hope to do was to get Mr. Davis safely out of the country, and then obtain such terms as had been given General Johnston's army, or, failing in that, make the best of our way to the Trans-Mississippi.[5]

Davis had a solid knowledge of the West, having formerly directed the western railroad surveys of the 1850's as secretary of war. He had also been to Mexico during the Mexican War. We now know that General Kirby-Smith definitely planned to help President Davis escape to Mexico. In a confidential letter to the General, written many years after the close of the Civil War, the chief of his Trans-Mississippi "secret service" accounted for five thousand dollars given him in the closing days of the war to spirit the Confederate president out of Havana and into Mexico.[6]

Davis, by the spring of 1865, saw the Confederacy collapsing almost everywhere around him, except in the West, but he could not quite bring himself to declare it extinct.[7] When Kirby-Smith heard that Davis planned to move southwestward in disguise, he prepared his command for retreat into Mexico with the Confederate president and made specific confidential overtures through his already mentioned agents in Mexico.[8] Almost simultaneously

[5] Basil W. Duke, "Last Days of the Confederacy," in *Battles and Leaders,* IV, 764.

[6] This agent ultimately surrendered the five thousand dollars to Union General E. R. S. Canby at New Orleans. See Ernest Cucullu to E. Kirby-Smith, January 29, 1891, Kirby-Smith Papers, University of North Carolina Library.

[7] See Rembert W. Patrick, *Jefferson Davis and His Cabinet,* 354.

[8] See Kirby-Smith to Robert Rose, *OR,* Series I, Vol. XLVIII, Part I, 1359. In

Kirby-Smith engaged in a general withdrawal from the loose Confederate Mississippi River "line"; indeed he found it impossible, to use his own words, to defend positions even along the Red River, "with the slender means at my disposal."

As dictator of the Trans-Mississippi region, he informed the Mexicans that his forces would most willingly enter into an agreement based upon mutual protection from a common enemy—the American Union. The General assured Maximilian's northern representatives that his war-tested soldiers, who hated Yankees and their Juárists allies, could be of great service to an imperialist Mexico. Also, Kirby-Smith asked his Mexican agents to inform Maximilian that if he received refuge he might influence as many as sixty thousand of his own soldiers, plus nine thousand Missourians (driven by warfare from their homes), to settle in Mexico. As permanent residents these men, of course, would be useful to the Emperor's hard-pressed regime in its fight against Juárez.[9]

All through May and during part of June, 1865, Kirby-Smith and his subaltern, General Simon Bolivar Buckner, commander of Confederate forces in Louisiana, delayed surrender of their commands to advancing Union armies in order to marshal troops for escape into Mexico. The final nature of that escape was not determined until almost the last moment. Kirby-Smith had promised Texas Governor Pendleton Murrah that he would not lay down his arms unless the Union offered an honorable peace, guaranteeing freedom of action to him and his men. But holding the Trans-Mississippi command together became increasingly difficult. Demoralization proceeded rapidly as large sectors of the Confederate eastern front gave way, frequently without the last-ditch battles Shelby and the hotspurs had anticipated. Entire companies and brigades became disorganized mobs, and Kirby-

---

this letter Kirby-Smith tells Rose that he wishes to offer Maximilian his services if the Confederates should be defeated.

[9] Hanna, *Flight Into Oblivion*, 80–81; *OR*, Series I, Vol. XLVIII, Part II, 1292. An excellent description of wartime Matamoros is Delaney's "Matamoros, Port for Texas During the Civil War," *Southwestern Historical Quarterly*, Vol. LVIII (April, 1955), 473–87.

Smith fast became "a general without an army." It was only a question of time before he would have to surrender his ragged troops.

On May 13, 1865, at a conference held in the lonely wooden home of Senator Louis T. Wigfall at Marshall, Texas, Kirby-Smith invited the governors of Arkansas, Louisiana, Missouri, and Texas to give him their counsel. The "confab" was also attended by such Southern generals as Shelby, Alexander T. Hawthorne of Arkansas, Buckner, William B. Preston of Kentucky, and John G. Walker. The main question at issue was: Should the vestiges of the Confederate Army in Texas make a stand at the Brazos River and fight on or surrender to advancing Union forces? The governors, who had already drawn up surrender terms, advised Kirby-Smith to accept them. But the General hesitated. We can be sure that, because of disrupted telegraphic communications, he could not have known that Jefferson Davis had been captured three days before, on May 10.[10] Furthermore, in spite of the general demoralization of his command, the General must have been sensitive to the fact that many of his soldiers by no means felt defeated yet. Writing from Louisiana after Lee's surrender at Appomattox and a few days before the capitulation of Kirby-Smith, a soldier confided to his wife:

> 'Tis useless to disguise the fact that Gen'l Lee has sold the Confederacy. A wholesale proscription will follow and I will have to leave my country on your account. Were I a single man I would fight them forever but you are dearer to me than any country. . . . If President Davis would come over here and take command and issue a heart stirring proclamation I think with the recruits he could get in a short time he could hold out for ten years and worry the Yankees into a recognition of the Confederacy. Would I were in Kirby Smith's place, my name should rank beside that of Washington as a 2d Pater Patriae. (May 5, 1865).

Five days later the same soldier wrote his wife again:

[10] See Joseph H. Parks, *General Edmund Kirby-Smith, C.S.A.*, 472–75. The Trans-Mississippi Department's communications with Richmond were mostly through the Union blockade by the end of the war.

I fear me the next thing we shall hear will be the surrender of
Kirby Smith. . . . My poor downtrodden country! What can thy
sons do who are true to thee. Exile alone awaits them. In a foreign
land dear we will have to make an asylum. . . . When shall our
sorrows have an end?

A final note of regret over Kirby-Smith's impending surrender
went to this soldier's wife on May 13, 1865:

Everybody but me is whipped. . . . I don't think all is lost by
any means yet, if Gen'l Smith would only prove equal to the
emergency he might inscribe his name highest on the Roll of Fame.
Oh if I had his opportunity . . . . I hope Gen'l Smith will not surrender though I sadly fear he will be compelled to for want of
currency. If we had a few million in specie we could certainly win
our independence. We hear Pres. Davis is in Shreveport with a part
of his cabinet & Commodore Semmes.[11]

At this point Shelby became prominent in determining the future course of the remaining Confederate troops in the West. At
a separate rump strategy session, held nearby in an abandoned
private residence, a number of younger officers, including Shelby,
decided that if the Southern governors wanted Kirby-Smith to
surrender or if their commander stayed on in Texas (as opposed
to going into Mexico), such action need not bind them. Some of
these young rebels even dared hope Kirby-Smith would turn
over his command to another general, one more determined to
fight below the Brazos River and beyond if Texas could not be
held. After Shelby expressed his desire to carry on the war in
Mexico, he was chosen leader of this group of dissidents at Marshall. By May 15 they began to plot their escape from "Kirby-
Smithdom." These men reasoned that wholesale flight was the
only way to avoid surrendering to the Union forces about to over-
whelm Kirby-Smith. If the old fool insisted upon staying behind,
let him do so. Meanwhile they would act as they saw fit.

Brigadier General Alexander Watkins Terrell, an associate of
Shelby's, wrote a short reminiscence, entitled *From Texas to*

---

[11] Edwin H. Fay, *This Infernal War*, (ed. by Bell Irvin Wiley), 422–46.

Mexico and the Court of Maximilian in 1865, which portrays the
state of mind of the hot bloods about to follow Shelby into Mexico.
Terrell, a regimental commander, was among those who

> . . . had agreed that each of us would address his own command,
> and ask for volunteers to cross the Rio Grande . . . and take the
> country up to the Sierra Madre mountains. The French forces then
> occupied no further north than Monterrey.

Shelby and Terrell for a short time actually wanted to *take* part
of Mexico itself, to use it for a future base or springboard from
which to reinvade the South. Terrell tells how, as "a set of free
companions," he, Shelby, and their fellow officers proposed to
seize the country ahead of them and even possibly to set up their
own government. "The example of Texas was before us," Terrell
explains. "It was believed that an army of two thousand five hundred or three thousand unmarried men could be secured if we
acted promptly. . . . Depots of flour and bacon were on the road
to Mexico at Corsicana, Austin, and San Antonio. We had abundant ordinance [*sic*] stores and could move a small army to the
Rio Grande."

Terrell, Shelby, and their colleagues had to notify Kirby-Smith
of these ambitious plans. This they knew would be a painful experience. When they called upon their commander as a delega-
tion, they told the "old man" that it had become idle to talk of
military discipline and of holding a line against the Union, at least
in Texas, and that they wanted to flee to Mexico with as many
men as they could muster. The gaunt, balding Kirby-Smith—a
West Pointer—listened "with evident pain," visibly shaken by
these plans for open defection of his junior volunteer officers.

Despite the fact that he, too, had quietly made plans to go into
Mexico, Kirby-Smith explained that he still wanted to keep as
many troops as possible together. His purpose is not entirely clear.
Weeks later, on his way to Galveston to sign the documents of
capitulation, Kirby-Smith stopped in Houston and delivered a
speech which perhaps throws light on his motives. He declared
that by disbanding itself, the Trans-Mississippi Department had

45

lost its only chance to negotiate better peace terms. Furthermore, he would not surrender without a direct order from Mr. Davis or without news that Davis had surrendered. One should remember that when Lee surrendered in Virginia on April 9, 1865, there were still more than 150,000 Confederate troops under arms farther west. The war, indeed, continued to be fought, albeit on a reduced scale, in outlying scattered regions. After Appomattox, General Nathan B. Forrest was still poised near Memphis. General John S. "Gray Ghost" Mosby was readying another of his mad-dog attacks on Union rear areas. Shelby's Missouri Division, though badly bruised, was relatively intact. Foreign ships still ran the Union naval blockade along the Texas coast. The Confederate raider *Shenandoah* would, albeit futilely, sink almost a dozen more ships.

One commander wrote that his men, then fighting in Alabama, "were ready to fight for the Confederacy to the last gasp under General Kirby-Smith. . . . It would have been an easy task for five thousand men at that time to traverse Arkansas and Texas on horseback. All the Southern states were then full of returning soldiers. The few gunboats on the Mississippi would have been no real obstacle." This officer explained how his men had long been used to taking care of themselves, to "moving rapidly with no more baggage or equipment than they could carry on their horses," living off the countryside and reassembling at distant points one thousand miles away. His men, he explained, were, even at the end of the war, "ready to fight to the last gasp, if fighting was possible. They were just then what the Emperor Maximilian most needed."[12]

What, meanwhile, was happening to President Jefferson Davis and his plans for a last-ditch stand? Within the Confederacy's eastern perimeter, the grimness of the attacks upon Richmond, Atlanta, Charleston, and Charlotte had chastened most of the major commanders, including Lee. Some of the Commander-in-Chief's officers suggested, before his surrender at Appomattox,

[12] W. E. H. Gramp, *The Journal of a Grandfather*, 116–17.

that they scatter to the mountains and continue guerrilla warfare. General Lee replied that this would entail an unnecessary loss of life.

Kirby-Smith, nevertheless, had reason to expect that if Davis escaped from Danville, Virginia—which he left on April 10, 1865, after he heard the news of Lee's surrender—he might order a stand in Texas against the pursuing forces of Union Generals Canby, Sheridan, Stoneman, and Wilson—most of whom were still miles from the heart of "Kirby-Smithdom." Indeed, Jefferson Davis had definitely hoped to join Kirby-Smith. This fact is fully verifiable. Before he held a negative cabinet conference on April 12 at Greensboro, North Carolina—with Generals Johnston, Bragg, and Beauregard in attendance—Davis hoped to move with a sizable force to meet the forces of Confederate General Richard B. Taylor in Alabama. Together he hoped they would proceed toward Kirby-Smith's command. In a letter of April 19, 1865, General Wade Hampton, who had been fighting General Johnston in South Carolina, encouraged Davis to continue armed resistance. He offered to furnish an armed escort under whose protection Davis could cross the Mississippi to continue resistance in Texas.[13]

Taylor, whose authority extended over Confederate forces in East Louisiana, Mississippi, and Alabama, did not, however, believe in such a plan. Earlier, when President Davis had visited him at Montgomery in 1864, Taylor "warned him of the danger of listening to narrators who were more disposed to tell him what was agreeable than what was true." General Taylor considered all the talk "about setting up a government west of the Mississippi, uniting with Maximilian, and calling upon Louis Napoleon for assistance" to be "much wild nonsense." He also warned Davis that "there would not be another gun fired" in the Trans-Mississippi Department "for the Federals had withdrawn their troops east of the river" toward the end of the war, as Sherman pummeled Confederate defenses from Chattanooga in the west to Atlanta in the east. Taylor thought the area beyond the Missis-

---

[13] Robert McElRoy, *Jefferson Davis, the Real and the Unreal*, II, 489 ff.

sippi simply outflanked by a war whose focus had changed as Sherman conducted his great raid through the heartland of the Confederacy. Yet, Taylor pointed out to his troops, even after Lee's surrender, "We owed it to our manhood, to the memory of the dead, and to the honor of our arms, to remain steadfast to the last." On May 8, 1865, Taylor was to surrender to General E. R. S. Canby at Citronelle, forty miles north of Mobile.[14]

Farther west, however, the lesser Confederate hotspurs Shelby and Terrell, who had earlier wanted to make such a stand, knew that time was running out as Kirby-Smith procrastinated, waiting for news from Davis. "We answered this," General Terrell later wrote, "by saying that he [Davis] could not cross the Mississippi with an army, and, if he came without one to continue the struggle here, it could only end in disaster and ruin." But Kirby-Smith and several of his aides still waited for the impossible and hid horses in the swamps of East Texas in hopes of hearing that Mr. Davis had crossed the Mississippi to join them in escape.

The Confederacy's president, however, made slow progress during his flight into the Carolinas and Georgia. Over roads flooded by spring rains his party bumped along in a miscellaneous collection of old wagons and other noisy carts. At Greensboro, Davis received the discouraging counsel of Johnston and Beauregard that further resistance would be folly. Despair reigned in their encampment, and a conviction that the South was beaten settled over the Confederate high command. Davis could not counter this feeling with talk of continuing the war, and, on April 24, 1865, he acceded to the peace terms thrust upon Johnston's North Carolina forces by General Sherman. Only on May 2 did Davis reach Abbeville, South Carolina, fiercely hunted as a fugitive by Federal forces. Even with a price on his head and with time rapidly running out, Davis believed he could still make a stand with Kirby-Smith in Texas. About this relentless faith in the Southern cause one historian has written: "If there was any single personality which contributed to this dogged continuance,

---

[14] Richard Taylor, *Destruction and Reconstruction* (ed. by Richard B. Harwell), 250–51, 272, 276.

it was that of Jefferson Davis. He refused to believe that he was beaten . . . ."[15] Whatever plans Davis may still have cherished ended on May 10, 1865, when his party was captured while bivouacked in some woods near Irwinville, Georgia. The South's "Lost Cause" came to a genuine stop that day.

Out west, meanwhile, General Kirby-Smith's indecisiveness over whether to go into Mexico or not nearly proved fatal to the success of Shelby's expedition. Terrell describes how after May 15, within one short period of forty-eight hours, thousands of troops, confused by the indecision and inaction of their unit commanders, ended their military service by slinking off into the night in small groups. Few commanders posted guards each evening or held roll calls or ordered formations. Military life deteriorated radically. Without a sizable army Shelby's "dream of taking a slice from Mexico was now ended," Terrell wrote. Yet Shelby's dissidents had already decided they must at all costs leave Texas, whatever the size of their force or whoever joined them. As Terrell put it: "We all felt that an era of oppression was before the people . . . and we sought a foreign country with feelings reckless of consequences." Terrell had himself hopefully sewed a letter of introduction to Maximilian, wrapped in silk oilcloth, in the lining of his boot, and, bidding good-by to those troops who chose to remain behind, he rode off with Shelby, about May 18, for the Big River.[16]

---

[15] Charles H. Wesley, *The Collapse of the Confederacy,* 104. The details of Davis' attempted escape are in Nash K. Burger and John K. Bettersworth, *South of Appomattox,* 95, 312–15.

[16] Alexander Watkins Terrell, *From Texas to Mexico and the Court of Maximilian in 1865,* 3–6.

❀

CHAPTER V

The Troubled Border

THE outwardly calm General Kirby-Smith, still nominally in command of the Confederate West (although he had turned over much power in Louisiana to Buckner), faced problems that would have tried the souls of even bigger men. The General's military zone could be likened to a thin shell unable to sustain the prolonged attacks made upon it. As one after another of his generals disbanded their troops and left him behind, Kirby-Smith moved his headquarters, on May 27, 1865, from Shreveport to Houston in Texas. Further desertions in large numbers were taking the heart out of the remaining western troops. Then came the news that General John G. Walker's brigade of Texas Infantry had actually mutinied and disbanded on May 19 and that General John Bankhead Magruder's forces in Texas, New Mexico, and Arizona had also given up their military entity. "Prince John" Magruder, commander of the Trans-Mississippi Department before Kirby-Smith, was a cantankerous but valued officer who had, in January, 1863, spectacularly recaptured Galveston and the Union revenue cutter, *Harriet Lane*. With Magruder at his side, Kirby-Smith finally accepted the hopelessness of their predicament. On board the Union steamer *Fort Jackson* at Galveston harbor on June 2, 1865, the two agreed to final surrender terms and handed over their swords to the Union commander, General E. R. S. Canby. Some days earlier (on May 26) Buckner had surrendered "his part" of the Trans-Mississippi Department to Major General Peter

J. Osterhaus at New Orleans. At first Buckner had thought of going to Mexico, but ultimately he returned to his native Kentucky.

Upon surrendering, Kirby-Smith obviously knew that he would leave behind both chaos and bitter disappointment. One eyewitness account reveals the feelings of the troops in the Trans-Mississippi Department when they heard of the plans for surrender:

> The soldiers were gathered in groups everywhere, discussing the approaching surrender. Curses, deep and bitter, fell from lips not accustomed to use such language; while numbers, both officers and men, swore fearful oaths never to surrender. . . . The depth of feeling exhibited by compressed lips, pale faces, and blazing eyes, told a fearful story of how bitter was the hopeless surrender of the cause for which they had fought, toiled, suffered for long years. The humiliation was unbearable.[1]

"With this news," wrote a Confederate colonel, "fled the hopes of the last Confederate soldier." This officer further stated that had he anticipated Kirby-Smith's surrender, "instead of ordering my men to report to me at his headquarters at Shreveport, I would have taken them to the Rio Grande . . . straight to Maximilian and Mexico." Another soldier, upon hearing the rumor that Kirby-Smith had surrendered, could not believe it and confided to his diary: "If so, a HEMP ROPE should be his support through life; the idea of giving up to the Yankees, and they are at least 5 or 6 hundred miles off, is simply disgraceful." His solution: "We should make one mighty, determined effort. . . . I say to the Trans-Mississippi Department, 'A LONG PULL, A STRONG PULL AND A PULL ALTOGETHER.' "[2]

Unfortunately for the writer, the time for marshaling a unified

---

[1] Joseph P. Blessington, *The Campaigns of Walker's Texas Division*, 307; Frank Cunningham, in *General Stand Watie's Confederate Indians*, 194, discusses the sequence of events leading to surrender.

[2] See Gramp, *The Journal of a Grandfather*, 114–16, 124, and Heartsill, *Fourteen Hundred and 91 Days in the Confederate Army*, 243, for the above quotations. For an appraisal of Kirby-Smith's errors of command see Ludwell H. Johnson, *Red River Campaign: Politics and Cotton in the Civil War*, 282.

spirit of co-operation to save Texas had passed. Five years of continuous warfare had left the Trans-Mississippi area exhausted, devastated, and confused. Practically every semblance of military discipline had gone. In these last days of the Confederacy a telegram sent by Union General J. J. Reynolds to General John Pope, commander of the Military Division of Missouri, read: "The thing is going to pieces so fast that one cannot count the fragments."[3]

A military aide who was with Kirby-Smith in the final days before surrender scribbled a fragmentary diary in pencil which reveals how hopeless conditions seemed to him and to his superior:

> Left Huntsville, [Texas] Wednesday, 24 [May, 1865] and reached Houston [25 May, 1865]
>
> Message to Buckner: Just arrived. Texas troops all disbanded. Public Property all seized. Galveston probably occupied by enemy this morn. No supplies for maintaining troops. Discharge them and send them to their homes. Inform Genl. Cooper. comdg Indian Dept. of the condition of things & advise accordingly. When shall I expect you? Will any troops accompany you? If you have not left, start all who wish to come immediately, under escort if practicable. Otherwise they must protect themselves.
>
> . . . Soldiers having seized all descriptions of Govt. property . . . having taken all ambulances, waggons, & animals belonging to Govt., was advised to secrete the transportation by which we're traveling. I sent it to the brush.[4]

With the exception of a few units, mostly from Missouri, which rather surprisingly awaited proper discharge by their officers, the Confederate units had begun to plunder the countryside before Kirby-Smith's surrender. Poorly clad soldiers—some old men, others young boys forcibly conscripted into Confederate service —proved unmanageable. Many of these troops had not been paid

---

[3] Arndt M. Stickles, *Simon Bolivar Buckner,* 274.
[4] David Wendell Yandell, MS Diary, May 22–25, 1865, in Eldridge Manuscripts, Box No. 47, Huntington Library.

for months. Before departing for their homes without official discharges, such soldiers divided up regimental properties and stores among themselves. Many a footsore "Johnny Reb" helped himself to a stray horse or mule or stole animals out of government corrals and private pastures. Soldiers, civilians, Negroes, and children, all joined in sacking and pillaging Confederate warehouses containing anything of value.[5] Some filled their duffel bags with sugar, coffee, and other delicacies to which they had long been strangers and took home anything they could to hungry families. Although he had ordered saloons closed and guards posted around supply depots, Kirby-Smith had been increasingly powerless to prevent such looting. He had dreaded the prospect of a reign of anarchy. Civilian and military authorities alike generally stopped performing their functions, relying upon the incoming Union armies to stabilize public order.

Once he had completed dismantling the headquarters under his command, Kirby-Smith decided "to place the Rio Grande between myself and harm," and crossed at Eagle Pass on June 26 with a small party. Ironically, his crossing preceded Shelby's, whose march was much slowed down by the increasing number of adherents flocking to join him. Described by a biographer as "mounted on a mule and dressed in shirt sleeves with a silk handkerchief tied around his neck 'a la Texas' and armed with revolver and shotgun, the former commanding general of the Trans-Mississippi Department rode into Mexico."[6]

Many years later, Kirby-Smith reminisced about all this in a letter to the editor of *Century* magazine. The General felt that he had acted decently as commander of the Trans-Mississippi Department. He stated that, as its commander, his powers were "supreme" and that, although he could have lived like an "emperor," he had acted abstemiously, even "personally raising vegetables" served at his dinner table. "When the war ended I could have, unquestioned, laid my hands upon thousands in gold. After my

[5] Ramsdell, *Reconstruction in Texas,* 34.
[6] See Parks, *General Edmund Kirby Smith, C.S.A.,* 482; Louis J. Wortham *A History of Texas from Wilderness to Commonwealth,* IV, 364–65.

army disbanded, I rode some 800 miles, across the Rio Grande to Monterey [*sic*] in shirt sleeves, with an empty purse but a clear conscience—light at heart, having been relieved from vast responsibilities and unlimited powers."[7]

The party with which Kirby-Smith traveled did not proceed southward without trepidation. The heat of the cactus plains through which they journeyed, the ever present danger of Indian attacks, and the fear that Mexican bandits would intercept their passage made the trip a torturous one. On their march the dust floated like puffs of clouds onto the tops of the maguey plants, casting an endless veil over the cacti and other flora of the deserts.

At Monterrey, Kirby-Smith found "a 100 or more 'Confederate censorians,' fault finding and dissatisfied," the names of whom we will never know, and, on July 5, boarded a horse-drawn diligence to Mexico City with Governors Thomas C. Reynolds and Cadmus M. Wilcox. Kirby-Smith was more than a month traversing the twelve hundred miles of territory from Texas to Mexico City.

Toward the flat, windy Texas delta country Grant finally sent his top cavalry aide, the doughty Major General Philip Sheridan, devastator of the Shenandoah Valley. On June 28, 1865, Sheridan reported:

General: I have just returned from a hurried trip along the coast of Texas. The following is, to the best of my knowledge, the condition of affairs there: The Kirby Smith and Canby surrender was, for the most part, a swindle on the part of Kirby Smith & Co., as all the Texas troops had been disbanded or had been discharged and gone home . . . . Kirby Smith, Magruder, Shelby, Slaughter, Walker, and others of military rank have gone to Mexico. Everything on wheels, artillery, horses, mules, etc., have been run over into Mexico. Large and small bands of rebel soldiers, and some citizens amounting to about two thousand, have crossed the Rio Grande into Mexico, some allege with the intention of going to Sonora.[8]

[7] E. Kirby-Smith to Robert Underwood Johnson, March 8, 1887, Kirby-Smith Papers, University of North Carolina Library.

[8] *The Present Condition of Mexico. Message from the President of the United States*, in 39 Cong., 1 sess., *Senate Exec. Doc. No. 6*, pp. 49–50.

In time, Grant made Sheridan his new commander in the West and gave him an entire army corps with which to patrol the Río Grande. Although Sheridan would have preferred to attend the Washington festivities that followed final surrender of the Confederacy, he headed west to establish his new command, believing that this "Army of Observation" formed a crucial part of the Union's emerging postwar foreign policy. "Little Phil," very short, stocky, and the soul of command, now poised his forces for hundreds of miles along the winding river. It was a time for no further mincing of words. Sheridan would close in on escaping Confederates in a big way. His was to be an inflexible barrier.

Secretary Seward's cautious policy was now supplanted by a policy of power. By 1866, Sheridan was in command of 52,000 troops. In April, 1866, Grant issued an order which prohibited embarkation from ports in Louisiana or Texas of anyone not possessing a permit from Sheridan's headquarters. Sheridan claimed later that this order "led ultimately to the failure of the Confederates who wished to emigrate to Mexico."[9]

Sheridan's vigorous patrolling of the border also proved a great encouragement to those *Juaristas* who wanted to depose Maximilian. One of Sheridan's first acts was to demand of Maximilian the return of munitions shipped over the border by the Confederates. We do not know whether this was done, but in the winter and spring of 1866 Sheridan furnished Juárez *liberales* thirty thousand surplus muskets from the Union Army's Baton Rouge arsenal. In fact, only what Sheridan termed Seward's "slow and poky" caution kept Sheridan's forces from seizing what he called a "golden opportunity to cross the border and clean up on the Confederates and Imperialists."[10] Sheridan urged this course

[9] U. S. Grant to P. H. Sheridan, May 17, 1865, reproduced in P. H. Sheridan, *Personal Memoirs,* II, 209–19; see also pp. 224–26.

[10] Regarding conditions on the border see Sheridan, *Personal Memoirs,* II, 202–19; Rister, *Border Command,* 20; and the stylized but convincing picture in Paul Horgan, *Great River: The Río Grande in North American History,* II, 841. Also see statement by the attorney general of New York reprinted in *Diario del Imperio,* June 29, 1865. Sheridan cracked down on Confederate dissidence in New Orleans by removing its mayor and the attorney general of Louisiana. Still

upon Grant, who, in turn, informed the Secretary of State that the War Department wanted the Mexican border sealed off even more firmly and that the French should, furthermore, be forced to withdraw from Mexico posthaste.

Accordingly, Seward relayed to Napoleon a series of increasingly stiff warnings about United States displeasure with the French puppet regime in Mexico. This pressure would weaken Maximilian diplomatically and thus affect the insecure Confederate exiles.[11] If Maximilian and the French were to be forced out of Mexico, the Confederate exiles would be at the mercy of Juárez. Ultimately, therefore, the action of Sheridan and Grant helped determine the fate of Shelby and his fellow exiles. But no Union force could possibly stop Shelby and the hundreds like him who had already crossed the border.[12]

---

later Sheridan removed from power the governor of Texas. See Fletcher Pratt, *Stanton, Lincoln's Secretary of War,* 449, and William B. Hesseltine, *Ulysses S. Grant, Politician,* 84.

[11] See the revealing diplomatic correspondence in 39 Cong., 1 sess, *House Exec. Doc. No. 1,* 356–410.

[12] The importance which Grant attached to stopping the escaping exiles appears in his *Memoirs,* II, 546. Grant therein ascribes the ultimate failure of the French in Mexico to his sending Sheridan to the Río Grande. "From that day the empire began to totter. Mexico was then able to maintain her independence without aid from us."

CHAPTER VI

❦

Shelby Moves South

SHELBY'S NEUTRALITY in the bitter Mexican struggle was tested
almost as soon as he had crossed the border. The area controlled
by the Juárists, through which Shelby would have to pass in order to reach Mexico City, ran irregularly along the United States
border at a width of from fifty to three hundred miles. Juárist
authorities naturally wanted to know Shelby's future plans and
political sympathies. He was, to them, an armed invader whose
forces could conceivably help tip the balance between victory
and defeat in Mexico's internecine struggle. Much to the General's surprise, Governor A. S. Biesca (sometimes Viesca)—Juárez' commander-in-chief of the provinces of Coahuila, Tamaulipas, and Nuevo León—proceeded to offer him military jurisdiction over these three states. If we can believe Major John N.
Edwards—Shelby's "official historian," who later wrote two books,
now almost forgotten, about his experiences with Shelby, *Shelby
and his Men* and *Shelby's Expedition to Mexico*—this power was
offered Shelby upon condition that he swear allegiance to Juárez.
According to Edwards, Biesca asked Shelby to become a *jefe
político,* or political chieftain, under Juárez. It is possible that
during this period when the Juárists were relatively hard pressed
for arms, they tried to enlist every possible source of aid. Whatever the offer to Shelby was, he declined it after a consultation
with his men.[1]

[1] These events are described by Terrell, *From Texas to Mexico,* 19; Parks,

The General was reluctant to prejudice the plans hopefully entertained by some of his men to seek asylum with Maximilian. Major Edwards was one of those who regretted Shelby's decision to turn his back on Juárez' offer. He wrote in 1867 that the *Juarista* proposal would undoubtedly have made Shelby "powerful in the politics of Mexico today."[2]

However, about July 17, 1865, after having marched only some fifty miles below the border, at the Mexican village of Pedrosney, Shelby did choose to sell some of his weapons and munitions to the barefoot *Juaristas*. Although he was not sympathetic to Juárez, Shelby was running low on money and decided to dispose of his heaviest cannon and ammunition. Such unwieldly arms were of less value to him now than he had anticipated. Dragging this equipment over sandy, washboard roads was especially hard on the party's horses. Its horses also pulled ramshackle, heavy commissary wagons, some of which still bore the old "U.S." marking of the Union Army. The Juárist *liberales* gave Shelby $16,000 in silver and about twice that amount in practically worthless Juárist script for his heavy equipment. The General distributed the money from this sale to each man in the party. There are conflicting stories about how much money Shelby received: one source says it amounted to only $82.00 a person. The General then tried to avoid further contact with the *Juaristas*.[3]

Years later some light was thrown upon the confusion concerning Shelby's sale of arms to the Mexicans. In 1896 the journalist George Creel, then a cub reporter, saw much of the General and a group of "Independence colonels" whom he interviewed for the Kansas City *World*. He wrote in his autobiography: "Not a one of my Independence colonels but had a story, and where any more thrilling epic than General Joe Shelby's reckless dash across the Rio Grande after Appomattox?" About Shelby's sale of equip-

---

General Edmund Kirby Smith, C.S.A., 482. Box, in "End of the War," *Confederate Veteran*, Vol. II (March, 1903), 122, states that Shelby's flag was sunk into the Río Grande on July 1, 1865, the party having reached Eagle Pass on June 26.

    [2] Edwards, *Shelby and His Men*, 547.

    [3] *Ibid.*, 543; O'Flaherty, *General Jo Shelby*, 247–48; Box (p. 122) says Shelby received only $3,200, "part in scrip and the rest in cash."

ment—according to Creel for $60,000, of which $20,000 was in cash and the rest in Juárez script—he recorded the following conversation:

> "But General," I exclaimed when this was told me, "the Juaristas outnumbered you five to one, according to your own admission. And you just told them you were going to join the enemy. When they got your artillery, what was to prevent them from taking back the money and annihilating you?"
>
> "You seem to forget, sir," was his icy reply, "that we still had our side arms."

Creel also tells the story that when Shelby and his men started to leave Piedras Negras, "some Mexicans went up to Ike Barry and insolently claimed the horse he rode. 'You don't say so!' laughed the Missourian. 'Well, you'll have a hell of a time ridin' him.' With that he swung his heavy sword and severed a Mexican's right arm at the shoulder. In the fight that followed many were killed, and the Southerners recaptured the artillery they had sold that morning."

By June 20 it was clear to General Shelby that he could expect no further recruits from across the river in Texas. Those armed Confederates who planned to join him had either already done so or had entered Mexico on their own. Shelby therefore came to a crucial decision regarding his future course. Before crossing over into Mexico, he and his men had contemplated fighting their way back into the South. But after Shelby learned more about the extent of the political confusion in Mexico, he decided it was futile even to hope for aid in this project from the seriously divided Mexicans or from the French troops of Napoleon III.

Shelby saw also that he must, above all, avoid conflict in Mexico. He must care for his band as a sheep dog cares for its flock; he must conduct himself with tact and caution. To remain the idol of his men, to serve his cause and theirs, he must try to soften past command jealousies and even sectional rivalries. Yet Shelby announced that, although his men were all on an equal footing, he would insist that they act and look like soldiers instead of rene-

59

gades. Doing so, he explained, would help improve the way they would be treated in Mexico. By election he was their leader, and he had a right to speak frankly.

Shelby had little information about the best route to Mexico City. The plan of march with which the troops had started out had to be altered by the light of each night's campfire, in accordance with the roughness of the terrain, the condition of the animals, and especially the scarcity of water. The men were constantly exhorted to look for wells unpolluted by the corpses of animals. Indeed, the march each day was almost from water hole to water hole, and their canteens were sometimes empty. Although in the villages there were wells, the group never ceased to fear impure water with its threat of typhoid and dysentery. A march of fifteen miles a day was good progress. As the group veered southeastward through a series of dusty crossroads on the route to Monterrey, they traded excess supplies of tinned jellies, coffee, and highly salted and smoked bacon for fresh beef, green beans, and *mantequilla,* Mexican butter. The last was frequently as rancid as the bacon of which they had grown so tired.

When the supplies ran low, each man volunteered to go on half-rations every other day in order to conserve money and food. This self-imposed regimen was similar to the group's posting guards—each soldier in the command stood one six-hour watch every other night. Officers also volunteered to keep fires burning until dawn. These frightened away coyotes and gray Mexican *lobos,* or wolves, as well as prospective looters.

The group usually camped outside the towns through which it traveled, principally to avoid trouble with the natives. Shelby had to be especially careful to keep his men away from local women, and to discourage the camp followers they sometimes attracted. He had to do this without disturbing morale or arousing edgy tempers. Rather than prepare his men for new battles, Shelby began to conceive of his role as that of a guide; his job was to reinstill a sense of hope in the future, to lead his men in peace, if possible, toward their new homes, wherever those might be.

But peace does not come readily to those labeled as foreign invaders. The very *liberales* who had sought Shelby's heavy arms almost immediately gave him trouble. They treacherously halted his band and produced the trumped-up charge of some *cholos,* or border-toughs, that Shelby's own horse and other animals ridden by the Confederates had been stolen. The General was unable to hold back his men, who were now spoiling for a fight over this accusation, and he could only pray that the Mexicans would back down. Luck was with him, for when his men threatened to open fire, the opposition suddenly dispersed. Perhaps the Mexicans realized how used to pulling triggers the Confederates had become. Shelby's men were accorded more respect thereafter. Word was passed along that, if pressed, the Confederates would fight.

The party encountered many travelers on the trails of Mexico —drivers with heavily loaded burros, long files of trotting, jingling pack mules, broken-down hay carts, ox drivers who whipped thin, bony animals ahead of them, and tattered walkers accompanied by dogs. Some of these travelers called out half-friendly greetings; others simply looked at the ground to avoid the embarrassment of eye-contact. . . . A strange and melancholy land, this Mexico.

Shelby held firmly to his basic tactic—to avoid trouble whenever possible. Shelby's men were more wary of the unknown expanse that lay before them than they were of the people who inhabited it. Wild gusts of wind, carrying sharp grains of sand, pelted them unceasingly, blowing tumbleweeds around the sore legs of their horses. Even at night the stars seemed to burn hot. The heat of the day was endurable only in the early sunlight hours after their camp was made. And the full blaze of day left their heads pounding and a feverish shiver running through their bodies. As they made camp each day and thoughts turned to the next unknown lap of their trip, their spirits sagged. They had plenty of food, but it took more than food to live in the wilderness. At night, reminded of relatives left behind in the South, it was a consolation to have their precious cache of "sipping liquor."

As Shelby slogged his way toward Mexico City, he did not know how many other Southerners had been trickling into the capital before him. Not all the Americans who traveled below the border were military men—or even avowed Confederates. North of Monterrey Shelby encountered a most controversial American indeed. This was the Honorable William McKendree Gwin, once United States senator from California. Gwin, who was traveling north, was an enigmatic proslavery advocate with a shady past, a real intriguer, and the owner of a long bony face, tinted by a deep tan by the sun and wind. Gwin was described by contemporaries as most "charming over his wine," but few persons trusted him and he trusted no one. Terrell, Shelby's fellow exile, saw Gwin as "a venerable looking man with a long snow-white beard, who . . . cautioned us not to trust the French . . . having just been ordered to leave the Empire." The Senator had a devious and fascinating story to tell Shelby and his men.

Gwin had recently come to Mexico from France with unsubstantiated claims that in 1864 Napoleon III had made him a duke, granting him "letters-patent" for colonization and exploitation of the province of Sonora. In Paris he had become acquainted with the notorious José Mariá Gutiérrez de Estrada, a designing Mexican royalist who had won French support for the establishment of a European throne in Mexico and who represented that rightist coterie that had deceived Maximilian into thinking the Mexican people wanted him to rule them.[4]

Gwin told Shelby how, through the efforts of Gutiérrez de Estrada, Pierre Soulé, a former senator from Louisiana and a Confederate brigadier general, had obtained from Napoleon a promise that the French Army would seize from Juárez the four north Mexican states of Durango, Chihuahua, Sonora, and Sinaloa.

According to Gwin, Mexico's northern provinces were to be peopled by Confederates and other immigrants from Europe, South America, or even Gwin's state of California. Such migrants would not only strengthen the economy of Mexico by

---

[4] Gutiérrez de Estrada, once *ministro de relaciones interiores y esteriores* of Mexico, wrote a short work entitled *México y el archduque Fernando Maximiliano de Austria* which argued for use of Maximilian's empire as a buffer against U.S. intervention in Mexico.

developing the mines of Sonora, they would also act as a buffer against the *Yanquis* of the north. Gwin was to reign over this fief as "Duke of Sonora." Some eight thousand French troops were supposedly to give Gwin the military solidity his dukedom needed to get on its feet.[5]

Whether Napoleon ever made any such agreement is uncertain; Count Egon Corti, an Austrian historian who later studied the diplomatic correspondence between Maximilian and Napoleon III, concludes in his *Maximilian and Charlotte in Mexico* that "Napoleon committed himself very deeply to Gwin."[6] Although Gwin was actually never ennobled, newspapers in the States spoke of his acceptance of a title of nobility and of his influence upon the French emperor. The New York *World* for June 19, 1865, in an article entitled "Emigration to Mexico," stated that Gwin was on the verge of clinching his plan. That same month a correspondent of the New Orleans *Times* wrote:

> The Confederates still continue to flock to Mexico. There is no doubt Dr. Gwin will get his project through. It only awaits the signature of Maximilian to become a law. He goes out as director general of emigration for the States of Sonora, Chihuahua, Durango and Tamaulipas, with extraordinary powers and *eight thousand* French troops to back him. The emigration is to be strictly southern, or Confederate. Ten thousand confederates are to be armed and paid by the empire, but kept in the above-mentioned States as protection to the emigrants. Strategical points are to be fortified and garrisoned on the frontier. Dr. Gwin's son has applied for and will get an exclusive privilege for all the railroads in Sonora. The southerners are elated and golden visions float before them.[7]

[5] See Lawrence F. Hill, "The Confederate Exodus to South America," *Southwestern Historical Quarterly*, Vol. XXXIX (October, 1935), 118; also James Morton Callahan, *The Diplomatic History of the Southern Confederacy*, 217, 258–59; Rippy, "Mexican Projects of the Confederates," *Southwestern Historical Quarterly*, Vol. XXII (April, 1919), 312–15.

[6] Egon Caesar Corti, *Maximilian and Charlotte of Mexico*, I, 326–27, 341; II, 449, 459, 498, 578; Amos A. Ettinger, *The Mission to Spain of Pierre Soulé*, 473.

[7] *Message of the President of the United States of March 20, 1866, Relating to the Conditions of Affairs in Mexico*, 39 Cong., 1 sess., *House Exec. Doc. No. 73*, 537.

However, the plans which Gwin submitted to Napoleon for the organization of his new "state" were vetoed by Maximilian and his cabinet. For a time Maximilian had not voiced open disapproval, and his silence may have been taken by Gwin to mean the Emperor's consent.

On June 26, 1865, Maximilian's official newspaper, the *Diario del Imperio*, made it clear that the Emperor had no intention of giving away part of Mexico to foreigners. He had also incidentally stopped shipment of the highly prized, stone Aztec calendar from Mexico City's *Zócalo* to a Paris museum.

It seems strange to think of Maximilian as a Mexican nationalist trying to preserve Mexico. Yet, in many respects he was an idealist who was dedicated to the interests of his indifferent subjects. The Emperor thought of himself as redeemer of Mexico. An autocrat he remained; nonetheless, he had written two tracts against slavery following a visit to Brazil a few years before coming to Mexico.

Gwin was informed by Mexico's self-righteous emperor that he did not desire the "coquetries of Empire before that Empire had an army, a bank account and a clean bill of health."[8]

The French intervention had contemplated colonization from the beginning, and Maximilian had consistently invited immigrants to Mexico from the United States and Europe. But the idea of a competing American province in northern Mexico, whose inhabitants would protect their independence with Spencer rifles and Bowie knives, was out of the question. Shelby, on his way to the Emperor's court, listened closely to Gwin's discomfiting account. Gwin's vision of building an empire had proved as illustory as had the early dream of the Seven Cities of Cíbola in Spanish colonial times, another legend with its roots in the very region where Shelby and Gwin met.[9]

[8] Copies of Gwin's plans to colonize northern Mexico submitted to Napoleon are in the Gwin correspondence, Bancroft Library, Berkeley, California. See also Edwards, *Shelby and His Men,* 49; also Callahan, *American Foreign Policy,* 313–14.

[9] Hallie M. McPherson, "William McKendree Gwin, Expansionist," (Ph.D. dissertation), 268; Gwin's arrest is mentioned in *MT,* October 28, 1865. Un-

A typical scene of the area in which the Confederates settled
on the eastern slopes of the Mexican cordillera.

General Edmund Kirby-Smith, C.S.A., about 1885.

Courtesy Huntington Library

When the two took leave of each other north of Monterrey, the former senator went on toward the States. He feared re-entering the South, but had no other place to go. At New Orleans he would be arrested by the decisive Sheridan. In two countries, his own and Mexico, Gwin gambled with loyalty and lost.[10]

As he made his way inland, Shelby met, in addition to Gwin, a tribe of Indians also migrating from the States. These were Kickapoos, who, confused by the Civil War, had, like Shelby's Confederates, left their homeland, to find new homes in Mexico.[11]

About July 28, at the Salinas River, some 180 miles south of Eagle Pass, Shelby's march southward was roughly one-quarter completed. Located some twenty miles north of Monterrey, this stream is one of many north Mexican rivulets that become raging torrents overnight when off-season rains strike. The

doubtedly the pressure exerted upon the French government by United States Minister John Bigelow had much to do with getting the French to withdraw sponsorship of Gwin's colonization plan. See Bigelow to Seward, July 13, 1865, and Seward to Bigelow, August 10, 1865, in 39 Cong., 1 sess., *House Exec. Doc. No. 1*, Part III, 518–21; J. Fred Rippy, *The United States and Mexico*, 245–48; Hallie M. McPherson, "The Plan of William McKendree Gwin for a Colony in North Mexico, 1863–1865," *Pacific Historical Review*, Vol. II (December, 1933), 384–85 describes Gwin's relations with the Mexican Confederates. See also Simon J. Ellison, "An Anglo-American Plan for the Colonization of Mexico," *Southwestern Social Science Quarterly*, Vol. XVI (September, 1935), 42–52; Beckles Willson, *John Slidell and the Confederates in Paris, 1862–1865*, 218.

[10] A letter written in 1865, from Mexico expressed Gwin's fear that a victorious North would "massacre" the South: "It really makes me sick," he wrote, "when I think of the bloody agony that awaits the southern people." Gwin told his wife that the "startling" surrender of the South had "made the blood of every southern sympathizer run cold with horror. No one will be safe in our native country. How I thank Providence that I have cast my lot elsewhere . . . . My policy is on every man's lips as the only one that will save this empire." See 39 Cong., 1 sess., *House Exec. Doc. No. 1*, Part III, 513. Grant called Gwin a rebel of the most virulent order," and ordered Sheridan to arrest him on authorization of President Johnson. Official Washington was enraged over an American citizen's conniving with Napoleon III in the face of a resolution by the United States House of Representatives (of April 4, 1864) deploring the French occupation of Mexico.

[11] See Appendix C below and Charles Blanchot, *L'intervention française au Mexique*, II, 285–86. August Santleben, *A Texas Pioneer*, 128–29. See Annie Heloise Abel, *The American Indian Under Reconstruction*, 76 n.; 39 Cong., 1 sess., *House Exec. Doc. No. 1*, 376–410; and James Farber, *Texas, C.S.A.*, 219.

party rode along it, their horses casting elongated shadows over the stream's bed. Large pools of water, not yet dried up by the summer heat, gleamed peacefully in the sun. While the members of Shelby's column were in the midst of crossing the Salinas near one of these pools, a group of Lipan Indians and half-blood guerrilla-bandits fired upon them from behind cottonwoods growing along the stream's banks. The suddenness of the attack forced them into a deep, slippery quagmire. The purpose of this ambush was to exterminate the entire party. Shelby's men fortunately possessed superior firepower, and, although the water was up to the saddle girths of their horses, they answered the marauders with a hail of lead that caused one observer to write that "the attack was a hurricane," indeed almost a massacre: "The Mexicans first broke, and after them the Indians. No quarter was shown . . . and the roar of the revolver volleys told how the Americans were at work." Despite their marksmanship, twenty-seven of Shelby's men were killed and thirty-seven wounded. Eight of the dead could not be buried, having been shot or drowned in the stream whose waters "closed over them until judgment day." The others were loaded on their wagons and buried nearby. By this time Shelby's force was probably reduced to less than four hundred men.[12]

The attackers were free partisans loosely associated with the forces attracted by Juárez. This blow was followed by another attempt to massacre the party at Lampazos a few days later, about which we know little. Shelby raced away from such ambushes at a gallop, the fury of his horse's hoofs seeming to stir up his determination to stay alive. The constant threats caused most of Shelby's men to wonder what manner of security could possibly be gained by siding with such disparate *Juarista* bands. Juárez was making no promises of help to the Confederates. In fact, his warnings to intruders were proving deadly serious.

Shelby knew that his movements were also being watched by the imperialists. The French Army still had reason to suspect Shel-

[12] Rister, "Carlota," *Journal of Southern History*, Vol. XI (February, 1945), 39.

by of being pro-Juárez. He had, after all, sold arms to the *Juaristas,* an act known to the French and highly irritating to them. How to prove to them now that he wished to ally himself with Maximilian? How to prove to anyone that he and his men would not sell out to the highest bidder for their services?

Just outside Monterrey, some 250 miles from Eagle Pass, at the end of one long day's march, Shelby decided to poll his men. Much to his relief, most of them agreed that they should shed their pseudo-neutralism and firmly declare for Maximilian and the French. They therefore authorized Shelby to inform the imperialists of their willingness to fight for Maximilian as a unit. This authorization was important to Shelby; he was now approaching an area of greater French control in Mexico. Rather than write to Maximilian of his group's loyalty to the empire or rather than send a messenger to Mexico City, he decided to await physical contact with the French.

The French, who garrisoned a series of thinly spread frontier outposts in northern Mexico, wondered how far they might allow the energetic Confederate general to march without some supervision. Maximilian's French commander in the north was General Pierre Jeanningros, a bushy-faced, corpulent veteran of the Crimean War and of fighting in China. His headquarters was at Monterrey. Jeanningros decided to allow Shelby's armed band to proceed no farther than that town without examination of its motives and armaments. Jeanningros may well have hoped to force Shelby to return home. On August 3, 1865, Jeanningros, with several thousand French legionnaires and Mexican auxiliary troops, threateningly encountered Shelby outside Monterrey. Acting for Shelby, Generals Hindman and Price called on Jeanningros. They were older men, and it was believed they might best explain the reasons for their march. Straightaway the Frenchman, his sharp eyes and prying nose pointed at them, made one thing clear: He would not permit further fraternization of any kind with the *Juaristas;* Jeanningros had obviously heard of Shelby's sale of arms to his enemies. After completing his conference with Shelby's emissaries, the French general began to maneuver his cannon and soldiers into an encircling arc around Shelby's meager forces.

This was hardly the welcome Shelby had expected from an important representative of Maximilian. Obviously Seward's dispatches to Paris were having more than a casual effect on French military conduct in Mexico. Jeanningros had been warned by his superiors to show the escaping Confederates no courtesies. In fact, he was to discourage them from proceeding farther. After all, these refugees bore a great resentment against the Union government to the North and had entered Mexico in defiance of it. By encouraging men who were hostile to Washington to settle in Mexico, Maximilian and the French were certain to incur the wrath of the United States. Maximilian and the French wanted, instead, friendship with the Union.

When Shelby's two colleagues returned to camp after their interview with Jeanningros, the young general was angered. He drew his dwindled Iron Brigade up closer to Monterrey and drafted a sharp memorandum to Jeanningros (translated into French by a member of his party). In this document he explained that he and his men, penniless and homeless, had been forced to sell the bulk of their ammunition and weapons to the *liberales* to survive. But he made it clear that if he were not allowed to proceed, he had no alternative but to attack with what weapons remained—even though he had a number of sick and wounded. "Shall it be peace or war between us?" Shelby asked the startled Frenchman. This note he sent to Jeanningros under a white flag of truce. Had Jeanningros refused him permission to continue inland, Shelby intended to organize an outright assault.

Jeanningros responded unexpectedly. He received Shelby's explanation of his predicament with military correctness—and also with unusual sympathy. He returned a note of his own, inviting Shelby to a personal conference at his headquarters within Monterrey. This meeting was a sympathetic one. Himself a man of iron discipline, Jeanningros liked what he heard about Shelby's regrouping his forces after the recent Juárist ambush at the Salinas and congratulated him upon his soldierly courage. After they had quaffed a number of draughts of absinthe together, Jeanningros gave Shelby and his officers a banquet and then allowed them to move on, commenting that Shelby was the only foreign general who had ever entered his lines. The Frenchman honored a pledge made him by Shelby to join the forces of Maximilian upon arrival at Mexico City. After several days in Monterrey, Shelby next marched to Saltillo, camping near the old Mexican War battlefield at Buena Vista where Zachary Taylor had made the reputation that took him to the White House.

But Shelby wanted it known that he was not trying to emulate Taylor or any other invader, that he was a refugee, not a conqueror. Yet Shelby's men were in part cast in the role of liberators on at least one occasion. Five days from Parras two of them, James Wood and Yandell Blackwell, picked up a tale about a beautiful young American girl who was being held as "a slave in the harem of a Spanish *hacendado*," Luis Enrico Rodríguez, who owned the hacienda Encarnación. This was Inez Walker, daughter of a California goldseeker and an Indian mother. Wood and Blackwell, who carefully concealed their intentions from General Shelby, determined to liberate the lass from her master. They gathered together twenty comrades and launched an attack upon the hacienda one night during a heavy storm. After occupying Encarnación's stables, they used a log as a battering ram and broke down the main door of the manor house. "One by one, the *hacendado*, Rodríguez, and his retainers were killed in the hand-to-hand fighting, and when Shelby arrived the place was a shambles." At first Shelby swore that every man involved in this episode would be executed. But after Wood explained the plight of Inez Walker, "her wishes were accepted as commands," according to a fulsome admirer of Shelby. Actually Mexico seems to have been her home. The woman joined the expedition, in what capacity this adherent does not specify.[13]

[13] George Creel, *Rebel at Large*, 30. The event is also mentioned in Edwards' two books on Shelby but is overdramatized.

Near Parras de la Fuente, a day's march southwest of Saltillo, about August 7, 1865, Shelby encountered Colonel Depreuil, the local French commander, who demanded an explanation of his presence in the country. Obviously Depreuil had not been in touch with Jeanningros. When Colonel Depreuil, furious and insulting and "far gone in liquor," began to curse Shelby and his men as "murderers and robbers," the General stated: "I imagined that when an American soldier called upon a French soldier, he was visiting a gentleman. I am mistaken, it seems. At least I can keep my hands clean, and I wash them of you because you are a slanderer and a coward." Creel claims that a duel was about to be fought when Depreuil shouted, "Off with your hat!" to Shelby and the General answered coldly, "Only to beauty and to God. . . . To a coward, never!" Shelby "already wounded in his right arm," was unable to handle a sword at this point, but Depreuil agreed to pistols. Then General Jeanningros arrived and forced Depreuil to apologize to Shelby, a duel being only narrowly averted.

Shelby headed farther south, and a few days later reached the outskirts of a larger Mexican city, San Luis Potosí. There General Felix C. Douay, another French commander who had not heard of Shelby's encounter with Jeanningros, sent the Southerner still one more tart message, demanding to know what Shelby's objective was in Mexico. Douay believed Shelby's men to be bushwhackers who might join the *Juaristas*. Indeed, by this time they looked the part. Their faces were burned hard by the sun and they wore long, straggly beards; their boots were full of dust and covered by a frosting of caked mud; and their clothes were badly torn by the sagebrush and cactus. Nonetheless, after one of Shelby's officers told Douay that—with the assistance of Shelby—the French might recruit as many as fifty thousand escapees for the imperial army, the French general endorsed Jeanningros' authorization for the Americans to proceed inland. He also made contact with Marshal François Bazaine, chief of staff of the French Army in Mexico, who sent an order allowing Shelby to move on to the capital. There occurred one further bit of French courtesy. According to George Creel, "Marshal Bazaine, appreciating their straits, generously dipped into his military chest and gave each man fifty dollars."[14]

[14] *Ibid.*, 32.

❦

CHAPTER VII

La Ciudad

AFTER SIX WEEKS of travel through the rock-strewn brushlands of northern Mexico, Shelby's men gave thanks for the cooler breezes and greener vegetation of the Mexican highlands. The climb left them short of breath, as few of the men were used to the higher elevation.

Finally, in mid-August of 1865, the hero of the Iron Brigade led his bedraggled party into Mexico City. *La Ciudad*, as it was called by Mexicans, seemed to sparkle, and the church bells welcomed the Americans as they marched along the tree-lined Alameda on that late-summer Sunday morning.

Nestled more than eight thousand feet above sea level, Mexico City, with its view of the snow-topped volcanoes, Popocatepetl ("Popo") and Iztaccihuatl ("the Sleeping Woman"), seemed remote from the violence and confusion farther north.

The people who strolled along the *Zócalo* looked with dismay upon the remnants of Shelby's armed column as they led their half-shod weary mules and horses down the city's *avenidas* in the direction of the government offices of Maximilian's regime. Crowds of such persons followed the little procession, craning their necks and grinning at the strangers. As the cathedral's bells tolled their call to mass, the tired and hungry foreigners may have been struck by the serenity of the Mexicans.

This composure obviously did not come of economic well-being. Most of those whom Shelby's men passed on the *paseos* wore no shoes. Their feet were as tough and gnarled as the bark of an old tree. They drew their rags closely about them, as if they might at any time fall off their bodies. Frequently they had no covering on their shoulders except dirty woolen serapes, and many appeared to be living on the edge of malnutrition. Like the Confederates, they were unkempt, but unlike them, they were at home. These were a stolid people who had not yet realized that their capital might become an armed camp.

Shelby's men also passed wealthier persons, members of *la gran sociedad*, who made their own way down the cobblestone streets in clanking and jogging carriages. Those men who rode by on horseback clad in silken finery, hats ornamented in gold, with embroidered velvet jackets, pantaloons adorned with silver buttons, and stamped-leather boots, and the women, with their black mantillas, gowns, earrings, and brooches, were separated by a wide gulf from the ragged *peones*. Yet both classes seemed proud of their metropolis and its way of life, and they stood apart from the Confederates in culture and outlook. The Confederates had much to learn about this city of Montezuma and of Cortés whose possession was being contested between Maximilian and Juárez.

Shelby inquired first about the location of the combined French-imperialist high command. The palace towards which he and his men were directed was a dilapidated, rambling two-story colonial edifice of dirty pink sandstone with a double doorway large enough for a coach to drive through. Two large iron gates protecting its doorways swung open as they approached it with their animals. The General and his men soon found themselves inside a large rectangular patio paved with uneven cobblestones and surrounded on all sides by several tiers of open corridors and balconies. These were supported by columns once whitewashed but now a greasy brown, the troops which had for decades used the building as a barracks having soiled the columns with their presence. The place had a smell of urine about it.

Under one of its portals, near a worn staircase leading up to the first balcony, was a long black table, lighted by an overhead oil-lamp chandelier, at which sat the commandant of the building

73

and of some adjoining barracks where the enlisted men in Shelby's own group later stayed. He eyed these foreigners with a suspicious air. Shelby produced his battered letters of authorization from Generals Jeanningros and Douay to enter Mexico City and asked to see the Emperor. The barracks commander promised to relay Shelby's documents to higher authority. The brigade was meanwhile given temporary shelter in the adjoining barracks of the Mexican and French army while Shelby and other high-ranking officers moved into several local hotels. They had finally reached their objective and now had only to be patient and await the interview with Maximilian.

The crucial audience with Maximilian took place on August 16, shortly after their arrival. It was held in "the far-famed halls of the Montezumas," as one of Shelby's associates called Chapultepec (the Aztec word for grasshopper) Palace. Maximilian and Carlotta had made this vine-covered hilltop castle their official residence even though the monarch drove daily into the National Palace, located at the *Zócalo* in the center of Mexico City. Chapultepec was magnificent. From their majesties' European castle, "Miramar," located on the Adriatic near Trieste, they had imported gilded chairs and tables, French tapestries, chandeliers, ottoman rugs, and damasks with which to line the walls. A sense of regality pervaded the place.

The Emperor kept Shelby and his associates waiting for a while on some cool marble benches located alongside the potted palms and jardinieres of ferns that lined the hallway leading to his study. Finally a guard opened one of the double doors at the far end of the long hall, and a French captain of cavalry, named Eduardo Pierrón, approached. Shelby and his aide, Major Edwards, removed their hats and followed the Captain inside to the private sitting room of the Emperor. Major Edwards described the Emperor as "nearly six feet high; his complexion fair; he wore side-whiskers; and his hair, which was light on top of his head, was parted in the middle. His features were refined, his eyes grey, and his form symmetrical."[1]

---

[1] The story of this interview is in Edwards, *Shelby and His Men.*

Maximilian knew some English, but it was the Empress, Carlotta, who acted as his spokesman and who assured Shelby of their majesties' sympathies over the misfortunes of the Confederates. She expressed the hope that they would find new homes and new friendships in Mexico. She and her husband wanted to be of help. To tender protection to exiles was in the best European tradition, she explained.

Shelby now learned why French officials in northern Mexico had acted so coolly towards him when they first met his party. Maximilian crisply told him that his group, *as an organized band,* was not welcome in Mexico. They might stay as individuals but not as soldiers. The Emperor hoped they would become farmers. He was willing to set aside land for them on which they might found agricultural colonies. He wished to give further thought to where they might most profitably be settled. Meanwhile, other Confederates would surely appear, and he wanted to learn the wishes of such later arrivals.

Shelby explained that he sought only asylum for his men, that he was already resigned to the breaking up of his command, if the Emperor had no further use for it as a military unit. But, if the Emperor so desired (according to George Creel), "Shelby laid down a plan to recruit forty thousand Americans against the time when the French soldiers would be withdrawn." He also pointed out to Maximilian that with the American Civil War over, the United States would enforce the Monroe Doctrine and that "France would have to get out of Mexico or fight."[2] Maximilian then terminated the interview with good wishes for the future. The tone of the meeting had been friendly but firm.

Shelby now realized he had no alternative but to disband his group. And at one last rally he did so. As he might have anticipated from hearing Gwin's story, the Emperor would never countenance an armed force in Mexico aside from his own troops and the French garrisons already there. Maximilian did not yet know the total number of Confederates in Mexico and feared establishment of colonies, similar to Gwin's proposed one, near the north-

[2] Creel, *Rebel at Large,* 31.

ern frontiers where opportunities for disaffection toward him would be stronger than farther south.

As the Confederates were not the first colonies welcomed to Mexico by Maximilian, they had to conform to the immigration pattern already established. Shelby could only guess how his soldiers would react to becoming colonists under this regime. A few of his recalcitrants, upon hearing that the Emperor did not want them as soldiers, slipped out of their quarters at Mexico City for Sonora, where they joined various Juárist chieftains in the north, an act which did not improve the position with Maximilian of the exiles remaining with Shelby. Certain of these rustic escapees had become so accustomed to a barracks-bag environment that civilian life, especially in Mexico, now became unthinkable. When the Paris high command notified the French Army in Mexico that scattered foreign enlistments would be permitted, provided no prominent personalities were engaged, some of Shelby's men enlisted with the French. Most of them were eager to join a counter-guerrilla organization under French Colonel Achille Dupon.[3]

These men were out to avenge the murder of Missouri's General Monroe M. Parsons, who, about the tenth of July, 1865, was killed at Toro, between Matamoros and Monterrey, with Confederate Colonels William Standish and William Conrow and three privates. Making their way toward Mexico City, they had been stripped naked and shot by assassins apparently in league with *Juaristas*. Their murders caused a high pitch of resentment among the Confederate exiles, and now their fellow countrymen meticulously sought out the culprits responsible. The *Mexican Times*, Mexico City's American newspaper, had complained bitterly: "General Parsons and his companions were not killed in a fight between Liberals and Imperialists. They were basely assassinated by a band of red-handed robbers . . . ."[4]

[3] He is sometimes mentioned as Colonel Charles Dupin. See Kathryn Abbey Hanna, "The Roles of the South in the French Intervention of Mexico," *Journal of Southern History*, Vol. XX (February, 1944), 17.

[4] Standish seems to have been Parson's assistant adjutant while Conrow was

Eighty-two of Shelby's restless men quickly moved to avenge the murders by massacring twenty-six Juárists suspected of the killings. The Juárists were captured in the vicinity where Parsons had been found dead; the imperialists had been pleased to allow Shelby's avengers to travel northward in order to carry out their retribution. Such harshness, however, scarcely ingratiated the Confederates with Juárez' men in the future. In fact, it was almost unthinkable to return homeward toward the United States through Juárez' effective border barrier. Furthermore, few Confederates yet wanted to return to the South.

Therefore, some of Shelby's avengers made their way back to Mexico City. Now that they were firmly cut off from their homeland, Shelby had a hard time keeping his most untamable men in line during the month or more when they were supposed to remain at the capital. Many could not forget the smoke of battle, and some of the youngest, unable to settle down, thirsted for new excitement. More of them would have fought for Juárez had they been able to arrange to do so.

A handful of Shelby's young stragglers obtained from Marshal Bazaine permission to march to the Pacific slope of Mexico, possibly to embark for the Orient; they disappeared from sight in and around Guaymas and Mazatlán. Others left Mexico City to hunt gold northwest of San Luis Potosí, while some slinked off for California, the Sandwich Islands, British Honduras, Brazil, and even Japan. Writes Major Edwards, "Perhaps fifty took service in the Third Zouaves," a crack African regiment operating with the French in Mexico that saluted its officers without the required French tradition of doffing the hat. Doffing the hat was definitely onerous for a Confederate exile. Thus, hats proudly on their heads, few Rebs marched back to the French garrison at Monterrey.[5]

a former member of the Confederate Congress. See *MT*, October 15 and November 4, 1865.

[5] French Captain Eduardo Pierron, secretary to the Emperor Maximilian, supervised the departure of a few Confederates to Monterrey, according to Edwards, *Shelby's Expedition*, 96–97. For mention of a party of sixty-five former soldiers of Shelby's who went to the Pacific Coast and Mazatlán under a Colonel

Shelby, especially after his interview with Maximilian, hardly favored the departure from *La Ciudad* of his youngest and strongest men. Rather than see them join other disparate military units, in war-torn Mexico, he advised them in fatherly fashion to await a place in one of Maximilian's projected agricultural colonies. But most exiles found it hard to loiter around Mexico City waiting for a strange emperor to determine their future. Not all the members of the former Iron Brigade took the General's advice. Some of the more reckless ones never returned to the United States at all. These were already lying in hastily dug Mexican graves.

Elliott, see Box, "End of the War," *Confederate Veteran*, Vol. II (March, 1903), 122.

❦

CHAPTER VIII

The Hotspurs Forgather

OF THE MEN IN GRAY who followed Shelby into Mexico, the record of most has been lost. We can only imagine their experiences —the thirst and fatigue, the ever present danger of banditry, and the making and breaking of camp amid the dark of night in a strange, forbidding land.

As he whipped up the mules drawing his old army ambulance toward Mexico City, Tennessee's former governor, Isham G. Harris, could not forget how hard it had been for him to leave home. Harris was still sought by the radical government of "Fighting Parson" William Gannaway Brownlow, notorious Reconstruction governor of his state. General Richard Taylor, Harris' wartime commander, knowing that he was a personal enemy of Andrew Johnson, had "urged him to leave the country for a time, and offered to aid him in crossing the Mississippi River." Harris had been "very unwilling to go," according to Taylor.[1] During the month of May, 1865, Harris and General B. H. Lyon of Kentucky, with two servants, had made their way, largely under cover of darkness, through the canebrakes and backwoods of Arkansas and Louisiana. After the capture of Jefferson Davis, Sheridan's net of military power drew tighter. The small group used a frail bark which they kept hidden from Federal authorities who were taking over large sections of the country through which they traveled. They poled this boat through the bayous and stagnant back-

[1] Taylor, *Destruction and Reconstruction*, 273.

woods escape routes into the lower South. When they reached Shreveport, Harris' party was able to rest only a few days. At Shreveport they surreptitiously bought horses from Confederate sympathizers and pressed on toward Texas.

The former governor reached the Red River country, to which he had taken the precaution of sending some of his Negro slaves and plantation stock. At San Antonio he learned of Shelby's plan to cross the Río Grande. On June 15, 1865, Harris and his small party, equipped with baggage and cooking utensils strapped on pack mules, set out to overtake Shelby. At Monterrey, Harris ran across a heavily armed party of about twenty haggard Missourians, who had entered Mexico before Shelby, and combined forces with them for the journey to Mexico City.

It is ironic that Shelby himself—though he had been the first to announce his desire to enter Mexico, was at the very heart of the movement to do so, and led the largest of all the Confederate parties that entered Mexico—did not cross the Río Grande until July 4, days and even weeks after other Confederates such as Harris, Terrell, and Kirby-Smith.

By the time he arrived in Monterrey, Harris was exhausted after fifteen hundred miles of almost continuous horseback riding. His bad humor was relieved, however, when he celebrated the Fourth of July regally with old friends who had recently arrived in Monterrey. Not since the Mexican War had the place seen so many Americans. Monterrey's newspaper *La Gaceta* reported that by the end of July, 1865, an estimated four thousand Confederate refugees had reached that city and that only slightly less than that number were at the border, planning to enter Mexico.[2] An exquisite banquet and the fine wines consumed during that Fourth of July evening cost three hundred dollars and were paid for in Confederate gold brought to Monterrey by General Magruder—the dashing "Prince John" of the

---

[2] Hanna and Hanna. "The Immigration Movement," *Hispanic American Historical Review*, Vol. XXVIII (May, 1947), 234, who cite this journal, estimate that only about one thousand Confederates migrated to Mexico from 1865–67. Their figures may be low, just as four thousand may be too high.

Commodore Matthew Fontaine Maury, C.S.N., after his return
from exile in Mexico and England.
From *The Journal of American History*, Vol. IV (1910).

Sketch of Governor Henry Watkins Allen of Louisiana,
by Harry Coughlin.

Courtesy Clayton Rand

Confederacy—who distributed small sums of money among those assembled there. Magruder loved pomp and ceremony, and during the ensuing celebration he proposed that toasts be drunk to "The Lost Cause, to Lee, Jackson, and to the Sovereignty of the States."

Afterwards Harris exchanged his saddle horse, harness, spurs, and bandelier for an animal-drawn Confederate ambulance to which he hitched his mules. He then handed the reins over to a Negro servant and reclined within the wagon, with a newly purchased dictionary in hand, to study the Spanish language. As his noisy contraption jogged and clanked along the deeply rutted roads, Harris repeated over and over to himself the mellifluous language he would soon be using to earn his living in a new land.

The journey from Monterrey to Mexico City was made in segments of only about twenty-five miles a day. Harris later called this trip "one of the longest, most laborious, and hazardous of my life." The extreme contrast between the heat of the day and the cold of night proved particularly bothersome. In the daytime a man's clothes seemed too warm; at night it was necessary to wrap blankets around one another's heads to keep from freezing.[3]

General Alexander Watkins Terrell had an even more spectacular story. In later years he loved to regale friends with his account of how, after receiving his letter of introduction to Maximilian from Texas' Governor Murrah, he formed at Austin, Texas, a small group of escapees (including Generals William P. Hardeman and Clay King, as well as Colonels George Flournoy, M. T. Johnson, and Peter Smith) which, about June 25, 1865,[4] headed toward Mexico on horseback with a few mules as pack animals.

They avoided the main roads in order to escape attention, and their trip was accordingly a less easy one. In Texas they were pursued by Federal soldiers and later, in Mexico, by rebel guerrillas. When the party reached the Nueces River, which crosses

---

[3] The record of Isham G. Harris' adventures is from 39 Cong., 1 sess., *House Exec. Doc. No. 1,* 528–29.

[4] This and other dates used in this and the following chapter are not fully verifiable approximations, inserted in order to achieve chronological continuity.

southern Texas, they found it swollen by recent rains and nearly out of its banks. After swimming the river several times to make their lariats fast across it, they quickly constructed a haphazard log raft with which to ferry across their provisions and camp equipment. Two members of the group who could not swim operated this raft. After their last crossing, the group abandoned their contraption and again took to their horses. As they galloped southward they heard Federal cavalrymen everywhere around them and through fieldglasses saw soldiers trying to catch wild horses less than a mile from the border.

Finally the party reached the Río Grande, their last barrier to freedom. Because Federal troops were already patrolling that river to prevent Confederates from escaping, Terrell's men drove their mounts at full speed along its banks while looking frantically for a suitable crossing. About every thirty minutes, however, the party had to rest their panting animals, stopping to remove saddles and blankets before remounting. Without such stops the lathered horses would have collapsed.

Eventually they found a crossing (Alamo Crossing, about two miles from Roma, Texas) and spied a small craft, formerly used as a ferry, on the Mexican side, onto which they could load as many as four horses and mules at a time. At that season of the year the river was full and its waters almost ice-cold. It had been a raw and windy season, and even in June the river was enveloped by a damp, chilling fog. Because they did not want the horses to cramp in the water, Terrell and his men undressed and swam across, retrieved the boat, and took it to the Texas side. Just as the stark-naked men started to load their horses on the boat, two half-drunken Mexicans, full of *mescal* and fresh from carousing at a local fandango, or dance, appeared on the banks of the river and excitedly reported that Union troops were pursuing them. Terrell's party obviously had no time to spare. As he and his men, after several frantic boat trips, got their last mule to Mexican soil, the Federals fired a series of volleys across the river. No one was wounded, and the Confederates fled.

The danger was not over. After they had ridden into Mexico

only a few miles, Terrell's party stopped to rest. Almost immediately they were surrounded, in a movement that was threatening though not overtly violent, by twenty or thirty fierce troops. These new adversaries were members of General Juan Nepomuceno Cortina's guerrilla band, who had spent the night at the fandango near the ferry crossing. This "rough looking set of scoundrels," Terrell said, was "hardly to be trusted." Their commander, the "Red Robber of the Río Grande," headed most of the "liberal" forces along the border between Mexico and Texas. Cortina's *renegados,* or hoodlums, had murdered General Parsons and his party, the massacre which Shelby's troops avenged. Cortina, like his rival *jefe político* Santiago Vidaurri, was a powerful frontier chieftain, whose loyalties vacillated like a weather vane in a windstorm. Eventually the notorious guerrilla teamed up with a group of Negro deserters from above the Río Grande and pillaged the former Confederate supply center at Bagdad.[5]

Cortina has been called by Texas historian J. Frank Dobie "the most daring as well as the most elusive Mexican bandit . . . that ever wet his horse in the muddy waters of the Río Grande." At a time when Mexico's northern frontier was in a state of confusion, her countryside swarmed with *jefes de guerrilla* of Cortina's type who harassed any and all travelers. Such *jefes* usually assumed power after a long series of political battles during which they won the leadership of several hundred men; they were then in a position to treat with either side in future power struggles. Eventually they might find a proper bidder to whom they could be persuaded to sell out their position. Once a Cortina or a Vidaurri did sell out, he assumed the honorary title of colonel or general and became respectable, either at the capital city or in the provinces.

After surrounding Terrell's party the Mexicans gave them green corn for their horses, but the Confederates remained cautious. Terrell ordered his companions to feed their animals in a circle with their heads out; every man stood near his bridle in readiness to attempt escape. Each of the Confederates was armed

[5] On the Bagdad raid see *MT,* March 24, 1866.

with a rifle and two six-shooters; this armament attracted the attention of the brigands, who lived by the use of such weapons and saw a chance to reap a harvest of arms. The Mexicans nudged steadily closer about Terrell's circle of horses and men and then tried to finger their guns. Refused the privilege, they requested surrender of Terrell's weapons. But the Americans had an answer ready. Terrell told the Mexicans that his men would gladly deliver their arms to the commander of the nearest town plaza if such a duly constituted official were to order them to do so. Cortina's men, anticipating an armed duel if they tried to disarm the Confederates, grudgingly agreed—and then dispatched several of their number into the nearest settlement to stir up trouble.

This small, bedraggled town, called Mier, was at the head of navigation of the Río Grande about three miles above where the Río Alamo flows into that river. During the long period when Texas had fought bitterly for its independence from Mexico, Mier had been celebrated for the fury of its fighters. On Christmas Day of 1842, a foolhardy band of Texans who had invaded Mexico during the "Mier Expedition" were chained, whipped, and shot there with no show of mercy. Now at this very spot Cortina's renegades spread word that Terrell and his men had butchered innocent Mexicans and ravished their women in several border settlements shortly before their arrival in Mier. If Cortina's men could not directly control Terrell by physical force, they determined to do so by influencing the local *alcalde,* or mayor. When they entered Mier, the Confederates found their situation desperate. As the General later wrote, "When we arrived at a high hill overlooking the town we heard the town bell ringing, and saw people running wildly about the streets, while a troop of Mexicans dressed in green uniforms were parading on the plaza."

Furthermore, a menacing crowd of angry civilians pressed in closely upon the gringos, moving them by physical force down the street to the local *calabozo,* a slimy-looking hovel of a jail whose white calcimine exterior was peeling off the adobe walls beneath it. Mob feeling was on the point of incarcerating Terrell and his men—an action that would, incidentally, have been quite legal, because of a regulation prohibiting armed foreigners from entering Mexico. Then Terrell had a stroke of good fortune. He chanced to look out across the town plaza over the hostile crowd of faces that surrounded his party and saw a man "coming up the hill at a gallop." In an instant he recognized the fellow. Terrell later wrote that this *hombre,* one Narciso Leal, "threw himself in true Mexican style on my bosom, calling me his 'amigo.' " He was a Mexican interpreter who had worked for him at San Antonio, where Terrell had been a judge before the war. Although the Confederate had already been ordered to surrender his arms, this Mexican, acting now more as a friend than as Terrell's interpreter, earnestly explained to the town's *alcalde* that the *Americanos* were upstanding gentlemen who had come as voluntary exiles to claim the hospitality of the "magnanimous Mexican nation." After the newcomer swore that Terrell's group bore arms only in self-defense and denied the rumors spread by Cortina's men, the Confederates were allowed to rest—but not before depositing rifles, knives, pistols, and other weapons under lock and key in the mayor's office.

Terrell had escaped outright imprisonment, but he was aware that he and his men were undergoing a form of more polite incarceration. They were housed in the local barracks for the night. Considering how he might get his weapons back, Terrell could not sleep though the night was warm and quiet. To use his own words, he lay thinking that this was "a town where the very name of Texan had long been more execrated than anywhere else in Mexico." Close Texan friends had been massacred in the very stone building where Terrell's party was lodged after their guns were taken from them. As these thoughts raced through his mind, Terrell continued to fear the arrival of Cortina himself, which would surely lead to permanent confiscation of both horses and arms, if not the execution of his party before a firing squad. Finally Terrell could stand the anxiety no longer.

Although his men had already ridden more than one hundred miles in a day and a night, he decided they must try to escape as quickly as possible. After midnight he shook them one by one out of their blankets where they had fallen asleep on the damp dirt floor, their heads pillowed on their saddles. After considerable grumbling, Terrell's men silently crept outside on all fours. They could see the long empty street, white by moonlight, spread out before them. It pointed the way toward freedom. A bell tower stood etched against the tops of the brown trees, and a gentle wind swept the sky clean except for a few specks of dust in the air. Stealthily they advanced on the mayor's office. Breaking into the city hall, where their weapons had been deposited, they quickly repossessed pistols and knives. After bribing several nocturnal Mexican loiterers with some double-eagle gold pieces, they recovered their horses and hastily obtained food. Being careful to avoid the town streets, they escaped by riding up the steep but sandy bank of a nearby arroyo which opened onto the unbroken deserts to the south.

As they galloped through the sage toward still uncertain safety, Terrell's men experienced a pardonable fear of being recaptured, either by Cortina's forces or by those of Mier's *alcalde*. Only after they had ridden steadily into the wind for several hours could they be sure that they had not been betrayed by the persons whom they had bribed. After leading his horsemen onward for some hours, Terrell finally held up his hand and slowed the small column to a walk. As they stopped to breakfast on roasted rabbit meat, the light set stirring the sounds of early morning. Their escape had been successful.

Now the countryside began to take on a hint of green. The next night they made camp in a fold of hills dotted with scrub oaks that murmured in the windy dark. A few days later, much to their relief, the heavily bearded party reached Monterrey.[6]

When the various groups of Confederate exiles finally arrived at Mexico City, they, like Shelby, found that they had to wait until Maximilian decided what to do about their presence in Mexico. Scores of such former Confederates had arrived on horseback and by every stagecoach from the north. They passed the time

[6] Terrell, *From Texas to Mexico*, 8–18, contains his original account of the trip from Texas to Monterrey on which this section is based.

in the smoke-filled rooms of the Hotel Iturbide, Confederate headquarters at the capital. This was the former residence of General Augustín de Iturbide, who had once proclaimed himself emperor of Mexico; it was so large that a diligence could be driven through its huge brass double doors. The ornate, velvet-covered chairs in its gilded lobby were now occupied by Americans—some still clad in Confederate gray—who for hours on end read or talked about the roads they had traveled, the highwaymen they had encountered, the campaigns they had experienced, or listened to Colonel Slayback burst into rhyme about the hegira to Mexico, which reminded him of the march of Xenophon's ten thousand.

The exiles also worked steadfastly to persuade Maximilian to award them land tracts. But the Emperor wanted to take ample time to decide the matter. After Maximilian received first one and then another of them, the Confederates felt they were making headway. They found themselves invited to such court functions as a memorial service for King Leopold of Belgium, Carlotta's father, and to teas, receptions, and musical affairs sponsored by Maximilian and Carlotta.

Nevertheless, this enforced period of exile was not only costly but frustrating. As their hotel bills mounted, the Confederates became increasingly anxious to settle down either in an agricultural colony or in a business. Where their great adventure would lead them was a question to which all wanted a quick answer.

While they awaited an answer, some took to the fleshpots of Mexico City. Some danced the fandango or gambled at monte each night by the light of smoke-filled bistros teeming with *señoritas* anxious to be bought. Flushed with drink, they boisterously accompanied these women home through streets flooded by moonlight. Lingering for a moment in a doorway, some young Confederate quietly removed the *rebosa,* or all-encompassing shawl, which his lady friend wore around her shoulders. In addition to arousing the enmity of jealous lovers, the exiles depleted precious financial reserves.

By arrangement with the government of Maximilian, General

Shelby shipped some men off from Mexico City for a few days' work in the sun in order to rehabilitate their slender purses and sagging spirits. But the younger men would inevitably bolt the supervision of Mexican overseers and head back into the capital to seek further excitement.

A Confederate who felt more at home in Mexico than the others was General Magruder, who had fought there with Stonewall Jackson twenty years before, during the Mexican War. On this second visit Magruder was determined to make Mexico his new home. Settling down in Mexico City, he became one of the most articulate Confederates and was even able to influence the Emperor's taste for clothes. Magruder was once considered, especially when he wore full regimentals, perhaps the handsomest officer in the Confederacy. Mutton chops and all, here was a man who knew both how to write love songs and how to love women. He was bound to make a good adjustment to Mexico. As commander of the Peninsula Campaign before Richmond, he had earned a reputation as a scrappy fighter. Later in the war he had swept down upon Galveston, Texas, and with only a few fieldpieces, which he lined up along its wharves, boldly attacked a heavily armed Union naval squadron and two river steamers and recaptured the town for the Confederacy. Later Magruder had, however, been "exiled" by General Lee to the Trans-Mississippi Department, where he relieved General John G. Walker of his command over troops in Texas, New Mexico, and Arizona. From their headquarters in Houston both men had gone to Mexico. But all this was in the past.

Magruder's fellow exiles appreciated the boost in morale which his presence gave them. "Prince John," as he was called, was still a dapper general with bushy sideburns, dressed in "a cutaway suit of salt-and-pepper color, with a tall dove-colored hat, and patent leather boots." Magruder suggested that his fellow exiles invest in similar wardrobes if they wanted to be noticed by the Emperor. Terrell and his friends had to confess that this was good advice, especially when they "saw the Emperor Maximilian dressed exactly as General Magruder was." Magruder stayed on in Mexico

City to help the Emperor with immigration problems while Terrell, Harris, and others were entrusted with the job of actually settling the Confederates on the land assigned to them.[7]

On September 5, 1865, Maximilian finally issued the long-desired land decree. This edict officially rededicated Mexico to a still larger immigration and colonization program. The Confederates were authorized to move eastward from Mexico City to the region surrounding Vera Cruz, where several Confederate colonies were to be set up. Maximilian assigned a tract of 500,000 acres of land for this purpose. Years before, Juárez had confiscated this land from the church, which had itself taken it from earlier owners. Now, much to the surprise of the clergy, the supposedly pro-clerical Maximilian confirmed Juárez' earlier confiscation decree and set the abandoned tract of land aside for those American settlers who wished to farm it.

A list of regulations pertaining particularly to the Confederates was prepared by Harris, Price, Perkins, and other leaders at the request of Maximilian. The fact that they were given an opportunity to help plan for their future made them feel the imperial government wanted them as permanent settlers. The *Diario del Imperio,* Maximilian's government journal, reassured the Confederates of his friendship toward all foreigners in its edition of September 19, 1865.

> Suplicamos en consequencia a nuestros amigos que han venido a Mexico con l'intención de buscar aquí un hogar, que esperen con paciencia el resultado de los trabajos de estos señores, asegurádoles que las miras del gobierno son altamente generosas, y que dentro de poco tiempo verán ampliamente recompensadas las privaciones a que muchos de ellos estan hoy sometidos.[8]

Roughly translated, this told the Confederates that they should be patient as the government sought to help them create new homes and a future in Mexico. Maximilian wanted to assure

---

[7] *Ibid.,* 45; Richard B. Harwell (ed.), *The Confederate Reader,* 184; O'Flaherty, *General Jo Shelby,* 284–85, 287, 293, 309.

[8] In its issue of November 3, 1865, Maximilian's *Diario del Imperio* published his land decree in full.

them that his intentions were most generous and that after a short period of privation their efforts would be crowned with success.

As they journeyed from Mexico City to the new land colonies, Harris, Shelby, Perkins, and Terrell were reunited with many old Southern friends, including Commodore Matthew Fontaine Maury, General Sterling Price, the two former governors of Louisiana, Henry Watkins Allen and Thomas O. Moore, and Governor Pendleton Murrah and Edward Clark of Texas.

The principal refuge to which the Confederates were heading they decided to name after Maximilian's consort, hispanicizing her name. The exiles felt Carlotta to be their best champion. They sensed that the Empress, as a fellow exile, had a special warmth for them. She, too, knew what it was to be far from home. In Mexico, especially, Carlotta seemed secluded and lonely. Both she and Maximilian seemed almost to crave the affection of their subjects.[9]

Maximilian traveled into various parts of the country, ostensibly to observe local conditions. Of his interest in the plight of the Mexican *peones,* there can be no doubt. He announced a program calling for the "regeneration of Mexico." He also did much to improve the capital city and busied himself daily with new plans for its renovation. The *Paseo de la Reforma* (to use the name a later ruler bestowed), leading out from the castle at Chapultepec toward Cuernavaca, was planned by Maximilian and was acclaimed a monument to his taste and public spirit. But it was a road that took him away from Carlotta. While the picture of the royal household given out to the public was one of total devotion to the Empress by her Max, there were indications that all was not well with their marriage. Rumors kept recurring that the Emperor maintained a secret love at his Cuernavaca retreat, the enchantingly beautiful Borda Gardens.

---

[9] Dressed sometimes in native costume, the young emperor and empress enjoyed the semblance of popularity afforded them by the groups of people along the streets of the capital who sometimes cheered them as they passed down the streets.

There was a suggestion of despair about "Our Carlotta," as some Confederates called her. Terrell claimed that she nodded gently whenever she caught sight of one of the Confederates through the window of her jogging wooden carriage with its familiar leather side curtains. The exiles believed the Empress was trying to let them know that she could tell they were not native Mexicans. Perhaps her poor disordered and diseased mind was already beginning to give way under her troubles.

The new community of Carlota was only a few miles off the imperial highway from Vera Cruz to Mexico City, then completed as far as Paso del Macho, about ten miles away from the main Confederate settlements, Carlota itself was some seventy miles west of the port of Vera Cruz, near the present town of Paraje Nuevo.

The road leading east into the Carlota region drops down for almost ten thousand feet through the oaks and pines into a zone of palms, ferns, and banana trees. To reach it one travels downward out of the cool, wild mountains of Mexico's heartland into a tropical belt flanked by the blue horizon of the Carribean.

Almost incessant Gulf rains beat down upon the exiles as their carts and animals rumbled along the winding roads toward the Mexican tidewater. The *tierra caliente* did not always jibe with the effusive travel literature about Mexico which many of them had been reading. The mosquitoes were thick and, because of the humidity, breathing difficult. In these half-million acres of well-watered cotton, sugar, and coffee land, the Confederates hoped to build a little South—a cluster of towns, quite apart from rude Mexican settlements nearby, to be modeled after their ideal of gracious agrarian life.

❦

CHAPTER IX

Carlota, Queen of the Confederate Colonies

WE DO NOT HAVE A FULL PICTURE of the Confederate colonies in Mexico, mainly because virtually nothing is left of them. The largest, most representative, and most important was Carlota. The town was built partly in the valley of Aconcinga on the ruins of an old Mexican village and partly on land hewn out of the jungle at the order of Maximilian. The town founders hoped that Confederate hotelkeepers, druggists, carpenters, blacksmiths, and bakers would flock there to build a beautiful city. Instead, ugly half-built blocks, too often consisting of shabby clapboard rooming houses, crumbling adobe offices, and ramshackle shops, arose everywhere out of the slimy, vine-infested surroundings. Crisscrossed by red dirt roads that exuded mud in April and dust in July, "downtown" Carlota never lost its air of impermanence. Heavy clouds bulging with unspilled rain seemed perpetually to hover menacingly over the town and its swampy hinterland.

Upon his arrival, Harris became *alcalde*, or mayor. In order not to confuse prospective immigrants, the colonists introduced an approximation of the American land system. A man with a family was allotted 640 acres, for which he paid one dollar an acre. Those without families were entitled to 320 acres at the same price. A town lot in Carlota usually was assigned each settler with the larger grant of rural land.[1]

[1] The best monographic account of the colony is Rister, "Carlota," *Journal of Southern History*, Vol. XI (February, 1945). In manuscript, the *Papeles*

The makeshift colony was quickly populated by a small number of people. If it was to succeed on a long-term basis, however, the town needed a steady flow of colonists from the States. But because of the expense of going to Mexico and the effectiveness of Sheridan's border patrol, this flow was never large. Some families eluded the barrier by sailing from New Orleans or Mobile to Havana, Cuba, and re-embarking at Havana for Vera Cruz. In a few cases Maximilian went so far as to offer poorer immigrants free passage by sea to Mexico and then a travel allowance of ten cents a league to the site selected for each family.

To attract large numbers of colonists, land prices should have remained cheap at Carlota and in the surrounding Confederate colonies, but they did not. From the start many thought prices too high and simply squatted upon or rented other lands. Some were gouged by fellow Confederates who bought tracts for pure speculation—an old American frontier practice. Only a limited number of 640-acre tracts, surveyed to sell at one dollar an acre, remained available. One could buy good land back in the States, particularly out west, for prices comparable to those charged at Carlota. Maximilian's original land prices were fair enough, but through speculation the land became ridiculously expensive. For a former Confederate soldier, who might have relatives partly dependent upon him back in the South, the inflated prices added to the high cost of clearing muddy jungle areas were an impossible responsibility to assume. Young couples in particular were unable to shoulder a financial burden of this sort, but many felt forced to do so because they had already sacrificed part of their earnings to reach Mexico.[2]

Various other small Confederate towns near Carlota were, if

del Imperio de Maximiliano, Archivo de la Nación, Mexico City, contain fragmentary material which I do not cite because of its eclectic nature.

[2] Land prices generally varied from plot to plot as did surveying costs. According to a letter at the Missouri Historical Society (St. Louis) from Thomas C. Reynolds to W. A. Broadwell, dated March 6, 1866, land surveying was estimated as costing from one-half to eight cents an acre. For land costs see Harmon, "Confederate Migrations to Mexico," *Hispanic American Historical Review,* Vol. XVII (November, 1937), 473.

anything, even less promising. At nearby Orizaba, General James E. Slaughter and Captain Herbert Price, General Price's son, started a steam sawmill, and General Hamilton P. Bee attempted to raise cotton. William Marshall Anderson, a visitor in 1865, estimated Orizaba's population at ten thousand and wrote: "The stores and private dwellings are nearly all of one story. The low walls, the iron grates of the windows, and the dull, rusty red of the tile-covered roofs make it look like an immense collection of private jails." At Orizaba and elsewhere native competition was severe, and foreigners, who tried to encourage more commercial and efficient methods of agriculture, were scarcely welcomed by competing Mexicans. Cordova and Omealco followed the building pattern of Carlota and remained makeshift orphan communities constructed on the remnants of earlier Mexican villages. Only occasionally did the other colonies provide more than basic shelter for their inhabitants. With all its defects, crude Carlota was in a sense the queen of the Confederate colonies.

An exception to the drabness in which the exiles lived was the largest hotel in Cordova—the Confederate. This ramshackle, two-story brick structure came to mean much to the immigrants. It was the only accessible social center within hundreds of miles, and the colonists met there to play cards or sip coffee. Patrons who sought escape from daily chores often engaged in gambling games in the hotel parlor. The proprietor, W. D. Johnson of Texas, organized dancing cotillions on Saturday nights. The scarcity of American women made it necessary for Southerners to escort heavily chaperoned young Mexican *señoritas,* who often grew tired of hearing about the empty life of some Confederate whose true love was back in Texas. Most men usually adjourned permanently to the gentleman's drawing room where they could smoke cigars, savor a quiet but expensive drink of imported Kentucky bourbon in an atmosphere clouded with smoke, or call for a julep at the ornate bar tended by one of Stonewall Jackson's mess boys. This was *the* place to exchange local gossip, to learn who had died or who was getting married back home, to swap disgusting details of the carpetbag onslaught on the South, to

94

damn the Radical Republicans and the Congress of the United States, or to argue interminably as to future lines of action.

All types of persons showed up at Carlota, including a Kentucky clergyman, the Reverend T. E. Holeman. According to William Marshall Anderson, "The Revd. Mr. Holeman of Frankfort . . . refused to marry a Yankee man and a Secesh gal." Because he had not taken an oath of allegiance to the Union back home, he "was informed on and expelled."[3] The arrival of this Southern minister to preach to the exile community at prayer meetings was most welcome. Because the Confederates did not insist upon pursuing occupations similar to their status in the South, the minister became only a part-time man of the cloth. Similarly, former Senator William Oldham of Texas, once chief justice of the Lone-Star State, was content to set up a business at Carlota as a photographer. Wives and sweethearts back home asked for pictures of their men and the land on which they had settled, and Senator Oldham filled their orders.

Some Confederates tried to work the soil, planting cotton, sugar cane, coffee, and field crops, much as they had done at home. At the same time they attempted to cling to traditions. They organized picnics, staged square dances and hay rides for the young, and sewing bees and literary circles for the ladies. Some even imported their own pianos and tried to encourage group singing. A few envisioned a transplanted Southern homeland yielding such secondary crops as rice, corn, pineapples, melons, and bananas—an economy so rich that it would eventually boast schools, conservatories, colleges, and their own newspapers.

The exiles counted heavily on growing and exporting coffee. As it would take three years to bring a coffee crop to maturity, they waited out that long period by cultivating sweet potatoes, corn, and beans, and by distilling cane juice into a passably explosive beverage. It proved hard to farm a region so overgrown with vegetation. Jungles, gnarled with bamboos, banana trees, and white-blossoming coffee bushes, were everywhere. Today,

[3] "Letter Regarding Colonization," 39 Cong., 1 sess., *House Exec. Doc. No. 1*, 531–35. *MT*, February 3, 1866.

Mexico's camellias, azaleas, gardenias, orchids, and gladiolas are flown to large cities of the Western Hemisphere, but no such markets then existed. The exiles could not live on the scent of flowers. They fortunately exploited fields of pineapples, papayas, and mangoes that already grew between the ruins of former haciendas. More familiar fruits, such as oranges, figs, and bananas, also came from the groves of previous tenants. But these were hardly staples. The colonists craved meat, rice, beans, and flour.

Maximilian wanted the Confederates to be responsible for operating their own colonies; he sought their co-operation as civilians in helping to combat widespread native disorders. As donor of their lands, he counted on them to help stamp out native unrest on their own plantations. Although they were nominally exempt from military service, the colonists were to help subdue the country in which they settled, and for this purpose Maximilian planned to build a series of small blockhouses and forts along the proposed railroad line from Mexico City to Vera Cruz.

He had hoped to reconcile the various factions (church, army, and *peones*) and to consolidate them in one imperial party, but he found all three factions drawing off from him one by one. As revolutionary feeling grew, he was forced to rely increasingly on the detested French army, thereby drawing upon himself even further hatred from the people of Mexico. The Confederate colonies faced an ever-increasing danger of harassment by the natives, and Maximilian could offer them little actual protection.

As a personal courtesy to Shelby, Maximilian's government allowed him to pre-empt a superb hacienda two miles from Cordova. He paid a modest sum for this expropriated acreage, as did other colonists to whom the government assigned such lands. The tile-roof hacienda, flecked with red poinsettias, had belonged to the notorious Mexican politician, General Antonio López de Santa Anna (then in exile). It stood amidst tropical vegetation at an elevation of only about one thousand feet.

The owners of such plantations might normally have been pleased to place their management in the hands of experienced planters. But Maximilian's government usually assigned such properties against an owner's will. The New York *Herald* of April 19, 1866, reported that there were about a dozen old haciendas, although run-down, available to the Carlota colonists because of expropriations by Maximilian. The improvements made on these plantations by previous owners sometimes ran into hundreds of thousands of dollars.

To his new plantation Shelby brought his wife and their two boys, Joseph and Orville, early in October. According to the *Mexican Times* of October 14, 1865, Mrs. Shelby and her sons had been living in Lexington, Kentucky. Somehow they had been able to sail from New Orleans to Vera Cruz. The General had not seen Bettie since 1861. Upon her arrival he found her considerably worn by her experiences. He was heartened beyond measure to be reunited with his family and to hear news of old friends in Waverly, St. Louis, and Lexington, the places where he had once lived and worked. To his wife's surprise, Shelby still did not have a gray hair in his head. Neither the war nor subsequent hardships had quashed his zest for life.[4]

Life at Cordova soon presented serious problems for Shelby, his family, and those former soldiers who settled nearby. By October, 1865, the General finished planting twelve acres of land in coffee only to have it looted by bandits who descended on the plantation while he was off visiting friends. The cagey Shelby quickly came home, held a conference with the leader of these bandits, and struck a bargain whereby the *hombre* became—for a confidential financial consideration—the guardian of his hacienda. He advised his former soldiers to make similar arrangements with the natives whose huts surrounded their small plots of land. In some cases these plots of land had been seized from their owners by the government on behalf of foreign colonists. The relationship between these natives and the new owners was bound to be difficult.

In the summer of 1865, Shelby joined a Major McMurtry in a freighting business which operated for a time out of Cordova,

---

[4] O'Flaherty, *General Jo Shelby*, 296. Bettie bore Shelby a third child in Mexico. They eventually had eight children.

using ten-mule wagon teams from Paso del Macho to Mexico City. The Mexican rail net extended only from Vera Cruz to Paso del Macho; Shelby's wagon line covered the remaining distance to Mexico City. Like his other enterprises, this business suffered from the confusion and violence then prevalent in Mexico. Shelby's freight line, however, did a thriving business supplying the French outposts. Thus Shelby became unmistakably identified with Maximilian's hated protectors. Strategically, as well as ideologically, this was a perilous position, for the French were perpetually under attack by the *Juaristas*. On one occasion, in February, 1866, Shelby, while engaged in freighting supplies for the French, was traveling northward from Mexico City with a handful of former Confederate soldiers and eight wagons full of army supplies. Suddenly his advance guard, under Captain James Kirtley, drew fire from behind some bushes off the road. A quick decision had to be made to keep the tiny contingent from being wiped out by Juárist guerrillas. Shelby scrambled for cover and characteristically decided to put up a defensive fight. After a short exchange of shots, Shelby, acknowledging the superior firepower of the *Juaristas,* ordered his men to give their horses full rein. His small fleeing group reached the French lines at San Luis Potosí only by firing with pistols over their shoulders.

At a later date, in March, 1866, while fighting the *Juaristas* near Cesnola, Shelby successfuly took part in the rescue of Colonel Depreuil, the French officer who had halted him at Parras the year before. Now Depreuil expressed his regret to Shelby "for the rude things said and done at Parras." But Shelby answered that the French colonel had had every right to question the purposes of himself and his suspicious-looking party.

Still later in 1866, from behind rudely constructed earthworks, and under clouds of smoke, Shelby, along with Confederates James Kirtley, Thomas Boswell, and George Hall, commanded the French evacuation of Cesnola. His greatest admirer, Edwards, commented that he did all this without "even so much as a red sash around him as insignia of rank or authority."[5]

[5] Edwards, *Shelby's Expedition,* 113; O'Flaherty, *General Jo Shelby,* 305.

98

Shelby was not fully clear in regard to his future course in Mexico, but there was one thing he was determined not to do: return to the United States. A letter of November 1, 1865, to a friend, Frank Lilly, back home, expresses the General's deep bitterness at those in the South who had stopped battling the Yankees in order to save their properties from destruction. Shelby, who had left his Missouri and Kentucky properties behind, could speak with fire on this subject:

> I am here as an exile; defeated by the acts of the southern people themselves. And why? Because they loved their "niggers," their estates, more than principle . . . . Let them reap what they deserved, *eternal disgrace*. D——n 'em, they were foolish enough to think by laying down their arms they would enjoy all the rights they once had . . . . My heart is heavy at the thought of being separated from you all forever; but I am not one of those to ask forgiveness for that which I believe *to day* is *right*. The party in power has manifested no leniency.[6]

[6] Printed in *Message of the President of the United States of January 29, 1867, Relating to the Present Conditions of Mexico*, 39 Cong., 1 sess., *House Doc. No. 76*, 502.

99

🏵

CHAPTER X

Sterling Price, Model Citizen of Carlota

AMONG CARLOTA'S RESIDENTS was Shelby's former military companion, stiff old Lieutenant General Sterling Price. The Virginia-born general had known Mexico as a young officer in 1846 when, with Grant and Lee, he had fought his way to the top of Mexico City's Chapultepec Hill during the Mexican War. Later, Price had gone on to become important in the politics of Missouri. Then the war had come, and with it the necessity of taking sides either for or against disunion.

As governor of Missouri, Price had originally stood for Unionism. He was one of those men who might have become just as staunch a Union leader as he was, later, a Confederate loyalist. However, he came to feel that too much pressure was being put on him to give his public utterances a more pro-Northern shading. Consequently, Price thought that Missouri and the other Southern states were being forced into a degrading position. For a time he had tried to keep an open mind about slavery, secession, and the value of ideological competition between the North and the South, but each month found him siding more with the South. Although influential Northern friends did their utmost to halt the steady shift in his allegiance, Price went off to war and became a Southern general. Later, one of his friends, James S. Rollins, a Missouri legislator, wrote to President Lincoln stressing Price's past loyalty and requesting pardon and liberal treatment should he return and recant. Lincoln, in a little-known letter, replied as follows:

EXECUTIVE MANSION
WASHINGTON D. C.
AUGUST, 1863

Hon. James S. Rollins: Yours in reference to General Sterling Price, is received. If he voluntarily returns and takes the oath of allegiance to the United States before the next meeting of Congress, I will pardon him, if you wish me to do so.

Yours truly,

A. LINCOLN[1]

Congressman Rollins had felt that Price would renew his allegiance to the United States if he could count on a pardon. But Price never for a moment intended to return.

Price was far from a professional soldier, yet he established his own soldierly code. He thought so little of West Pointers that he once inserted a notice in the papers denying indignantly a rumor that he had received a military education. Price did what he could to shape up the miserably equipped, poorly organized Missouri militia forces. His men often fought without uniforms or proper weapons (some had only old flintlocks and shotguns) and used smooth stones and rusty chains as artillery projectiles.

Nevertheless, Price's First Missouri Militia won notable victories early in the war at Lexington, Wilson's Creek, and elsewhere. Then Price sustained a serious defeat during his famous armed raid, of September, 1864, into southeastern Missouri. He had attempted this operation in company with Shelby's cavalry, the Iron Brigade. The raid had been considered daring from the standpoint of distance from its base, the amount of country traversed, and the scope of its general objective—to capture central and upper Missouri. He had intended to seize St. Louis, partly as a counterpoise to Sherman's threatening march through Geor-

[1] See James S. Rollins, *Letters and Speeches*, (n.d.), Plate No. 12, a collection of letters and memorabilia bound together, in the Missouri Historical Society in St. Louis.

gia. When he crossed into Missouri, Price counted upon its people to rise and join his invasion force.[2]

But he had overestimated both his own equipment and the rebel spirit in Missouri. Furthermore, some critics charged, his tactics were poorly chosen. The Union Department of Kansas inflicted grave losses on Price: 3,700 men killed and wounded, 3,000 taken prisoner, and many pieces of his artillery and wagon trains destroyed or captured.[3] After a humiliating retreat under withering fire toward Indian Territory, he ended up in the Trans-Mississippi Department, chafing and disillusioned.[4]

Down South he was severely criticized, mainly for his fussy slowness and caution in attack. General John Bankhead Magruder, one of the South's most popular generals, and not a close friend, however, congratulated him on the raid, claiming that "it stopped the siege of Mobile and diverted many men from Sherman."[5]

In the fall of 1861, Price's wife had moved southward from Missouri to Texas, driving a pair of white mules and a wagon. She received an official act of welcome, passed by the Texas state assembly—the only instance of such a welcome ever accorded a woman by a Southern legislature. Later in the war, as the Confederacy dissolved, it was wholly natural that General Price should follow her to Texas. After Texas fell, the General was attracted by the prospect of colonization under Maximilian.[6] He had no desire to go back into Missouri, the scene of his defeat. Like many other exiles, Price decided to leave his family behind until he could establish a secure residence abroad. In October, 1865, a Missouri newspaper wrote of the General: "Nothing was left him from the wreck of war, all his property had been con-

---

[2] See Lucy Simmons, "The Life of Sterling Price," (M.A. thesis), 103; also Richard J. Hinton, *Rebel Invasion of Missouri and Kansas and the Campaign of the Army of the Border Against General Sterling Price*, 5; and *Missouri's Republican*, September 30, 1867.

[3] Simmons, "The Life of Sterling Price," 103.

[4] Jay Monaghan, *Civil War on the Western Border*, 307–45.

[5] *OR* Series I. Vol. XLI, 1053; Simmons, "The Life of Sterling Price," 103.

[6] *Missouri Republican*, January 28, 1865.

fiscated by the United States Marshal of the Western Division of Missouri." The journal describes how some "thirty Confederates— General Price among them—moved into Mexico from San Antonio, Texas," to establish an American settlement.[7]

When Price first went to Mexico, he firmly believed that it was not only a safe retreat but that the government of Maximilian was strong. Although he later learned how wrong he and other Confederates were, Price steadfastly claimed he did not want to return to the States "either to share in the reconstruction of the South or to ask pardon of the Union for the part he had played in rebellion." Price and his fellow exiles still had serious apprehensions regarding a future life back home, especially "because of the emancipated Negro."[8] He felt that going to Mexico was the best possible course open to him, an alternative choice he would have repeated again under similar circumstances. Price secretly hoped, however, that Maximilian's regime would be recognized by the United States. But this never happened, on account of the continuing enmity of Washington toward Maximilian's government.

After arriving at Mexico's capital, Price was among those who worked hardest to induce Maximilian to issue the original decree establishing the Confederate colonies. The St. Louis *Missouri Statesman* for October 20, 1865, reported that Maximilian had appointed General Price to act as one of several commissioners of colonization and immigration. He helped conduct the sale of public lands and was himself given a large tract at Carlota. From this 640-acre grant Price donated the land on which the town actually stood.[9]

Sterling Price worked his precious land diligently. He culti-

[7] *Ibid.,* October 20, 1865.

[8] *Missouri Statesman,* July 28, December 15, 1865.

[9] Actually Matthew Fontaine Maury, discussed in another chapter, was largely in control of Mexican colonization. A circularized "colonization letter," issued by Maury on February 7, 1866, lists the district agents for colonization, and, although Price's name is not on the list, he acted as deputy to Maury. See Harmon, "Confederate Migrations to Mexico," *Hispanic American Historical Review,* Vol. XVII (November, 1937), 468–69.

vated crops by hand and played the role of a patriarch surrounded by plantations belonging to the remnants of the band
that had escorted him to Mexico. Price never lost the loyalty of
the men who served under him. And he loved their flattery. Together they faced the dangers of Mexico. His home was shielded
by a high adobe wall topped with a thick sprinkling of jagged,
broken glass. Situated near the railroad track running from Vera
Cruz to Mexico City, the house itself was little more than a mud
shack propped against the leaning wall. Fastened to the dwelling
was a faded canvas army tent in which Price kept his supplies.[10]

On January 16, 1866, a correspondent of the New York *Herald* described the Price cantonment as follows: ". . . I saw in the
plain extending before me a few tents scattered here and there,
and at about five hundred yards a cluster of a dozen unfinished
houses pleasantly situated along a brook, lined with a row of trees
and plants. 'What is this?' said I to my conductor . . . . 'This,' said
he, 'is General Sterling Price's settlement. Here are his tents and
those of his friends, and here the foundation of a city which, ere
long, will be as large as Richmond.' "

The General stood six feet, two inches in height and had long,
flowing, white hair. He was a peculiar combination of pride, dis-
cursiveness, and coldness. "Old Pap," as his troops called him,
could be dour and haughty, even mulish during moments of difficulty. In Mexico there was much to call forth his truculence, and
he frequently lectured his visitors, pointing a long bony finger at
them to punctuate his partisan convictions.

Price found it necessary to go frequently to the capital city to
seek defensive aid against marauders. In part this was because of
his insistence upon an exclusive attitude toward colonization. The
Mexican newspaper *El Pájaro Verde* quoted Price on this matter:

> We have around us some rich and intelligent families but we do
> not take as companions other than the ones who establish among *us*
> and speak *our* language . . . . The town will be composed exclu-
> sively of Confederate families.

[10] *Missouri Statesman*, January 26, 1866.

About Price's supercilious attitude this Mexican newspaper commented bitterly:

> It could not be said with more clearness that the good fortune in the Carlota colony is only for the foreigners and that not even the rich and intelligent Mexicans will have a part in it if they do not renounce their native tongue, that is to say, if they do not transform themselves in every possible way into North American foreigners.[11]

On July 2, 1866, he wrote his son, Edward W. Price,[12] about some particularly unfortunate disturbances at Carlota:

> I have now just returned from the city of Mexico after an absence of nearly three weeks. I visited Mexico at the request of our colony to see the authorities in relation to an outrage perpetrated upon a portion of the outskirts of the colony by a band of robbers claiming to be liberal troops and to make arrangements as would prevent such things from happening again which I think I have succeeded in having done. These robbers robbed and carried off thirty from the outskirts of the settlement taking them one or two at a time from their fields in rapid succession and running them into the mountains and holding them with the hope of being paid by other immigrants for their release; failing to get pay they have released their prisoners who have returned and an Imperial Military Post has been established in their midst.

The kidnapers were chastized by the French Army and Price wrote that their commander and twenty other robbers were killed. This incident and similar ones that followed did not immediately sour Price toward Mexico—if we can judge by his letters to friends. He continued to write almost exaggerated descriptions of the land's beauty:

> Every month that I live in Mexico satisfies me more and more that

[11] This and preceding quotation from Hanna and Hanna, "The Immigration Movement," *Hispanic American Historical Review*, Vol. XXVIII (May, 1947), 244-45.

[12] In a letter added to the T. C. Reynolds Papers at the Missouri Historical Society (St. Louis) only as late as December 11, 1948.

it is the best climate, the most productive soil and with a stable government would be the most desirable country I have ever seen . . . .
The Emperor becomes impatient and fretted when it is even doubted that his government is not a fixed and permanently established
government; he should know better than outsiders; my opinion is
that one more year will develop the fact . . . . I do not wish that any
of my letters or portions of them should find their way into newspapers.[13]

One observer wrote that Price "sat much in the shade of his
tent, telling the stories of the war and hoping in his heart for
the tide of persecution and proscription in Missouri to run itself
out." This friend believed that "politics was as necessary to his
mental equilibrium as sleep to his physical."[14] Although he disavowed it, Price no doubt dreamed of returning to public life in
Missouri after conditions settled down again. So did many other
exiles with him. But Price was proud and stubborn.[15] Furthermore, he harbored the thought that the Carlota and Cordova settlements were as near to the vital New Orleans and New York
markets as his Missouri homeland, and he joined other Confederates in the dream that new fortunes could be made from farming in a new country.[16]

When he had built, by his own hand, a bamboo and adobe
shack, the lonesome Price sent for his wife back in Missouri. Mrs.
Price left for Mexico as soon as she could raise the funds. Unfortunately the steamer on which she traveled was damaged by
high seas after leaving the port of New York. After returning to

[13] Sterling Price to Edward W. Price, Reynolds Collection, Missouri Historical Society (St. Louis). Another more widely printed Price letter, reprinted from
the *Missouri Republican* and dated December 16, 1865, is quoted by Rister,
"Carlota," *Journal of Southern History,* Vol. XI (February, 1945), 46.

[14] Edwards, *Shelby and His Men,* 105.

[15] Simmons, "The Life of Sterling Price," 109–10.

[16] *Ibid.,* 7. According to a New York *Herald* correspondent, Price claimed
to have exported five thousand dollars' worth of coffee by 1865. This seems incredible. See Harmon, "Confederate Migrations to Mexico," *Hispanic American Historical Review,* Vol. XVII (November, 1937), 469; and Hill, "The Confederate Exodus to South America," *Southwestern Historical Quarterly,* Vol.
XXXIX (October, 1935), 110, 120–21; (January, 1936), 161–99; (April, 1936),
309–26.

that harbor, she finally booked passage upon the ship *Manhattan*, and, following a second wind-lashed voyage, arrived at Vera Cruz in mid-1866 with several other ladies who were joining their husbands and sweethearts. These women must have been the most welcome of all the southern belles in history, as they stepped ashore in their finest crinoline dresses and flat straw hats.[17]

Mrs. Price was surprised at how the General had aged. He confessed that he had been ill during much of his stay in Mexico and had been losing weight steadily. His spirits were also very low, and the unceasing rains that knew no season were disturbing to his spirits as well as his health. After his wife's arrival, however, it seemed as though he was for the first time beginning to relax from the tensions of the war. Like Shelby, he was greatly cheered to see his family again.

Price spent his spare time studying a trunk full of staff papers he had brought to Mexico with him. He never lost a lively sense of his own importance and pored over these records, preparing various articles from them for publication. Many of the exiled generals, like Price and Early, published vindications of their past Civil war strategy in United States journals. In particular, the *Southern Magazine* featured such apologies during the 1860's and 1870's in a section entitled "Haversack." Later Robert Underwood Johnson would carry more of their serious explanations of battle tactics in his massive *Battles and Leaders of the Civil War*, a compilation of the military history of the war by its major warriors.[18]

[17] *Missouri Statesman*, September 7 and 17, 1866; *MT*, May 26, 1866.
[18] Colonel Thomas L. Snead, in a letter to Colonel John F. Snyder of Virginia written April 21, 1882, stated: "I was during the war General Price's most trusted staff officer—his only confidant and I have all his papers—he having taken them to Mexico and thence brought them here and given them to me—as a basis of a history of events." Several of the best Price letters are in the collections of the Missouri Historical Society (St. Louis).

CHAPTER XI

The Other Colonies

ALTHOUGH THE MAJOR COLONIZATION CENTERS were in the Carlota and Cordova region, the Confederates ventured beyond the beautiful valley of Aconcinga looking for other places to settle. Maximilian also opened areas northward and westward to them and assigned to each of the areas American colonization agents. Judge Oran M. Roberts and William P. Hardeman of Texas were stationed at Guadalajara, William M. Anderson and John G. Lux went to Monterrey, George W. Clark was stationed at Durango, Alonzo Ridley of California settled at Mazatlán, John Henry Brown at Mérida, and Y. P. Oropesa at Vera Cruz. Near San Louis Potosí, a Methodist minister from Missouri, F. T. Mitchell, established a 5,000-acre colony in the Río Verde Valley. Mitchell went into cotton planting on an extensive scale, leasing two large haciendas for a period of ten years. The New Orleans *Picayune* reported that cotton in that area "grows about six feet high with but little cultivation. We have seen an average stalk with one hundred and sixty well formed boles upon it."[1]

Still other colonies were planned in Chihuahua, at Saltillo, throughout Jalapa, along the Río Verde near Tampico, and in Coahuila, where Commodore Maury sent William Marshall Anderson on a surveying trip. Another popular spot that was being readied for settlement, once the fighting with Juárez ended, was

[1] Rister, "Carlota," *Journal of Southern History*, Vol. XI (February, 1945), 41; New Orleans *Picayune*, January 18, 1866.

the hacienda of Michopa near Cuernavaca, about seventy miles west of Mexico City. Maury also planned to develop the Laguna district, about one hundred miles west of Patos, on the borders of Coahuila and Durango, today one of Mexico's most important agricultural areas. Largely because of the warfare that raged in Mexico, these outlying agricultural colonies, offered to the Confederates at minimal prices by Maximilian, remained undeveloped. Wheat, cotton, and livestock would have eventually formed their major output. But we know very little about these colonies.[2]

One of those assigned lands to the north for colonization was Colonel David S. Terry, C.S.A. Terry had been a judge in California, involved first in vigilante disturbances and then in a political fracas that had made him notorious. Before the war he had fought a famous duel near San Francisco in which he had killed Senator David C. Broderick. Partly to bury this memory and also to escape public abuse, Terry had gone into the South to fight for the Confederacy. After the war he migrated from Texas into Mexico. At Guadalajara, capital of the Jalisco district, and at Mazatlán and Parras as well, he tried his hand at sheep raising and cotton growing on a tract of more than twenty thousand acres. As an agent of Maximilian he enticed other immigrants to join him. Terry was moderately successful, but he failed to settle the land with enough Americans to achieve the large colony he had planned.

Terry's experiences in Mexico were in some ways typical of those of other Confederates. In time he had to give thought to educating his children, a problem faced in common by them all. Mrs. Terry took them to California, and despite the fact that he had made plans to remain in Mexico for the rest of his life, Terry eventually admitted to his wife that if he did not come back to the States, he would clearly be derelict in his "duty as a husband and father."

The "anarchy, bloodshed, oppression and outrage" everywhere hastened Terry's departure. In mid-1868, Terry drove his re-

---

[2] Harmon, "Confederate Migrations to Mexico," *Hispanic American Historical Review*, Vol. XVII (November, 1937), 459, 481.

maining mules and horses to Mazatlán on the Pacific coast of Mexico, where he took a steamer for San Francisco.[3]

In the Tuxpan area, on the Caribbean coast of Mexico north of Vera Cruz, about a hundred colonists settled on the large plantations of Tumbadero and Zapotan (or perhaps Zapotlán). These were renowned for their choice coffee, sugar cane, corn, and tropical fruits. General Shelby was a leader in the Tuxpan enterprise. A European nobleman, Baron Enrique Sauvage, had interested him in the area. Maximilian had granted to the Baron and various associates a tract of land the size of Delaware near Tampico. The plot has since proved to be one of the richest mineral regions in the world. Years afterwards, great quantities of oil were discovered there.

From earliest times this fertile land had supported an efflorescence of wild Indian rubber and mahogany trees. Sauvage promised Maximilian he would settle three hundred families on his Tuxpan and Huauchinango grants within one year's time. The Baron was looking for partners to develop his land grants when he chanced upon Shelby at a time when Shelby was tiring of operating his precarious Carlota freighting business under adverse conditions. After being convinced that this Tuxpan grant was safe from marauders because, unlike Carlota, it lay in a relatively unexposed and remote northeastern corner of Mexico, Shelby agreed to dispose of his equipment and to enter the land-development and colonization business.

In time Sauvage turned his project over to Shelby and went off to join Richard L. Maury, the Commodore's son, in a plan to link Vera Cruz, Campeche, and Cuba by submarine telegraphic cable, having also obtained the right from Maximilian to operate overseas communication from Mexico. Shelby hoped to sell land in 320-acre tracts at one dollar an acre, and he engaged surveyors under Major R. J. Lawrence of Kansas City to lay out plantation sites. The colony founders envisioned a railway between Tampico and Vera Cruz which would serve the Tuxpan area, and

[3] Regarding Terry's Mexican activities see A. Russell Buchanan, *David S. Terry of California, Dueling Judge,* 139–49.

Maximilian pledged a beginning subsidy of $20,000 for the road.

Shelby's colonization venture attracted wide attention. The *Mexican Times,* the voice of the exiles in Mexico, took an interest in the General's experiment. At a time of disappointment with the progress of colonization at Cordova, the *Times* lauded Shelby: "We conscientiously believe that had the management of affairs at Cordova been entrusted to his keeping, today a great growing colony would be stretching its browned hands southward to the Gulf and northward to the border of Mexico . . . . With him there is no such word as fail . . . . The Tuxpan colony goes bravely on and the shares are in the market."[4]

To equip his colony, Shelby went to Havana, bought a schooner, and loaded it with provisions for some two hundred Confederates and Mexicans whom he employed to clear the lands and set up the new site. He hoped that thousands more would be attracted. It is not clear where he obtained financial backing for this venture. Mrs. Shelby may have brought him money from Missouri. At least part of it came from Maximilian, although the resources of the imperial government were failing increasingly with each month of the war against Juárez. In the face of continuing internal warfare, Shelby attracted few colonists to Tuxpan. Nevertheless the General flooded Texas and Arkansas with circulars promoting this latest immigration project. He stressed the value of Tuxpan's resources and its accessibility to the South. He even offered to transport settlers to the site—at the suggestion and expense of Maximilian. He also wrote to agents who might sell Tuxpan's lands at New Orleans, New York, Galveston, St. Louis, Chicago, and Baltimore. For a time Shelby operated his schooner directly between Tuxpan and New Orleans.

Shelby bought old smoothbore muskets, *pistolets de tir,* and ammunition at Vera Cruz from the withdrawing French Army and passed such weapons out to each new arrival. He suspected, correctly, that these hopefuls—who did not know their lands

[4] See *MT*, September 24, October 8 and 29, 1866. See also Hill, "The Confederate Exodus to South America," *Southwestern Historical Quarterly,* Vol. XXXIX (April, 1936), 323.

had been appropriated by Maximilian from the Toluca Indians— would be left unmolested for only a short time. Eventually the fierce Toluca Indians demanded the return of their mahogany forests and oil-rich beaches from Shelby's colonists.

Shelby fought these Indians in a series of bitter hand-to-hand skirmishes. They would appear suddenly from out of the ravines, thickets, and lagoons surrounding Tuxpan. Here Shelby again showed himself to be nothing if not a steadfast man of grit. During the height of fighting, Shelby was the mainstay of the colony. He was described as: "alcalde, magistrate, patriarch, contractor, surveyor, physician, interpreter, benefactor, autocrat, everything."[5] Unfrightened, he defended his colony against the Indians, the Juárist guerrillas, the jungle, and yellow fever. When the nearby French garrison at Corretzetla departed in haste, he and his dirty, ragged settlers were left exposed. Within days, sometime in February, 1866 (the date is uncertain), they were attacked by some two thousand guerrillas and Indians, who fought from behind the tangled and bush-enshrouded cover of the jungle. Shelby, as usual, would not surrender. For this he paid a high price.

The colony was destroyed almost overnight. The air thick with dust and smoke, the flames from their huts leaping skyward, the gunfire deafening them, Tuxpan's terrified immigrants attempted escape by sea. The countryside bristled with enemy guns. With few weapons, supplies, and practically no earthworks, the Tuxpan colonists grimly dug hasty defenses along the beaches. Their only hope was to put up a delaying action while they prepared an escape in their pest-ridden, leaky old scows. The situation became progressively more desperate. Some of the boats on which the Confederates hoped to escape were captured by hostile natives who put the colonists to the torch and threw their corpses into the ocean.

[5] Unfortunately the only source which pretends to give any thorough description of Shelby's colonization ventures is again John N. Edwards, whose writings must be considered at least partly unreliable. On Sauvage and the Tuxpan grant see Edwards, *Shelby Expedition*, 119, and *Diario del Imperio*, September 15, 1866.

A handful of sweaty, harassed stragglers, cursing Mexico, its mosquitoes, and its heat and suffering from perpetual *vómito,* landed at Vera Cruz farther south and took temporary refuge at Cordova. Almost before the Tuxpan colonists reached Cordova, long jungle vines began to cover their formerly rich fields. Would Carlota be next?

CHAPTER XII

❦

The Colonies Falter

AN EXILE WROTE HOME a realistic description of conditions at Carlota that is one of the few eye witness accounts available today. The writer speaks of house rent being "rather high, $25 per month for six rooms." He continues with a description of the foods available: "greenpeas, tomatoes, cabbage, turnips, eggs, chicken, fresh beef, pork, bananas, oranges, lemons, and one hundred other varieties of fruits and vegetables, fresh and in abundance." The writer concedes that although inconveniences undeniably existed, they were minor: "At first, on account of the language, my wife thought she never would like to live in the country, but necessity soon forces a person to learn to speak it." The writer's wife enjoyed Mexico's cheap labor perhaps most of all: "We have a female servant we pay $5 per month," her husband stated. Then he reported an important event with more than a touch of pride: "On the 21st of January, at 11:40 A.M., my wife was safely delivered of a fine healthy rebel child, a little girl, whom we have named Carlotta after the empress of Mexico, and deservedly so, because she has been and still is the true friend of true Confederates." The writer next excoriated those who were coming to Mexico with "improper motives," those who "imagined that they would be forthwith installed into some fat office, those who not being disposed to adapt themselves to temporary inconveniences would not labor, and to their shame went back to the dis-United States, like a dog returning to his vomit."[1]

This observer was more accurate than most of the Confederate correspondents. In general, the accounts of life at Carlota sent to the States by its colonizers scarcely gave any hint of the difficulties encountered there. Relatives and friends back home who had read about Carlota in letters from Mexico would probably not have recognized the site were they to have seen it. The Confederate exiles consistently reported that Carlota was a choice location from the standpoint of scenery, climate, and soil.[2] They did not mention the yellow fever during the rainy season or that eternal Mexican menace, dysentery, an affliction, known as "the Aztec curse," which wreaks havoc upon its victims. Their correspondence included no details about tired old cavalry mounts which foundered in a sea of mud on days when plowing a furrow of any kind proved impossible. Instead, they described Carlota's fertile fields as located spectacularly between the blue Gulf of Mexico and the ice-capped volcanic peaks of Orizaba and Popocatepetl to the west. They emphasized the spell which this region cast upon those who first saw it.

As its beauty could not obscure the menace of malaria, typhoid, and pellagra, nor could it reduce the serious, ever present inconveniences of life. Sanitary conditions were so primitive as to be nonexistent. There was a real contradiction in such a scene as that presented by ladies, dressed in silken finery for some social occasion, picking their way through mud puddles in the middle of the night in order to reach an outside privy deep in a rain-drenched clump of canebrakes. Not only were privies hard to find, but public conveniences of all sorts were missing. Transportation, vital in any community, was extremely limited. Wholesome, uncontaminated food was hard to obtain. There were no

---

[1] Benjamin Crowther to J. Calvin Littrel in *Message of the President of the United States of January 29, 1867, Relating to the Present Conditions of Mexico,* 39 Cong., 1 sess., *House Exec. Doc. No. 76,* pp. 514–15.

[2] *Missouri Republican,* July 28, September 28, 1866.

banks to which one could entrust his money. English-speaking schools or hospitals were nonexistent.

Nor was there a servile class to whom one might turn over one's burdens. General Thomas C. Hindman, commander of the Trans-Mississippi Department before Kirby-Smith, wrote home of his life in Carlota that it was "a harder country to make a start in than the United States" and that trying to introduce any form of slavery there was impossible. "All our Negroes," he reported, "decided to leave us upon our arrival here, and did so, except Charlie, whom I employed until I could get Mexican servants. He will leave tomorrow. Negroes are worse than worthless in this country. If you decide to come," he told a correspondent, "by all means bring Mexican servants with you from San Antonio—at least a cook and a washer and ironer." He also thought it a mistake to cart along furniture. His had been broken up en route, and he found local table ware, kitchen utensils and other items quite plentiful. "I would bring only my trunks," he wrote, "containing clothing, the bedding, cooking utensils for the road . . . a good wall tent with fly and poles, a good axe and hatchet, spade and pick . . . ."[3]

The formerly wealthy exiles found that life in Carlota had a certain leveling aspect. One observer described in these words the condition of the incendiary Judge Perkins of Louisiana: "He is well and pushing finely ahead with his new coffee farm. He blacks his own shoes, and feeds and curries his own horse."[4]

The Mexico of that day offered one further difficulty: the prevalence of robbery. Traditionally, Americans below the border have been considered fabulously rich, and the Carlota colonists seemed prosperous to the *peones* who everywhere surrounded them. Some Confederates arrived with gold fillings in their teeth and laden with trunks containing family heirlooms, silver, silks, and bone china salvaged from plantations. From the moment

[3] Hindman's letter was to J. E. Barkley of Cotton Gin, Texas, and was dated July 8, 1865. It is reproduced in Ted R. Worley (ed.), "A Letter Written by General Thomas C. Hindman in Mexico," *Arkansas Historical Quarterly*, Vol. XV (Winter, 1956), 365–68.

[4] Dorsey, *Recollections of Henry Watkins Allen*, 354.

the Confederates first set foot in Mexico, they were the victims of hundreds of thefts, some petty, others more damaging.

On occasion the local proclivity toward thievery became almost ludicrous. A susceptible Confederate victim was Colonel Beverley Tucker of Virginia. While traveling between San Luis Potosí and Mexico City, he was robbed no less than five times: "The first time they took his money, the second time his clothes, the third time they tried to get his money, but [as] he had none, they struck him on the head with a sabre, just over the right temple, which came near putting an end to his sight, if not his life." Tucker had refused to lie flat on the ground while the bandits rifled his belongings, including a gold watch. The victim was robbed for a fourth time when the stagecoach on which he protectively took passage was stopped and all the occupants were required to surrender their valuables. This time even his boots and much of his clothing were stripped off. As if this were not enough, a government report states, "twenty leagues beyond, towards Vera Cruz, the stage was again stopped, and Beverley Tucker was robbed for the fifth time."

During the war, as a Confederate agent in England, Colonel Tucker had read glowing accounts in the English press about colonization projects in Mexico. He had interested the London *Standard* and the Cincinnati *Enquirer* in sending him there after the war as a correspondent. He came with his wife and son James. The younger Tucker found work helping to construct the railroad from Vera Cruz to Mexico City, while the Colonel roamed the country recording journalistic impressions, trying thereby to earn additional money. His headquarters were in Cordova's Dixie Hotel, "a barn-like place without a single comfort."

After his five-fold robbery Tucker was impoverished. Near San Luis Potosí he found temporary employment on a large hacienda in Juárez territory. His wife taught school and later wrote her grandchildren about their condition: "One beautiful morning . . . after our breakfast of coffee, bread, and three turkey eggs (your grandfather laughed so heartily at my insisting upon dividing the odd turkey egg) the fact had to be faced that our last cent was gone." The proud Tuckers managed to keep their sense of humor, by then having replaced the Colonel's stolen gold watch with a "nickel watch larger and fatter than a biscuit," having virtually reached the end of his resources.[5]

Another problem which faced these men who had been leaders in the society from which they had fled was finding appropriate employment. Only a few attained positions of high responsibility in Mexico. Governor Henry Watkins Allen published the *Mexican Times*, and this satisfied him; others tried to "make work."

Disputes among the restless Confederates and the necessity of legal representation before the government created a larger than average need for attorneys at Carlota and the other Confederate centers nearby. General Thomas C. Hindman, former congressman from Helena, Arkansas, and long a member of the bar there, was only one of several exile lawyers at Carlota. Hindman, who had led a division at Shiloh and who, as has been noted, commanded the area from Missouri through Arkansas and Louisiana to the Red River, started a law practice that concerned itself mainly with the complex differences between the United States and Mexican legal systems. Dapper and only a shade over five feet tall, Hindman made up in energy and activity what he lacked in size.

Those Confederates possessing technical skills that made them valuable to Maximilian—in particular, railroad operators and land surveyors—were fortunate. Among them were naval Lieutenants Francis T. Chew and Thomas Scales. They were off the Confederate raider *Shenandoah*, which had continued to fly the Rebel flag months after Appomattox. A determined pair, they had come to Carlota from Liverpool, where the ship's master had finally surrendered the *Shenandoah* to the British Navy on November 6, 1865—but only after a dramatic voyage, tracking down Yankee whalers in the Pacific and dodging floating icebergs in the Bering

---

[5] The Tucker account is from *Message from the President of the United States Regarding Conditions in Mexico*, 40 Cong., 1 sess., *Senate Exec. Doc. No. 15*, p. 43. See also Beverley Randolph Tucker, *Tales of the Tuckers*, 42–48.

Sea. Fearing the consequences of capturing thirty-eight American ships and 1,053 Yankee prisoners in thirteen months, the *Shenandoah's* crew dispersed to all parts of the world, including Mexico—where Lieutenants Chew and Scales settled down as surveyors. Like General Walter H. Stevens,[6] once Lee's chief engineer (who became top engineer of the Mexican imperial railways), they worked for Maximilian.

Former Missouri Governor Thomas C. Reynolds was made superintendent of the country's shorter rail network. Superintendent Norris, formerly of the New Orleans and Jackson Railroad, also became an official of the Mexican railroads, as did Major General Waterhouse, a railroad contractor.

Maximilian's government would probably not have awarded Generals B. H. Lyon of Kentucky and John McCausland of Virginia posts as two of its principal surveyors if they had not enjoyed high rank and wide experience as military engineers. Similarly, General Oscar M. Watkins might never have been taken into the Mexican diplomatic service if he had not been a commander of unusual background. Not all former generals achieved this degree of success, and a few naturally harbored resentment whenever discrimination against them could be charged.

Unfortunately, most of the exiles were former soldiers, and although the Emperor could well have used their services in the army, he felt obliged in most cases to keep them out of uniform. Maximilian was anxious to obtain diplomatic recognition by the

[6] Edwards, *Shelby and His Men*, 105, mentions the men off the *Shenandoah*. See also George W. Groh, "Last of the Rebel Raiders," *American Heritage*, Vol. X (December, 1958), 49. General Stevens to General P. G. T. Beauregard, a.l.s., January 30, 1867, complains that in addition to his work as chief engineer of the Mexican railways, he was "practically performing the duties of President besides" and wanted to return to the States. On November 18, 1867, Mrs. Stevens, his widow, wrote to her sister about General Stevens' funeral at Vera Cruz: "The pall bearers were Gen'l. Barton, Col. Linsay Walker, Col. Myers, Capt. Turpin. Many ladies walked, showing that the memory of our Confederate dead is precious. . . . Albert [obviously a former slave] walked near our carriage and sorrow stricken beside us. He said Gen'l Stevens was more than a master to him—a Brother." Excerpts of both letters from Forest H. Sweet, *Autograph Letters, Catalogue 142* (1957).

United States. To employ former Confederates in his army would certainly jeopardize this goal.[7]

As a consequence, most of the exiles turned to the land. This was the wrong occupation for men so high-spirited and ambitious. It was a serious mistake to turn toward agriculture in a country where manpower meant so little and where rural life was debased. Mining would almost surely have offered more rewards to mechanically minded Americans. Although they would have required greater capital to exploit the mineral wealth of Mexico, the Confederates might have secured claims and knowledge of mines that proved lucrative later for other Americans. For example, little did the settlers of the Tuxpan region know of the rich oil deposits to be found beneath the lands which they had laboriously tilled.[8]

Once back at Cordova from Tuxpan, Shelby wrote his friend Major Lawrence: "One thing is certain, we must all get away from here or I will be damned if we don't starve—there is no joke about it." The General had sacrificed much in his disastrous adventure. He and his associates had even sold their wives' jewelry in order to buy arms and supplies with which to keep themselves alive. It is certain that he foresaw that it was only a matter of time before the Juárists would make a thrust at Carlota. Shelby, always concerned with more than his own safety, felt he had a duty to stand by the exiles whom he had encouraged to join him. For this reason he thought that talk of their leaders' abandoning the Confederate colonists in Mexico was unpardonable. When, on his return to Cordova from Tuxpan, he heard that Gen-

[7] General Magruder was one of the few Confederates appointed a major general in the Mexican Imperial Army. Generals A. W. Terrell and W. P. Hardeman were made *chefs de bataillon.*

[8] Attempts were later made to obtain title to the lands granted the Confederates in Mexico. The Juárez regime eventually acknowledged responsibility toward American citizens' investments in Mexico in a pamphlet entitled *Responsabilidades contraidas por el gobierno nacional de México con los Estados Unidos en virtud de los contratos celebrados por sus agentes, 1864-1867* (Mexico. 1867). But these were obligations toward Americans who had helped the government of Juárez, not Confederates who had sided with Maximilian.

eral Price had left for the States and that some fifty thousand dollars was being raised for the relief of Price, he was enraged. "They had better a damn sight appropriate that fifty thousand to the orphans and widows that were made by his damn blunders," he declared.[9]

Some of the exile leaders did not stay in Mexico even as long as Price. General Kirby-Smith found himself disappointed with Mexico after only a few days at the capital city's Hotel San Carlos (run by a former servant of General Buckner who had become wealthy). The devout general's particular grievance against Mexico was not shared by many of his fellows: he found life at the capital lax and immoral.

Within a few months the General went to Havana, hoping that it might soon be safe to return to his beloved South. On July 31, Kirby-Smith wrote his fellow West Pointer, Lieutenant General Ulysses Simpson Grant, "relying," as he put it, "upon the friendship of past years." He stated: "I arrived here [Havana] day before yesterday, having been frightened away from Texas by the reported indictment of Gen. Lee and the amnesty proclamation of the President. I understood that if I gave my parole I would not be permitted to leave the country, and would be liable to indictment for treason. On the urgent entreaty of my friends I left Texas untill the Government should have clearly determined upon the policy to be pursued towards the South.

"I am now abroad," Kirby-Smith continued, "with not more than sufficient means to subsist upon for ten or twelve months. I am separated from my family, who are dependent upon my exertions for their support. I must go to work and do not wish to live under a foreign government or to seek employment in a foreign land. Will you kindly write to me and candidly advise me what to do. I do not think I am asking anything that conflicts with your duty.

"I wish to return home, will give my parole, take the oath of

[9] J. O. Shelby to R. J. Lawrence, February 2, 1866, printed in *Missouri Historical Society Bulletin*, Vol. IX (January, 1953), 217.

alligeance [*sic*], and quietly and peaceably settle down .... I may go to Merida, Yucatan, where I understand I can live economically."[10]

Later Kirby-Smith advised Southerners not to leave the South for Mexico. He felt that "instead of seeking asylum abroad, their own destinies, and the triumph of the principles for which they fought are in their own hands."[11]

One of the most illustrious of Southern leaders stayed at Mexico City only a few months longer than did Kirby-Smith. It is interesting to speculate on the course of colonization in Mexico if one of the colonists had been this man—the Confederacy's Lieutenant General Jubal Anderson Early, controversial commander of the Shenandoah Valley Corps of the Army of Northern Virginia before Lee relieved him of command. Of one thing only can we be sure: If the colorful Early had been a permanent colonist, the Mexican episode would be better known today than it is.

General Early was the archetype of those Southerners who could not forget. Radical in thought and action, he never gave up his fight for the Stars and Bars. To the end of his life he was unwilling to admit his defeats of September, 1864, at Winchester and Fishers Hill at the hands of General Sheridan and his setback before General Custer at Waynesboro in March, 1865. In July of 1864, Early had also led an ill-fated raid on Washington, D.C.; this and the routs suffered in battle with the two generals cost Early his command. In contrast to Lee's conduct in the same area, Early gave the order to burn Chambersburg, Pennsylvania, to the ground before abandoning it to the "damn Yankees."

Early was strong tempered and vigorous, of medium build, intelligent, and full of grand talk. Douglas Southall Freeman described him as an intolerant and snarling man, dressed perpetually in a crumpled uniform and referred to by his troops as "Old Jube." People said that the tartness of Early came out in his

10 E. Kirby-Smith to Lt. Gen. U. S. Grant, July 31, 1865, a.l.s., Eldridge Papers, Box 47, Huntington Library.
11 Parks, 462–75.

flashing eyes and that he "cussed and swore awfully and drank liberally," but that he achieved a limited popularity with troops despite his "wicked ways." He was well regarded until his great defeat.

Divested of command and undaunted by the news of Lee's surrender, Early had started to move southward on horseback in late April, 1865. He still hoped to vindicate his reputation by fighting with Kirby-Smith's Trans-Mississippi Department. He rode through Virginia, North Carolina, Tennessee, Mississippi, across Arkansas, and on through outlying bands of guerrillas into Texas. We can imagine him as he traveled along, clad in his traditional dress, "his great white overcoat, his slouch hat with the black plume, his short gray beard and light hair, his red face, the large field-glasses and the inevitable canteen."[12]

When Early learned upon reaching Texas that Kirby-Smith had surrendered the Trans-Mississippi Department, he was amazed. He had not dreamed that Confederate authority in the West would vanish so quickly. Early in July, 1865, he left Texas via Matamoros for Mexico. By then whole squadrons of Union Cavalry were closing in on the Río Grande country. After some weeks he reached Vera Cruz in August by a most circuitous route through the Bahamas. "When I started," he wrote a friend, "I found it necessary to get off by water as the route over the Rio Grande had become impracticable, on account of robbers and guerrillas. It would have been worth my life to go on that route."[13]

As Shelby did for a brief period, Early next sought to determine if there was any prospect of a war between Mexico and the United States. He still hoped for a fight against the Union forces. Often hungry and speaking only two words of Spanish (both described as contemptuous), he finally arrived at Mexico City in the late fall of 1865. Finding there no possibility of a war against the Union,

[12] George Dallas Mosgrove, *Kentucky Cavaliers in Dixie* (ed. by Bell Irvin Wiley), 230.

[13] *DAB*, V, 598–99. See also Jubal A. Early, *Autobiographical Sketch*, 468; William D. Hoyt, Jr., "New Light on General Jubal A. Early After Appomattox," *Journal of Southern History*, Vol. IX (February, 1943), 113–17; Edwards, *Shelby and his Men*, 122; *Personal Memoirs of P. H. Sheridan*, II, 211–12.

Early became engaged in journalistic combat with his old rival, General Sheridan. On January 20, 1866, he published in the English-language *Mexican Times* the first of a series of bitter explanations of his wartime strategy against Sheridan in the Shenandoah Valley. In these articles (later reissued in book form) the battle-hardened, testy warrior not only gratified his feelings about Sheridan, Sherman, Grant, and many other Union generals, but also denounced rumors that he had asked for a pardon, in words which reveal the state of mind of a true Southern "fire-eater":

> I would not accept a pardon from the President of the United States if gratuitously tendered. . . . I have nothing to regret in the course pursued by me during the war. . . . I utterly disclaim all allegiance to, or dependence upon, that nation. I am a voluntary exile from my own country, because I am not willing to submit to any foreign yoke imposed upon it.[14]

The brevity of Early's stay in Mexico was in no way due, as in the case of Kirby-Smith, to a discovery of vice in the streets of Mexico City. Rather, it was Early's realization that Maximilian was altogether too anxious to gain the good will of the United States. In May, 1866, he sailed for Canada, via Havana, in disgust. "I found Maximilian's empire an infernal humbug," he wrote a friend from Havana on May 10 of that year. It is possible that if he had joined Shelby's force, he might have found his proper environment. But it is unlikely that he could have endured service under a junior commander and even more unlikely that such an individualist could have long remained part of colony life.

---

[14] Quoted in Hesseltine, *Confederate Leaders in the New South,* 99; Early's "defense," about which a correspondence with Thomas Caute Reynolds developed, was entitled *Memoir of the Last Year of the War for Independence in the Confederate States of America.* See "Letters of Thomas Caute Reynolds," *Glimpses of the Past,* 34–41; also Coulter, *The South During Reconstruction,* 277. In Cuba, Early acutally met his mortal enemy, Sheridan, which helps explain why he did not stay there longer. Also in Cuba for a short time was Confederate Secretary of State Judah P. Benjamin. At Toronto the next year the rebellious Early published another defense of Southern chivalry and his "bad luck" in retreating from Sheridan, which he later included in his autobiography.

✿

CHAPTER XIII

News from the States

By 1866 many of the expatriate Confederates were watching events in the American South with increased interest. Any of them who already were giving thought to the prospect of returning home could not have been encouraged by news from their homeland. From Unionized Kentucky came word that displaying a souvenir Confederate flag was punishable by a fine of from fifty to one hundred dollars. In some states, laws were enforced making it a penitentiary offense ranging from one to five years' imprisonment for unauthorized groups to hold meetings of a "suspicious" or "secret" nature. A rigorous oath was required of ministers of the gospel before they were allowed to perform marriage ceremonies. The South was at the mercy of radicals and carpetbaggers.

Within a few months of the war's end, it was clear that Lincoln's hopes of rebuilding the Union through a policy of clemency toward the South had been torn to bits in favor of the harsh reconstruction measures advocated by such Republican Congressional leaders as Henry Winter Davis, Benjamin F. Wade, Zachariah Chandler, Thaddeus Stevens, and Charles Sumner. The impetus of these men was hate, and their goal, to see to it that the South held as many black voters as possible and as few white ones.

For exiled Southerners the radical spirit of vindictiveness and retribution was all too obvious in such speeches as that made on the floor of the United States House of Representatives in 1865 by Indiana's former abolitionist advocate of Negro emancipation, Congressman George Washington Julian, when he spoke of their respected former leaders:

> As for Jeff Davis, I would indict him, I would convict him and hang him in the name of God; as for Robert E. Lee, unmolested in Virginia, hang him too. And stop there? Not at all. I would hang liberally while I had my hand in.[1]

The radicals entrusted the reconstruction governments down South to carpetbaggers or to persons whose partisan Unionism was a matter of provable record. Oaths of previous loyalty to the Union forces were required of those who wanted to hold federal offices. These oaths were nonsensical; it was common knowledge that practically every male from seventeen to fifty-five years of age had, in one way or another, been involved in the rebellion.

Honest men to whom the South looked for leadership were unable or unwilling to sign these oaths and consequently remained disqualified from public offices. Civil servants received letters such as those which Treasury Secretary Hugh McCulloch sent them: "On account of your inability to take the oath required by law, I am reluctantly compelled to suggest that you forward me your resignation."[2] The feelings of the Southerners were not assuaged when uneducated Negroes were placed in the vacated positions and when professors and ministers were kept from teaching and preaching.

In Missouri, from which so many of the exiles had come, the postwar state oath was even more severe than the federal test oath. Missouri officeholders had to swear their innocence of eighty-six separate acts of disunion. In order even to vote, former Confederates had to declare under oath that they had *never* acted in a hostile fashion toward any Missouri government.[3] Those Southerners who hoped for Presidential pardons faced signing an "iron-clad test oath" if they wished to hold federal

---

[1] Quoted in Hodding Carter, *The Angry Scar*, 25.
[2] The quotation is from Harold M. Hyman, *Era of the Oath*, 71.
[3] *Ibid*, 97.

office or to practice law in federal courts. As a result certain courts and offices in the South remained closed for years.

The oath became a device to insure Republican party supremacy in the United States Congress. By keeping Democratic former Rebels outside that body, Republican dominance was assured and "Radical Reconstruction" was perpetuated. Henry Winter Davis and Charles Sumner even spoke of depriving Southerners forever of their citizenship and office-holding rights. This Northern vindictiveness helps to explain why the Mexican exiles were reluctant to return home.

As early as July 31, 1861, an act of Congress had determined the penalties for conspiring to overthrow the United States government; this was a "high crime" to be "punished by a fine not less than $500 and not more than $5,000 or by imprisonment (for no more than six years) or by both such fine and imprisonment." Later, the Mexican exiles heard of more serious laws that called for the confiscation of property; eventually treasonable activity came to be punishable by death "or, at the discretion of the court," by imprisonment "for not less than five years and fined not less than $10,000."

True, there were amnesty proclamations issued by both Lincoln and President Andrew Johnson soon after the end of the war. But these were so restrictive that more than 150,000 Southerners remained excluded from the original amnesties. The amnesty proclamation of President Johnson required former Confederates who owned property worth more than $20,000 to make special application for amnesty. Their cases had to be reviewed by proper Union authority, and pardon had to come directly from the President. However, few of the Confederates in Mexico owned property in excess of $20,000. Furthermore, they resented asking a pardon for having done what they thought was their constitutional right to do—secede from the Union.

As military confusion in Mexico increased, most exiles hoped the United States Congress would eventually make if safe for them to return. But the requirement of an oath was to men like

Shelby a distasteful admission of Yankee supremacy, a stimulus to their still powerful feelings of defiance. The exile temperament was especially sensitive to any suggestion that the Union was in a position to hurt them. Many exiles were disappointed that President Johnson, a Democrat and a Southerner, did not provide some special dispensations for them. Johnson not only failed to make such dispensations, but added to President Lincoln's exceptions from amnesty rights still other classes of persons who could not qualify for pardons. Among these were included "all persons who left their homes within the jurisdiction of the United States to aid the Confederacy." In the classes of persons excepted from pardon, Johnson listed fifty occupations that included most upper class former Confederates abroad or at home.

In Washington, on December 19, 1865, Senator John Conness had introduced a resolution on the floor of the Senate requesting the President and any government department to submit specific information regarding the names and plans of "dissatisfied citizens in Mexico."[4] Such threats as these called forth all the exiles' defiance. At this time Missouri's former governor, Thomas Caute Reynolds, wrote General Jubal Early from Mexico:

> I quietly await the results of the contest [Reconstruction], consider myself still a citizen and resident of Missouri, and hope and expect, God willing and my life lasting, to return to it, as one of the ruling class. Meanwhile I wish success to all efforts to restore the South to equality and *power;* towards such as wish to oppress or injure Confederates, my attitude personally is simply one of calm, contemptuous, derisive defiance. The whole nation, from the President down, with all its fleets and armies, is powerless to hurt a hair of my head; and, if they think at all of it *they know it.*[5]

As he began to receive mail regularly, Shelby too showed bitterness about the South in letters sent home. When he heard about Reconstruction conditions, he became increasingly irritated. Friends reported that many families remained broken up after the war, that former soldiers and friends would have joined him

[4] 39 Cong., 1 sess., *Congressional Globe,* 77.
[5] *Glimpses of the Past,* 35–36.

in Mexico if it had not meant abandoning their relatives. Slaves, of course, were now gone, and poverty was everywhere apparent. Shelby's correspondents wrote that state Reconstruction governments were bringing out the evil in people, even stirring up the enmity of close friends towards each other. Deserters from Shelby's own brigade had turned into thieves, and formerly honest soldiers had become outlaws, driving off cattle belonging to their neighbors, stealing government grain, and defrauding one another.

With Yankee strangers in command of the Old South, Negroes too had been "made impudent" by their new status. Shelby heard stories about Negro troops being used against whites in the South. In Tennessee, Governor William G. ("Parson") Brownlow's Reconstruction militia was the prize example. In Arkansas, Governor Powell Clayton was also about to arm Negro troops in order to police whites. In Texas, Mississippi, Louisiana, North Carolina, and South Carolina, similar action had either been adopted or was contemplated.[6]

To a former Confederate who still looked to the past in spirit, such conditions were intolerable. All this did not make an exile like Shelby less defiant; he was confused and perhaps prone to exaggerate the dangers facing him back home. Unfortunately, what such a man thinks is happening in a given historical situation influences his behavior as much as what actually is happening. Imagined persecutions, tangled emotions, stubbornness, and humilation help create martyrs; imagined apprehensions help create reactionaries. And Shelby was becoming a reactionary who under tension reflected the insecurity of his awkward residence abroad.

Shelby and his associates were especially terrified by the experience of such "arch-secessionists" friends as Pierre Soulé, former United States senator and envoy to Spain, and Raphael Sem-

---

[6] In Texas, Governor Edmund J. Davis used Negro troops in 1871. In Louisiana, Negro troops were organized by Governor Henry C. Warmoth, in June, 1870, and placed under the command of Lee's former subaltern, General James Longstreet. See Otis A. Singletary, *Negro Militia and Reconstruction*, 13–14, 35–36.

mes, late commandant of the *Alabama*. Both had close connec-
tions with the Mexican exiles. Soulé was arrested at New Orleans
as early as 1862 by Union General Ben Butler and sent north to be
imprisoned. In 1866, Semmes was taken from his home at Mobile, imprisoned at Washington's Marine Barracks, and charged
with treason and acts of piracy on behalf of the Confederacy.
Although Semmes was promised immunity at the end of the war
as the Confederacy's greatest naval hero, he nevertheless had to
defend himself against a government prosecutor who boasted that
if Semmes had been tried immediately upon his arrest, he would
have been hanged.

When finally cleared of the charges against him after months
in prison, Semmes was elected a probate judge of his county in
Alabama only to be driven from the bench by an order of the
Secretary of War that declared him ineligible to serve—a plight
suffered in common by others of high rank. A tide of emotion
still ran high against Confederate officers in the States. As
Semmes himself had stated in a letter to President Johnson:
"We live in times of high party excitement, when men, unfortunately, are but too prone to take counsel of their passions."[7]

For such men as Shelby, Reynolds, or Early, still unwilling to
admit defeat, the idea of seeking "political rehabilitation" by
searching out persons of influence in the North, or relying upon
"pardon brokers" to intercede with the White House and the
Congress, would have been almost insufferable.

[7] W. Adolphe Roberts, *Semmes of the* Alabama, 245–51.

❦

CHAPTER XIV

Agent for the Emperor
Commodore Matthew Fontaine Maury

ONE CONFEDERATE EXILE was destined to play a large, albeit frustrated, role in Mexican colonization. Commodore Matthew Fontaine Maury, celebrated oceanographer, naval astronomer, and author of *Physical Geography of the Sea,* served the Confederacy abroad for most of the war. During the first part of the conflict, Maury helped to fit out such ships as the man-of-war *Georgia,* a new 500-ton iron screw vessel which in seven months of prowling captured nine Northern ships. On this ship his nephew, Lieutenant William Lewis Maury, raided United States shipping in the South Atlantic and off the coast of Africa. Later this Maury commanded the small Confederate Navy, while his uncle turned down repeated lucrative offers to establish himself in the service of the French and Russian governments.

As an intellectual as well as a naval officer, Maury could not resist the temptation to write a series of articles for the Richmond *Enquirer,* articles that complained of waste, inefficiency, and red tape in the Confederate high command. Partly to get him out of the way, his superiors decided to send Maury on a purchasing mission to England. As an agent for the Confederacy, he made London his headquarters, and, with James M. Mason, he frantically bartered contraband cotton for naval vessels, medicines, and foodstuffs. He also contracted for the construction of blockade runners and rams in English shipyards as well as continued his experiments with electronic torpedoes and mines.

After two and one-half years in England, Maury—a Virginian only five feet, six inches tall, almost sixty years old, and balding—became a major refugee of the Civil War. While clandestinely escorting supplies into the Confederacy, he learned in Cuba of the South's defeat; he could neither continue his voyage nor return to England.

This scholar-mariner, who was probably the South's most distinguished scientist, remained stranded on foreign soil, and, although he was without money of his own, Maury refused to touch a cent of the large sums officially entrusted him by the Confederacy.[1] He voluntarily abandoned in England almost $40,000 worth of torpedoes, telegraph wire, and other supplies which he had bought for the defense of Richmond. As he wrote his wife, "I did not want any of the $10,000 or $20,000 which they will bring, though someone will get it who has no more right to it than I have."[2] His various biographers claim that Maury's greatest concern lay with the plight of his beloved Virginia. When he contemplated surrender, he sent a letter to the officer commanding United States naval units in the Gulf of Mexico, a part of which read:

> In peace as in war I follow the fortunes of my native old state. I read in the public prints that she had practically confessed defeat and laid down her arms. In that act mine were grounded also. I am here without command, officially alone . . . and as I consider further resistance worse than useless, I deem it proper to formally so confess.[3]

Like other Confederate agents abroad, Maury was unfortunately excluded from the United States amnesty proclamations. For this reason, he was counseled by friends, such as General Robert E. Lee and Charles Francis Adams, not to return immediately to the States.[4] His brother-in-law, Dr. Brodie Herndon, advised him:

[1] Charles Lee Lewis, *Matthew Fontaine Maury*, 186.
[2] *Ibid.*, 187.
[3] *Ibid.*, 188.
[4] Lee counseled some Confederates aboard to come home. See T. C. Reynolds

In view of the state of the public mind in the North at present I think it would be decidedly unsafe for you to return to this country. . . . your prominence, and the earnest part taken by you in the cause, would make you the decided object of that "vengeance against leaders" so openly proclaimed and so plainly visible. In time, I hope, these vindictive feelings will subside, and then, and only then, would it be safe and prudent for you to return.[5]

But what was Maury to do abroad? How could he support himself? The answer to these questions lay in his own background and prestige. As early as 1842, at the age of thirty-six, Maury was superintendent of charts and instruments at the United States Naval Observatory. Before the war, in 1858, Maury had been decorated for his scientific work by Maximilian of Austria while the Archduke was commander in chief of the Imperial Austrian Marine, the navy of his brother, the Emperor Francis Joseph. A friendly correspondence had developed between the Archduke and Maury.

Maury's name was familiar to others in Mexico. During the American Civil War he had written General Juan de Dios Peza, for a time Maximilian's minister of war, offering to demonstrate the new electric torpedoes on which he had been at work. We do not know what happened to this offer, but we know that through Maury's lifelong interest in the natural history of Latin America and through his authorship of several scholarly articles on Mexico in the ante bellum period, he was recognized there as a scientist of distinction. As emperor of Mexico, Maximilian urged Maury to visit him; now that Maury was an exile, he gratefully accepted the invitation. Thus Maury, already a commodore in an age when admirals were commissioned sparingly, decided to give up returning to his own country, which had also honored him in the

to J. A. Early, a.l.s., May 10, 1866, Reynolds Papers, Missouri Historical Society (St. Louis).

[5] A description of Maury's colonization activities appears in Chapter XIII of Lewis' biography. See also the less well-done Hildegard Hawthorne, *Matthew Fontaine Maury;* Jacqueline A. Caskie, *Life and Letters of Matthew Fontaine Maury;* John W. Wayland, *The Pathfinder of the Seas;* and Frances L. Williams, *Matthew Fontaine Maury: Scientist of the Sea.*

past for his scientific services. Resolving instead to cast his lot with such cohorts as the rough cavalrymen Shelby and Price, he took ship for Mexico.

Maximilian regally celebrated Maury's arrival at Mexico City. The first notice of Maury's appearance at the capital was an announcement in the *Diario del Imperio*, on July 7, 1865, that the distinguished North American scholar Sr. Maury had assisted at the dedication of Maximilian's new academy of arts and sciences, one of several cultural and scientific organizations founded by the Emperor. This was followed by a gala ball at Chapultepec Castle. It is astonishing that Maximilian found time to devote to social and cultural pursuits in the midst of a perilous and draining conflict with his enemies. But he had been liberally educated, had traveled extensively, and desperately sought to introduce European cosmopolitanism to Mexico.

Today his regime appears to have been far more enlightened than it once was believed to be. Maximilian has long been stereotyped as a nineteenth-century reactionary monarch; yet his public pronouncements show a live concern not only for culture but also for social problems. Many of them dealt with the improvement of education, the elimination of poverty, the reorganization of government, and desperately needed prison reforms. Unfortunately, the founding of museums, academies, and libraries was scarcely in keeping with the spirit of the times in Mexico.

The illiterate mass of the Mexican people had little understanding of the new emperor's true motives. Even well-informed persons believed that Maximilian was less interested in social reform than in a veneer of culture and a desultory flirtation with the sciences, particularly astronomy and biology. It seemed curious to Mexicans that he should spend valuable time pursuing butterfly specimens and that he should cavort with foreign naval officers like Maury and appoint Professor Bilimek, a strange Austrian, director of Mexico's principal museum. Maximilian's collection of mushroom specimens and the butterflies collected by Carlotta and her ladies in waiting in the midst of a period of warfare seemed as eccentric to Mexicans as the royal fondness for foreigners. Commodore Maury's experimentation with Cinchona trees, which he imported from the Far East for the purpose of producing quinine, also seemed strangely out of place in a war-torn land.

On September 25, 1865, Maximilian named Maury the Director of the Astronomical Observatory in Mexico City. Although Maximilian's interest in Maury was understandable, members of the Emperor's entourage openly wondered about the value of a scientist and naval specialist to a regime whose chief problem was survival and which virtually had no navy. Mexicans, and even some Confederates, asked why Maury was the only person who could enter Chapultepec Castle by the door known as the "Gate of Honor" without first being announced.

On November 4, 1865, Maury inserted in the *Mexican Times* a notice which was his reply to rumors circulating at home to the effect that he planned to ask for pardon from the United States government:

> I have neither directly nor indirectly asked pardon nor any other favor from the President of the United States.
>
> M. F. MAURY
> *Honorary Counselor of State*

This new title was an indication of the Commodore's unequaled prestige at the court of Maximilian.

At this time Maury developed an interest in a subject that was especially close to the Emperor's interests—immigration. Both men came to believe that Mexico's future depended upon attracting craftsmen, artisans, and skilled laborers from Europe and the United States. An *émigré* himself, the Emperor was anxious to regenerate Mexico by assimilating large numbers of such talented immigrants; this hope was at the heart of plans to colonize new and backward areas of the country. He particularly desired colonization from the United States. Other nations had proved what could be done by utilizing ambitious immigrants. The successes scored in the 1840's and 1850's by large-scale European immigration to the United States were a model to follow. Yet, when he heard of this plan, Robert E. Lee expressed emphatic misgivings:

> We have certainly not found our system of government all that was anticipated by its original founders. I cannot, however, despair of it yet. I look forward to better days. The thought of abandoning the country is abhorrent to my feelings. I prefer to struggle for its restoration, and share its fate rather than to give up all as lost. To remove our people to a portion of Mexico which would be favorable to them would be a work of much difficulty.[6]

The problem of attracting immigrants from the United States, of allocating land to them equitably, and of establishing them in a new country had become increasingly difficult for Maximilian's government in the midst of the campaigns against Juárez. The Emperor needed an American to take charge of colonization who really understood Mexico's Confederates and who was also a person of some public stature in his homeland and abroad. He believed he had such a man in Maury.

Late in 1865, Maximilian appointed Maury imperial commissioner of immigration in addition to his other duties. This seemed a logical choice to the Emperor, even if various Confederates in Mexico jealously grumbled over the appointment.

The Commodore accepted his new assignment at a salary of $5,000 a year, then a relatively large sum. He wrote his son, Richard L. Maury, that he had also obtained a salary of $2,500 for him as his assistant. Given a section of land at Carlota, the elder Maury moved into a house at 13 Calle San Juan Letran. To get his first pay check, he agreed to obtain Mexican naturalization papers. Maximilian also gave Maury $150 with which to furnish his office, $500 for one year's expenses, and $1,500 for a clerk and messenger. He was authorized to appoint state colonization agents in Virginia, Texas, the Carolinas, Missouri, Louisiana, and Alabama.

---

[6] Quoted in Bernard Jaffe, *Men of Science in America*, 229. On Virginia colonization see A. J. Hanna, "The Role of Matthew Fontaine Maury in the Mexican Empire," *Virginia Magazine of History and Biography*, Vol. LV (April, 1947), 105–25.

Their salaries of $100 a month plus a yearly allowance of $300 were likewise furnished by the Emperor.

Maury launched an ambitious program. He hoped to build a "New Virginia" in Mexico to be inhabited by some of the leading families of the South and stated publicly that Maximilian's edicts governing immigration would attract as many as 200,000 Americans to Mexico.[7]

Back in his native Virginia there was little enthusiasm over Maury's plans, and even at Maximilian's court a French naval officer, Captain Chabonne, publicly joked about the Commodore's hopes to attract 200,000 immigrants. Some of Maury's relatives thought the old man had gone out of his mind. His fifteen-year-old son, Matsy, wrote the frankest of letters telling him that folks at home did not at all take to the colonization scheme. When Commodore Maury sent an in-law a notice that he asked to have published in a stateside paper, the man refused. He stated that everyone would think Maury insane if it were ever published.[8]

The Commodore, however, plunged on with his immigration project. His son Richard and daughter-in-law Susan joined him in Mexico during 1865. Maury's son did not hold the status of his father at first, but during the remaining months of Maximilian's regime, his influence on immigration policy grew.

Maury was also assisted by General Magruder as land commissioner. Magruder was given a salary of $3,000 a year and ostensibly outranked Richard Maury. Magruder brought part of his family with him. Maury, however, was shrewder as to the future and left his family in Virginia, except for Richard. Assisting Maury and Magruder was a third appointee—Governor Thomas C. Reynolds of Missouri. Reynolds was given no special title, which contributed to his discomfort when working with Maury. The trio were authorized by Maximilian to offer various inducements to immigrants.

Under the Emperor's edict of September 5, 1865, Americans

---

[7] Burger and Bettersworth, *South of Appomattox*, 67–68.
[8] Patricia Jahns, *Matthew Fontaine Maury and Joseph Henry*, 273–74.

able to circumvent General Sheridan's border check points on the Río Grande were allowed to bring into Mexico duty-free personal effects, farming equipment, and domesticated animals. Each immigrant was to receive a registered title to his land which was exempted by the government from taxes for the first year of occupancy. Taxes on property transfers were also suspended for immigrants. An immigrant could become a naturalized citizen as soon as he settled a land grant. He was also exempted for five years from military service, though required to join a local militia unit for protection of community properties. Freedom of worship was guaranteed. Although slavery was forbidden in Mexico, former slaves could be brought into the country as "servants." This concession provided an inducement to those settlers whose former slaves had remained loyal to them. Each employer, however, had to care for his peons as though he were their guardian. Only a few Negroes accompanied the Confederate exiles, despite the fact that a fully paid sea voyage for servants was promised to certain Americans whom Maury considered especially desirable.

For a very short time during 1865–66, Maury's colonization scheme attracted considerable attention in the States. In one mail alone, according to John N. Edwards, Maury received seven hundred letters asking for information about how to reach the Confederate colonies. He prepared a printed form letter describing the attractions of life in Mexico which was reproduced in newspapers throughout the United States. Intended to answer touchy questions about religious toleration in Mexico, the circular erroneously stated that such toleration was "sanctioned by the Pope." The letter also announced that new lands upon the Pánuco River ("30 miles west of Tampico . . . up to the table land") were to be opened. The circular discussed the granting of free alternate sections of land ("with a preemption right to the rest at $2 per acre"). Mexico's available land tracts were described in fanciful terms as places where one need only wait for a plantation of ripening red coffee berries to yield its crop. As for those persons who decided to cultivate the many green squares of sugar cane that already dotted the countryside, their fortunes were almost assured before they settled on the land, Maury promised.

Maury, together with J. O. Forns, a lesser-known Confederate colonizer, issued another circular captioned "Ho For Mexico!" It described as a land of milk and honey "Forn's Colony," a tract of some twenty-five square leagues (108,459 acres) on the hacienda of Limón located on the Pánuco River in the Department of Tamaulipas.[9] Maury took pains to praise other Confederate settlements also. In fact, because Carlota and Cordova were already well advertised, he wanted to pay more attention to lesser-known colonies. The colony at Omealco and a still smaller one at Río Verde were made to appear equally attractive.[10]

Maximilian also authorized various independent immigration companies to attract migrants to Mexico. An American and Mexican emigrant company was formed in December, 1865, and he gave it a charter to sell land grants. He authorized an Asiatic colonization company to bring Chinese labor to Mexico. Another company received permission to import French and Spanish emigrants. French soldiers whose Mexican enlistments had expired were encouraged to become residents. Maximilian also made provisions for his fellow Austrians to settle in Mexico, attempting by every means to give his empire new blood. The Emperor was anxious to work out an agreement with the United States to regularize the colonization of Americans in Mexico, and he sent several agents to see Secretary Seward in Washington. Although each of these envoys was rebuffed, the Emperor's interest in immigration continued at a high pitch throughout 1865.[11]

However, in the new year, Maximilian's position began to deteriorate. On May 31, 1866, Maximilian received word that Napoleon III intended to withdraw French troops from Mexico. He

[9] M. F. Maury, "Letter Regarding Colonization Possibilities," February 7, 1866, Huntington Library. The Forns Advertisement of February 9, 1866, is also in that library. The letter is reproduced in Appendix B of this book.

[10] 39 Cong., 1 sess., *House Exec. Doc. No. 1* Part III, 210. See Appendix D below.

[11] W. C. Nunn, *Escape from Reconstruction*, 49–50.

apparently was dissuaded from an immediate impulse to abdicate by the courageous Carlotta, who offered to go to France to plead with the French emperor to fulfill his treaty obligations to supply Maximilian with French arms and protection. She set out the very next day, June 1, 1866, on her mission.

From that moment Juárez' power continued to grow. His forces, formed of hitherto scattered and disunited bands of cutthroats, brigands, beggars in rags, and escaped convicts recruited off the streets of countless northern towns, rallied under the united command of General Mariano Escobedo, and converged upon Mexico City and Vera Cruz. Intent upon pillaging, laying waste, and destroying French forces in all the major centers of imperialist resistance, the Juárists began to force a general retreat upon the Emperor's armies in the south.

In such an atmosphere, popular rioting flourished. At Carlota, Cordova, Orizaba, or Omealco, the Confederates were pressed upon by hordes of destitute *peones* hungry for land, food, power, and revenge. With the smell of gunsmoke in the air, it was virtually impossible for Maury or anyone else to carry forward any organized program of immigration.[12]

One of the greatest hindrances to Commodore Maury's efforts was disapproval by the United States of emigration to Mexico. Maury's colonization agents throughout the South were so harassed by the federal government that they were forced to give up their posts. A radical congress was determined that Southerners should stay in the South. By April, 1866, Richard Maury, who for a time served as acting commissioner of immigration for Maximilian's government, was informed that the United States Department of State had absolutely terminated all movement of American citizens into Mexico for their own safety. This announcement followed the arrest of Maury's key agents by the United States government.[13]

---

[12] 39 Cong., 1 sess., *House Exec. Doc. No. 76*, 525; Arthur Howard Noll, *A Short History of Mexico*, 272–80.

[13] Richard L. Maury to O. G. O'Neal, April 10, 1866, in 39 Cong., 1 sess., *House Exec Doc. No. 76*, 527–28.

Because of Juárist pressure on Maximilian, plus Sheridan's firm sealing of the border and United States discouragement of immigration, the flow of Americans into Mexico virtually stopped by mid-1866. Even Maury's increased promises of travel money—to be repaid only when a new colonist could afford it—failed to attract immigrants.[14]

As a consequence, Maury's value to Maximilian decreased markedly. The Commodore became a sort of human curiosity piece in an atmosphere of siege and land warfare. His fine scientific mind and naval background did not serve him in his promotional activities. He was, furthermore, too distant, reserved to the point of being unable to mix and mingle freely with either Mexicans or lower-class Confederates, and too tactless to be popular among the Southern leaders with whom he dealt. Generals who already despised one another added Maury to their list of pet hates. Maury seemed especially weak in understanding the feelings of disappointed land seekers; he had, of course, made the mistake of promising them too much. The *Mexican Times* for January 27, 1866, reported that 260 immigrants had recently landed at Campeche and Tampico. Surely these persons had not been fully apprised of the war-torn state of Mexico and of the fearsome conditions they would encounter. Otherwise, they would in all probability not have sailed from the United States.

Maury had also asked for overly large amounts of money from Maximilian's deteriorating government with which to run his program. That regime eventually had to curtail instead of increase its expenditures on behalf of immigrants. Penniless exiles and the Mexican authorities alike were disappointed with the results Maury achieved: the immigrants because they did not gain the riches they had expected; the imperial government because not enough immigrants had arrived and because wartime conditions frustrated their effectiveness as colonists. Maury's colonization

---

[14] Maury's specific colonization instructions were printed in the *Diario del Imperio*, December 5, 1865. His plans are described in Mexico City's *La Sociedad*, December 7, 1865.

office found itself unable to obtain cheap land for settlement and was inactive in surveying such lands as it did secure.

While Maury publicly kept up a façade of confidence in his colonization project, he had genuine misgivings about Mexico. He wrote his wife that he would not like to see Tots (his daughter Mary) betrothed to "one of these dark-skinned Mexicans." Quietly, during the summer of 1865, he got his wife to sail to England. Still fearing to return to Virginia, he planned to join her in London. The news he heard from home all seemed bad. Maury could never quite believe that slavery was really over, though his son Matsy wrote "Pa" that his mother was happy to be leaving, if only to get away from their "free nigger" servants. He reported that the family had "run through" three cooks since Pa was home, an unheard of turnover before the war.[15]

Maury wanted his family out of the States, mainly because he feared reprisals against them. With Jeff Davis still in Fortress Monroe and Wirz of Andersonville certain to hang, Maury did not want to take chances with the Reconstruction regime installed in Virginia after the war. Even his favorite newspaper, the Richmond *Whig*, was attacking him. Maury was befuddled and confused. Hiding his true intentions, he made covert retreat out of Mexico his first order of business. Lonely for his wife and realizing that Maximilian's court might well fail, the Commodore soon slipped away to England.

On September 14, 1866, the government's *Diario del Imperio* announced that a new telegraph company headed by Maury's son Richard had received a ninety-nine-year contract to operate a prospective submarine cable linking the port of Vera Cruz with Cuba and the outside world. The planning and construction of this venture gave Maury a chance to withdraw from his deteriorating position. He therefore left on a mission to England, purportedly for Maximilian. As if to prove that he was going there only on a short visit, he left behind his son and daughter-in-law. Maximilian wanted Maury to stay on at the observatory but not in connection with colonization matters; and although he granted

[15] Quoted in Jahns, *Matthew Fontaine Maury and Joseph Henry*, 274, 284.

Maury a leave of absence to go abroad, he stopped his salary before he sailed from Vera Cruz for Liverpool in March, 1866. And even though Maury was now ostensibly a Mexican diplomatic agent, after he reached England, on April 19, 1866, Maximilian politely but firmly dismissed him by letter.[16]

Upon arrival in England, Maury was a white-haired, stooped, and dejected man. Nevertheless, outside London he set up a unique course of study in the use of land and underwater mines for visiting representatives of foreign nations. Swedes, Dutchmen, and Frenchmen alike attended his classes, and he garnered high fees for his tutelage in the arts of warfare. He stored away this money for future re-entry into the South. When his son Richard was removed as assistant Mexican immigration commissioner, his father obtained a job for him as an assistant manager of a mine in Javali, Nicaragua. Both men felt they could not yet return to the South. Dictating several textbooks on geography to his daughters Eliza, Mary, and Lucy, Maury awaited the time when he could sail for his beloved Virginia.

Finally, in July, 1868, it seemed safe to return, and Maury sailed for New York with his family. Although the United States was pressing Britain for damages wrought by the commerce raiders that Maury had helped provide while a Confederate agent in England, he, somehow, escaped widespread public notice.

The feeling about Maury in Mexico was not nearly so forgettable. In Mexico City it was common belief that he had been asked to leave the country after falling into disfavor with Maximilian. The *Mexican Times* on January 8, 1867, reported that a deficit of £72,000 had been uncovered in the operation of Maury's colonization office. The paper averred that he was "graciously permitted to depart" without further responsibility for the loss.

Maury suffered abuse at the hands of the Mexican press, some

[16] Reputedly Maury also went to buy scientific apparatus, for a contemplated study of Mexico's weather. In 1866, John Tyndall and other eminent scientists gave Maury a testimonial dinner in London at which he was presented $15,000 "for his disinterested service in the cause of science to the maritime nations of the world." See Jaffe, *Men of Science in America*, 229–30.

of it undoubtedly unjust. Although the *Times*'s language suggested dishonesty on Maury's part, it is more likely that the deficit resulted from the failure of Maximilian's government to anticipate the costliness of Maury's operations. *L'Ère Nouvelle*, a French paper in Mexico City, demanded that Maximilian disband Maury's inefficient colonization office. The paper complained that this bureau had attracted gullible American colonists who not only became burdens on the Mexican economy but who, because of their personal failures as colonists, gave Maximilian's immigration plan a notorious reputation abroad. After Maury's departure the Emperor dismantled the colonization bureau and threw its stranded employees into the disgruntled ranks of other unemployed foreigners in Mexico.[17]

Probably no departure caused as much bitterness among the remaining Confederates as did Maury's. His promises had created hopes and had brought many of them into a predicament that was daily growing more dangerous. He had also aroused jealousy by his closeness to Maximilian. A military man almost by courtesy, Maury was both respected for his scientific greatness and cursed for his role in Mexican colonization.[18]

[17] Burger and Bettersworth, *South of Appomattox*, 71–72.

[18] Maury wrote a series of secret (and quite gloomy) reports to Maximilian, often including information about the way members of the Emperor's government felt about the regime. The last of these reports was dated January 8, 1866. See Corti, *Maximilian and Charlotte of Mexico*, II, 539–40; also Hanna and Hanna, "The Immigration Movement," *Hispanic American Historical Review*, Vol. XXVIII (May, 1947), 239.

CHAPTER XV

Governor Reynolds, Dissenter

Resolute hardy men will keep coming here. Fat cavalry foragers . . .
who, like Maury, expected the immigrant to receive not only a farm
but a peon to work it, had best look before they leap into Mexico.
                    T. C. Reynolds, to Jubal Early, May 10, 1866

ONE OF MAURY'S LEADING CRITICS was Missouri's former governor,
Thomas Caute Reynolds. Diplomat, soldier, and a well-traveled
man of learning, Reynolds had journeyed overland into Mexico
with Shelby; he was on familiar terms with the many generals
who had come from Texas, most of whom admired him. When
he went to Mexico, Reynolds was fortyish, short, husky, bespec-
tacled, with a swarthy complexion and refined facial features. A
native of Charleston, South Carolina, this intense, pudgy man,
addicted to excessive cigar smoking, had enjoyed a varied career.
After a period as a student at the University of Virginia and
abroad at Heidelberg, Reynolds had joined the United States
diplomatic corps in 1846. Following service as secretary of lega-
tion at Madrid, he had entered political life in Missouri.

    This cosmopolite was one of the few politicians in the Middle
West, including Lincoln, who got along well with the large German population in and around St. Louis before the war. When
he went to Mexico, Reynolds was better prepared than most Confederates for accommodating himself to the ways of foreign people. He already knew the Spanish language well and was, indeed,
a fluent linguist.

Yet Reynolds' limitations were well known, the chief one being his quarrelsome disposition. Reynolds had been prominent in Missouri politics before the Civil War; but his career had been filled with excitement and, occasionally, violence. During the 1850's, when debate over the abolition of slavery reached fever pitch in that state, Reynolds developed a particular animosity toward Benjamin Gratz Brown, a strong Unionist and the virtual founder of the Free Soil party in Missouri. Brown later became Missouri's governor, and he was Horace Greeley's running mate in the Presidential election of 1872. Brown was editor of the *Missouri Republican,* in whose columns he blasted the institution of slavery in Missouri and advocated emancipation of Negroes. Reynolds was so little able to conceal his abhorrence for Brown that he permitted a conflict to develop, which could be resolved only by recourse to personal violence. In 1856 there was a duel, as a result of which Brown limped for the rest of his life.[1]

Reynolds carried his feuding with Brown and other abolitionist sympathizers into the Civil War period. He also found it difficult to tolerate certain pro-Southerners. An unpleasant relationship with Price developed at the time of Price's military defeats in 1864. Reynolds respected Price's ability, but their papers at the Library of Congress and at the Missouri Historical Society reveal that their animosity was a continuing one, even in Mexico. The self-important Price and the irritable Reynolds fought almost every time they met. If the Confederate colonies were to succeed, leaders such as these should have established a harmonious relationship, and yet they never did.

The origins of the Reynolds-Price dispute were buried deep within the circumstances in which both men found themselves at the close of the Civil War. The attitude which Reynolds developed toward Price at that time is sufficiently important to examine carefully, as it throws light on the characters of the two rivals who became fellow exiles. The evidence which follows comes entirely from Reynolds' letter books.

[1] *National Cyclopaedia of American Biography,* XX, 318; *DAB,* II, 105.

At the beginning of 1865, Reynolds had found himself, as the civilian governor of Missouri, heading a "government" in exile at Marshall, Texas. He deeply resented the fact that General Price, in his September and October, 1864, "raid" into Missouri, had failed, as Reynolds put it, to "redeem the state from its Union occupiers." Reynolds, furthermore, felt that Price had sought to keep General Shelby's military exploits from becoming better known and had blocked Shelby's promotion to major general. In fact, Reynolds considered that men like Price "infested the Confederate military service with drones and incapables."[2]

As Missouri's last Southern governor, Reynolds greatly resented Price's general popularity. He accused him in the columns of the Marshall *Republican* of trying to make scapegoats out of two subordinates, Generals John S. Marmaduke and William L. Cabell, both of whom had been captured on Price's ill-fated Missouri raid. Reynolds excoriated those "old ladies of both sexes, the spinsters of martial and marital propensities, idolizing an osculatory hero; the misses who might mistake a drum major for a field marshal" who were then "rooting for 'Old Pap' Price." Reynolds, paraphrasing Jefferson Davis, who had spoken of Price as the vainest man he had ever met, called Price "the haughtiest of Confederate generals."[3]

On January 18, 1865, Reynolds had written to Confederate President Davis to complain about some remarks that Price had made about him in both the Marshall *Republican* and Shreveport *News*. Price, having been appointed by Missouri's previous governor, C. F. Jackson, apparently viewed Reynolds, in his own words, as a "pretender" to the governorship of their common state. Reynolds had asked both President Davis and the Trans-Mississippi Department's commander, General E. Kirby-Smith, to remove Price from command of Missouri troops. He wanted all Confederate cavalry from Missouri placed under General Shelby.

[2] Thomas C. Reynolds to General Kirby-Smith, January 5, 1865, Reynolds Letter Books, Library of Congress.

[3] Thomas C. Reynolds to Major Henry Ewing, January 16, 1865, *ibid.*

Reynolds frequently referred to Price as an incompetent general and believed him prone to "slur over his disasters." On one occasion he called Price "a general whose reputation has been made by newspaper articles."[4]

Reynolds had actually persuaded Kirby-Smith to order an investigation of Price's conduct during the Missouri raid of late 1864. He charged that Price had maintained such slovenly discipline that he had even allowed his troops to scalp Federal soldiers, letting them, furthermore, ride through the streets of Boonville, Missouri, with scalps tied to the pommels of their saddles. The charge was never proved, but Reynolds carefully collected evidence against Price from a wide variety of correspondents. In one letter he called Price's Missouri campaign "a weak and disgraceful plundering raid" and quoted General Kirby-Smith as stating that Price was "absolutely good for nothing."[5]

Writing on February 25, 1865, to George G. Vest, a Confederate senator from Missouri, Reynolds had depicted his quarrel with Price as a "contest between order, discipline, and civil authority on the one hand, and military misrule and popularity-hunting on the other." But the investigation of Price's command apparently never occurred. As conditions went from bad to worse in the Texas of mid-1865, the Confederates became too preoccupied with their own withdrawal to complete proceedings against Price which had been ordered to begin at Shreveport, Louisiana, in April, 1865. Reynolds never forgot his quarrel with Sterling Price. Although he was to modify his feelings somewhat in later years, the fight with Price continued hot during their stay in Mexico.[6]

[4] Thomas C. Reynolds to Colonel J. R. Eakin, January 21, 1865, *ibid.*

[5] Thomas C. Reynolds to Waldo T. Johnson, March 2, 1865, *ibid.* Price had been an admirer of William C. Quantrill's illegal guerrillas and had even tried to justify their notorious killings of civilians, rape, and other acts of violence. See Brownlee, *Gray Ghosts of the Confederacy*, 133–34.

[6] Writing to Thomas L. Snead from St. Louis on February 16, 1887, Reynolds qualified his distaste for Price by stating: ". . . at the Confederate reunion at Roanoke Mo. in 1871, I stated in a speech to it that, whatever had been my difference with Gen. Price, I recognized him as 'Missouri's foremost soldier.'" Snead Papers, Missouri Historical Society (St. Louis).

Governor Reynolds got along even less well with Maury, under whom he worked in the colonization bureau. The Commodore haughtily pressed upon him a myriad of tasks which Reynolds considered unsuited to his temperament and background. Behind his superior's back, he accused Maury of lacking competence and good judgment in expending the large sums authorized by the Emperor for colonization purposes. Reynolds believed the Commodore's achievements confined to the concoction of misdirected, complicated, and naïve plans, incapable of execution. He also thought he knew more about handling immigrants than Maury. Reynolds had been governor of a large state, had come to Mexico before Maury, and resented having to work under him.

On the other hand, Maury's dealings with Reynolds revealed the Commodore's envy of Reynolds' close contacts with those military officers who had come with him to Mexico.[7]

Because he was openly embarrassed by Reynolds' criticism of Maury's colonization plans, Maximilian gave Reynolds other duties early in 1866. He was appointed superintendent of Mexico's only real railroad line, an English-backed enterprise, at a salary of five thousand dollars a year. This stipend, significantly, was equal to Maury's. Although Reynolds spent much of his time away from Maury's Mexico City colonization office, he resented the need to be out on the road supervising the broken-down equipment and incompetent laborers assigned to maintain the bedraggled Mexican railways. In addition to his railroad responsibilities, he was still called upon to help Maury in his colonization work.

In 1866, Reynolds signed a petition to join in founding a short-lived colony and port at the Bay of Banderas in Jalisco and executed this document in the capacity of *"El Director de la Agencia General en México de la Compañía Americana de Emigración*

---

[7] The *Diario del Imperio* for March 11, 1865, had listed Reynolds among a group of Southerners petitioning for 16,000 acres of land on which to establish a colony at the Hacienda de San José Buena Vista near Tehuacan. When this colonization venture fell through, Reynolds had gone to work for Maximilian and Maury.

a México." The Jalisco colony was another of the Confederate settlements in Mexico that failed.[8]

Reynolds did not retain this authority for long; more realistic than Maury, he knew that he was not the man to undertake a promotional program for Maximilian. Much conjecture about Reynolds' relationship to Maximilian occurred among the Confederates every time the former governor would back out of such schemes and commitments.[9] In 1868, he wrote Jefferson Davis from Vera Cruz that he had simply tired of filling the position of an "amenuensis in Maury's absurd colonization bureau" and that he was disgusted with officials in Mexico who sought to swindle the desperately earnest Confederates seeking lands there.

Reynolds, like other exiles, continued unabated his hatred of President Johnson. He believed the President lacked boldness and tact in dealing with his Radical Republican opposition. He called Johnson the embodiment of the poor-white spirit of the South and considered that it was this background which made the President "side against secession, because the wealthier classes supported it," and which "originated his $20,000 amnesty exception" and also his stand for Negro equality. Although he "despised Andy Johnson" and would ask no favors of him—including the right to return home—an air of nostalgia and homesickness pervades Reynolds' correspondence. Like Shelby, Price, and other exiles, he inwardly wanted to return but was afraid of the consequences.[10] Reynolds and his associates did not realize that most of them would have been quite safe in returning. In fact, by staying outside the country so long they took a chance that public sentiment against them might change for the worse. Reynolds wrote Davis that he had come to Mexico not primarily as an immi-

[8] The petition, dispatched via the Emperor's "secretary," Capt. Pierrón, is in the Reynolds Collection, Missouri Historical Society (St. Louis).

[9] Reynolds objected to the simulation of certain conversations with the Emperor Maximilian and others concerning colonization reported inaccurately in John N. Edwards' *Shelby's Expedition to Mexico*. In correspondence with Edwards, he called it a "romantic" book.

[10] *Glimpses of the Past,* 42, contains several important Reynolds letters, expressing his feelings about returning to the United States.

grant but as an exile, trusting to his knowledge of several languages to make a living. Whether he could continue to do so was at best hypothetical.

By the end of 1866 it was clear that Carlotta's mission in Europe was a tragic failure. In Paris her first efforts to obtain an interview with Napoleon III were rebuffed; when she finally succeeded in seeing him, Napoleon not only refused to give further aid to Maximilian and Carlotta but treated her almost brutally. She stayed at the French royal court only a few days. Carlotta next went to Rome to plead for aid from the Pope; when even the Holy Father refused her request for intervention to save Maximilian in Mexico, Carlotta collapsed. Suffering from the intense strain of anxiety, she was stricken with what papal physicians called "brain fever." By October 4, 1866, she was pronounced hopelessly insane and taken to the quiet surroundings at Miramar, Maximilian's ancestral palace. There and also in Belgium she remained in strict seclusion until her death in 1927. The Empress never again saw her Maximilian or the Confederates who admired her so much. The Confederates had lost forever their best friend and champion in Mexico.

In desperation, Maximilian allowed himself to be persuaded to issue new and fiercer regulations against the *Juaristas*. All persons bearing arms against the empire were declared bandits to be tried swiftly by courts-martial and condemned to death. Bazaine issued an order to shoot every Mexican found carrying arms who was not enlisted on the imperialist side. The order read: "Hereafter the troops will make no prisoners, and there will be no exchange of prisoners."[11] This fanaticism did severe damage to the imperialist cause. By approving such orders, Maximilian added popular fury to the opposition faced by his harassed, hard-pressed forces. Some of his staunchest adherents refused any longer to support an empire guilty of such cruel injustice. Clerics, alienated by Maximilian's secular reforms and by his failure to return church lands expropriated by Juárez, now helped plot his ouster. Mexicans impressed into the imperial army chafed at an

[11] Noll, *A Short History of Mexico*, 270.

especially unfortunate decree of October 3, 1865, in which Maximilian labelled the Juárists bandits subject to immediate execution if captured. Even Confederate exiles[12] were repelled by the butchery inflicted upon Juárists, a ruthlessness for which Maximilian, a lonely and forsaken historical figure, would stubbornly pay with his own life.

As Maximilian moved out of his capital in November, 1866, to spend two fateful months of indecision at Orizaba, the Juárez forces poured down from northern Mexico, having retaken Matamoros, Chihuahua, Monterrey, Guadalajara, San Luis Potosí, and other key centers once occupied by the French. Only now did the Emperor attempt to organize a corps of American defenders. By January, 1867, Bazaine's armies had formally begun their retreat to the port of Vera Cruz, fighting a desperate rear-guard action to save themselves from total destruction.[13]

While the French retreat was underway, Maximilian held a personal interview with Reynolds, who had inherited the mantle of Maury as his closest Confederate adviser and favorite American. Maximilian was undecided whether to abandon Mexico or to make a stand on his own. At that late hour few could in good conscience urge him to remain. Bazaine tried to impress the Emperor with the futility of attempting to carry on with a weakened, shaky force in a land in open rebellion against him. Before Bazaine left Mexico in March, 1867, he wrote Maximilian a final letter begging him to abdicate and offering him a last chance to depart for Europe. The young emperor's brother also wrote Maximilian, as reigning monarch of his native country, Austria. He appealed to Maximilian's ties with Europe and urged him to escape while there was yet a chance. According to George Creel, "Maximilian sent for General Shelby [too] and asked him if it was still possible to rally his countrymen." Shelby replied that it was "too late" and

[12] As the French withdrew, some Americans were on both sides of the fray. Juárez' personal bodyguard was reputed to consist in part of a picked detachment of former Confederates from California.

[13] For an account of the fierce battles in Mexico between imperialists and Juárists see Juan de Dios Frias, *Reseña Histórica de la Formación y Operaciones del Cuerpo de Ejército del Norte durante la Intervención Francesa.*

urged him to retreat to Vera Cruz and to get away in an American warship. Maximilian, again according to Creel, thanked the General for his candor, "took off the gold cross of the Order of Guadalupe that he wore and pinned it on Shelby's breast. The two then embraced and parted, never to meet again."[14]

Reynolds was among the few who reminded Maximilian of the "sacred duty" of a Hapsburg to fight on.

On February 19, 1867, Maximilian retreated to the village of Querétaro and made it his last official capital. Surrounded by a few foreign officers, mostly Austrians and Belgians, Maximilian personally assumed command of the armies that had been under the control of his major generals, Mejía, Miramón, and Marquez. We do not know whether or not Reynolds was there. By March 1, 1867, Querétaro was besieged by the Juárist forces. After an exhausting siege of the convent of La Cruz, Maximilian's imperialist headquarters, the members of his personal guard and the Emperor himself, refusing various opportunities to escape, were made prisoners on May 15. At sunrise on the morning of June 19, 1867, Maximilian and his aides were led up the hill of Cerro de las Campañas, outside Querétaro. After giving presents to the soldiers who were to execute him and asking them to aim at his body rather than his head, Maximilian gave a short speech which ended with the words, "*¡Viva México!*" He was then blasted off his feet by several bursts of rifle shots.

The advice of Reynolds may have confirmed the Emperor in his fatal stubbornness. It is somewhat ironic that the giver of such advice was a man who had fled from his own country and who would soon save himself by compromising with Maximilian's enemies.

Reynolds remained in Mexico for about four years. He was in Mexico City when the Republican armies forced its surrender on June 21, 1867. His diplomatic abilities enabled him to be one of the very few technical specialists retained by the Juárez government. Later, Juárez reappointed him as an inspector of the Mexi-

14 Details of Maximilian's movements after he left Mexico City are in Percy F. Martin, *Maximilian in Mexico*, 273-374; Creel, *Rebel at Large*, 34.

can railways. Reynolds achieved the difficult feat of staying in the good graces, successively, of Maximilian's imperial government, Juárez, and General Porfirio Díaz, later Mexico's perennial dictator-president.[15]

In spite of his singular political adaptability, Reynolds found no true rewards in Mexico. His bitter and, indeed, horrible memories of Mexico stayed with him till the end of his life.[16]

[15] Thomas C. Reynolds to B. Crawley, a.l.s., (contractor, Mexican Railway), January 9, 1869, in Reynolds Collection, Missouri Historical Society (St. Louis).

[16] Floyd C. Shoemaker, "Missouri—Heir of Southern Tradition and Individuality," *Missouri Historical Review*, Vol. XXXVI (July, 1942), 442–43.

CHAPTER XVI

✿

A Voice in Exile
Henry Watkins Allen and the Mexican Times

WHILE OTHER CONFEDERATES IN MEXICO had turned to farming, railroading, freighting, soldiering, and work for the imperial government, Governor Henry Watkins Allen of Louisiana established a newspaper. The exiles had found a welcome voice of exile in Allen's English-language journal, the *Mexican Times*. Its first issues were printed on the cumbersome old press of Mexico City's French paper *L'Estafette*. At its peak the *Times* was a daily, reaching possibly some two thousand readers.

The paper trumpeted all the favorite Confederate themes. Recurring constantly in its columns were justifications of the flight to Mexico, warnings against returning home, glorification of the Emperor and Carlotta, the recapture of dramatic moments of the war, and assurances of success for immigrants planning to come to Mexico. The paper also listed new arrivals, answered their queries and complaints, published news from the States, and printed the names of persons for whom the Mexico City post office was holding mail.

Throughout its lifetime, from September, 1865, to June, 1867, the *Times* brought profound satisfaction to its readers. In the journal's faded and yellowed columns, one perceives what the exile mind, in its peculiar defensiveness, seized upon as important and meaningful. The *Times* was subsidized by Maximilian and highly responsive to any preference he might express; in the main, however, it mirrored the basic impulses of the leading Confed-

155

erates. Chief among them was the compunction to explain and justify to themselves and to those back home *why* they had left for Mexico, and this theme was a major one in the paper's columns.

Perhaps the best reply concerning why the Confederates went to Mexico was written by editor Allen in answer to a "flippant and scurrilous" attack upon his fellow exiles by Horace Greeley, editor of the New York *Tribune*:

> You upbraid us and abuse us for quitting our native land and coming to Mexico, when you know very well that there was full many a Federal prison "gaping to receive us." When we left our country all the governors of the seceded States had either been arrested or orders to that effect had been issued . . . . We can safely say that if any guarantee had been held out that we would not have been disturbed, none of us would have expatriated ourselves.

Allen ended his defense by an attack on Greeley, that "poor demented old man," for whom the Confederates in Mexico wished none of the harm which Greeley had hoped would befall them. Allen wrote that he did not care if Greeley married "a black woman and became the father of a goodly number of black children." *"De gustibus non est disputandum,"* editor Allen commented.[1]

This sniggering reply to Greeley characterized the touchy reaction of Confederates in Mexico to reproach from the States. There was a good deal of such reproach, and some of it was from Southern newspapers. The exiles were quick to meet attacks against them with criticisms of their own. The *Mexican Times* was the only organ at their disposal for such replies, and they spoke up unhesitatingly in its columns. An editorial in the issue of November 11, 1865, regretted the attitude at home toward the Confederates in Mexico. The writer commented upon a recent article from the Richmond *Times*:

> It is written, we are pleased to see, in the kindest spirit towards all Confederates who are now in Mexico—This kind language, however, is not official. President Johnson does not use such language,

[1]*MT*, February 3, 24, 1866.

for we have positive information that all who have left the United States for Mexico are considered outlaws. In a letter from Mrs. General Shelby of Missouri to the General, now in Mexico, she says: "General Sheridan told me that you had outlawed yourself by going to Mexico." And we are also informed that every Confederate of note, who has returned to any southern state from Mexico, has been arrested.

"Why are there any Confederates in Mexico?" the *Mexican Times* asked. "Listen and we will tell you. Read, and you will agree with us that there was no other course to pursue." The writer continued:

> The gallant and distinguished gentlemen now in Mexico were told that they would be arrested and cast into a loathsome prison, there to be held for future humiliation and punishment. A reward in the public newspapers had already been offered for one of them . . . . Although chastened by adversity and saddened by the recollections of the past; although suffering much mental agony for a dear absent wife, or a tender-daughter, or a bosom friend, still, with stout hearts, they are "Buffeting the waves of misfortune."

The paper grew almost shrill as it complained of the plight of "exiles compelled, many of them in their old age, to begin life anew." Yet the *Times* did not seem anxious to take note of the changing attitudes toward Confederate exiles abroad that would soon make it possible for them to return without fear of recrimination. The Rebel leaders in Mexico were too deeply committed to the righteousness of their cause to admit that bitterness toward them back home might be subsiding. Only occasionally did their paper print news of the increasing number of pardons granted repentant Confederates. The *Times* did not want its readers to hear of pardon. In fact, it intensely disliked even the suggestion of attaining Northern justice through repentance. Instead, it inclined markedly toward the view that apologies were due to those who, like its editor, had been wronged at Union hands. The exiles clung to a sense of having been wronged, and some found that their justification for staying on in Mexico depended upon nursing this feeling tenderly.

The Confederate newspaper stressed the evils that awaited those who should foolishly decide to return home. It carried items certain to have a striking effect upon its readers. It warned of depredations against them by fellow Southern Democrats and scalawags and of impoverishment at the hands of impertinent "nigger robbers." The *Times* gave full attention to the hated "Beast Butler," Union commander at New Orleans and "insulter" of Southern womanhood. The Mexican exiles joined indignant Southerners everywhere in condemning General Butler's notorious wartime order proclaiming that any female insulting a Union soldier would "be regarded and held liable to be treated as a woman of the town, plying her avocation." There were also continuing attacks in Mexico's American paper at the accursed General William Tecumseh Sherman and his fateful march through Georgia. But, above all, the *Times* repeated allegations that return to the South would be only to expose oneself to personal violence.

The editors of the *Mexican Times* described such events as the arrest of Confederate General P. G. T. Beauregard at New Orleans—his home encircled by Yankees one night, he was taken from his bed and locked in a cotton gin until the following morning. The *Times* erroneously reported that Beauregard was arrested because of a rumor that he was sheltering General Kirby-Smith! The paper also deplored the incarceration of General John S. Mosby at Alexandria, Virginia.

The *Times* never ceased to feature protracted accounts of Northern intolerance and persecution, particularly the imprisonment of former Confederate President Davis, who, it asserted, had been made a scapegoat for imagined atrocities.[2] The exiles refused to forget how, "at damp Fortress Monroe," Davis had been clamped into irons and kept under the vigilance of a sentinel. The *Times* deplored the long two years during which Davis was imprisoned and not allowed to stand trial or to answer accusations against him.[3] It looked as though the North had intended

[2] See *MT*, October 7, 14, November 4, 1865.

[3] See *MT*, June 16, July 23, 1866, and Robert D. Meade, *Judah P. Benjamin, Confederate Statesman*, 342.

to see him killed, if not by hanging, then by deterioration of his health, the *Times* charged. The thought of Jeff Davis chained in his cell like a common criminal while Negroes sat in Southern legislatures created widespread indignation among the exiles.[4]

Few of them would ever have admitted what historian Rembert W. Patrick has called the astonishing moderation toward such leaders shown by the North after the war. As he points out, many who "expected drastic punishment, if not death," escaped harm. Only a few high-ranking prisoners actually had to undergo confinement, and for brief periods only. Yet for proud men such disgrace produced mental agony more serious than physical abuse.

That there could be no freedom under Northern military rule, the *Mexican Times* sought to prove by examining newspapers from home. It smarted over the suppression of the Richmond *Examiner* by the military commander of Virginia.[5] It carried headlines from the Memphis *Appeal* reading, "What A Brave And Proud People Cannot Endure." The *Times* extended sympathy to all who refused to yield to Northern reconstruction of the South. Its November 18, 1865, issue reported the execution in Nashville of the "celebrated and desperate guerrilla," Champ Ferguson whose last words were, "I die as true a Confederate as ever fought for my native South." Whenever it could find such symbols of resistance, the *Times* extolled them as worthy of emulation. The newspaper frequently included such selections as the following:

> Dr. Massie, late surgeon of the staff of General Walker, of Kirby-Smith's army, has just returned to Texas from a rapid trip to Virginia, his native state. He informs the Houston Telegraph that Virginia, and all other portions of the late Confederacy, which he visited, present an almost uninterrupted scene of ruin and desolation. . . . and many design going to Mexico and Brazil.[6]

Stories of unremitting migration out of the South recurred frequently in the *Times*. "It is authoritatively stated," the paper informed its readers on November 4, 1865, "that 8,000 Missourians crossed the plains this season en route to Oregon. Most of these,

4 See Patrick, *Jefferson Davis and His Cabinet*, 363.
5 *MT*, March 17, May 12, 1866.   6 *MT*, November 4, 1865.

having aided the South in the late war," the paper asserted, "are disfranchised under the new Constitution of Missouri."

The paper sometimes resorted to a form of racial hatred as subtle as it was effective. The *Times* left its readers with the definite impression that Negroes were largely in command in the Old South. Its columns were filled with stories about race, tales of Negroes caught stealing, Negro women advertising for white husbands, tension between whites and blacks, and perpetual mob violence. Other accounts poked fun at the South's new order, especially at those Negroes who "tried to put on airs."

A story entitled "On Her Dignity" is illustrative. It spoke of a certain "lady of color," a "veritable coquette," who "sashaid" into a Southern store one day after the war, "rustling her silks and sables" and giving the whites about her the impression that the new order was there to stay. When the white and very Southern store clerk who waited upon her called the Negro woman "Auntie," the Jezebel remonstrated: " 'How did you *redress* me?' I said, 'here auntie is something I recommend.' 'Well Madame I'll *deform* you dat's not my name,' the coquette said. 'My proper *distillation* is Miss ———.' " The paper went on to remind its readers that "Auntie" was a "perfectly proper" term for negresses in the *Old* South. This article broadly implied that the new Negro vocabulary was hardly an improvement on the old.[7]

By the use of such stories, often printed in Negro dialect, the *Mexican Times* took its readers' minds off other worries. The words, "Diabolical Acts of Negro Soldiers," headlined a lurid story on March 17, 1866, that featured the raping of a little white girl. The paper presented this as symbolic of totally new racial conditions under which returning whites would have to learn to live "at the mercy of the blacks."[8] Events back home confirmed its belief that the Negro deteriorated once he was given freedom.

To keep spirits up, the *Mexican Times* extolled the chivalry, acts of heroism, and wisdom of those wartime leaders who had come to Mexico. The paper, indeed, launched a journalistic *tour de force* to recapture the glory of the war and to memorialize the

[7] *MT*, January 27, 1866.   [8] *MT*, November 4, 1865.

General Jo. O. Shelby, C.S.A., about the time of the Mexican
adventure. From John N. Edwards, *Shelby and His Men.*

Confederate generals in Mexico. From left to right:
Cadmus M. Wilcox, John B. Magruder, Sterling Price,
William P. Hardeman, and Thomas C. Hindman.

Courtesy National Archives

Lost Cause.[9] A bitter piece entitled "The Character of Stonewall Jackson" was the first in a series, followed by Jubal Early's denunciation of his old enemy, Sheridan.[10]

But no story was more attractive to readers than "How General Shelby Captured a Gunboat," an account of his heroism while fighting in June, 1864, along the White River in Arkansas. The article reveals that, after the "brilliant" Shelby crept up on the iron-clad Union gunboat *Queen City*, "only a little blue band of water, smooth and pliant as a woman's necklace, lay between the lion and his prey." A Union sentinel paced his beat in the white moonlight, "little dreaming that Shelby and his fierce avengers of blood" were on his track and that four fully loaded cannon almost touched the sentinel with their "sinister muzzles." At the height of the drama someone lit the cannon fuses, and "again and again—the earth a volcano and the water red with battle light— did the helpless vessel receive in her vitals a hurricane of shot and shell." All this the "dashing Shelby" achieved without even so much as the loss of a man.[11]

The paper likewise obediently extolled the Emperor:

> With the peace he gives, comes prosperity. With his firm yet mild government comes national stability, national courage, and a desire to move forward in the great march of progress. Let us all, then, strengthen his hands—let us hold them up and help him in his arduous task, and deserve by our cordial support a portion of that protection and honor which he so nobly declares his intention of giving.[12]

The *Times* was equally enthusiastic over Carlotta. "Her majesty, the Empress," it exulted, "has endeared herself to everyone by her noble qualities as a sovereign and her many virtues as a woman. She is ever thoughtful of the suffering poor, and has been

---

[9] *MT*, January 27, 1866.

[10] *MT*, December 2, 1865; January 20, February 3, 1866.

[11] *MT*, January 27, 1866. Edwards' account of this same episode is in O'Flaherty, *General Jo Shelby*, 213. The full official story is in *OR*, Series I, Vol. XXVI, 413–32.

[12] *MT*, *ibid*.

princely in her charities." The Empress was not only "princely," she was also "the proudest, queenliest, noblest woman of the age . . . pure and stainless as a heaven-guarded child."[13]

The *Times* took every occasion to reassure English-speaking persons in Mexico that Carlotta and Maximilian were doing everything possible to keep law and order. The paper pointed, as example, to the costly measures taken by the government to protect civilians against guerrillas. Maximilian frequently used the *Times* to placate the fears of Americans and to propagandize persons who intended to come to Mexico.

On occasion the *Times*'s enthusiasm exceeded its accuracy. It represented life south of the border as uniquely tolerant of ideas, religion, and race. "You can select such society as you please. You can go to mass on Sunday morning and to the bull fight in the evening, and to the opera at night. Or you can go and hear a very good Protestant sermon in French . . . ."[14] Imitating Commodore Maury's promotional literature, the *Times* tried to coax immigrants over Sheridan's "fictitious" boundary line:

> The fortunes which you have lost can be regained here by a few years of industry and enterprise. Come then and bring with you your families and your household goods. Let the maid and the matron—the aged sire, the tender son, and the hired servants all come.[15]

At Maury's request the *Times* published a number of energetic testimonials by planters who were happy cultivating such crops as cotton, tobacco, and sugar cane.

Only rarely did the paper express distaste over conditions in Mexico, and then it linked the country's major problems to immigration. In objecting to the lack of a Mexican middle class, for instance, the *Times* believed a larger foreign population would help create a stable bourgeois society. It also spoke out for wider use of Confederate talents. It applauded the employment by the Mexican government of the engineer Henry Hirsch to help drain Mexico City of its excess water, a condition already causing the

[13] *MT*, November 4, 1865; November 14, 1866.
[14] *MT*, January 27, 1866.   [15] *MT*, September 16, 1865.

sinking of public buildings. The *Times* advocated even greater use of Confederates—particularly in the army—and once suggested that although the Mexican authorities had been kind to the exiles, they had failed to understand the military use that could be made of them.

When, however, immigrant complaints about the slow processing of their land claims or crop failures or native molestations became too strong, the paper sprang to the defense of Maximilian's government: "As Rome was not built in a day," it admonished complainers, "neither can large tracts of land be set apart and surveyed in an hour. We therefore repeat: have patience and you shall be provided for."[16] In contrast to Maximilian's official *Diario del Imperio*, the *Times* carefully avoided mention of the internal warfare in Mexico, seeking not to alarm prospective immigrants. Only occasionally did the paper permit itself to print adverse military news. Usually its headlines read, "Another Imperial Victory."

In the *Mexican Times* appeared detailed accounts on expected immigrants; one of these read as follows:

> Judge William G. Swan, a member of congress of the Confederacy, and others are about to immigrate from Columbus, Georgia. Major General John S. Williams of Kentucky, accompanied by sixty persons left Nashville last week and we are advised of one hundred and fifty families in West Virginia, who are preparing to make their home in Mexico.[17]

Many such immigrants crossed over into Mexico from Texas, but others quietly floated down the Mississippi from the border states of Tennessee and Kentucky on river boats and flatboats. After reaching New Orleans, they would try to book passage for Havana or Vera Cruz. This was a delicate undertaking as the New Orleans authorities had strict orders to stop all fleeing Confederates. If customs and immigration officials allowed an occasional party clandestinely to slip through the dragnet established by Grant and Sheridan, such officers had to be sure it was worth their while.

[16] *MT*, November 4, 1865; March 31, 1866.   [17] *MT*, March 3, 1866.

The "chief government detective" at New Orleans allegedly asked one group for as much as five hundred dollars. After clearing the hurdle of bribery, a ship broker took their passage money and herded them on a small, crowded schooner "of about 90 tons burthen with 4,500 feet of lumber until there was barely room for a man to crawl between the floor of the deck and the lumber; he [the ship broker] filled the space fore and aft with barrels, boxes, etc., which made the trip anything but agreeable or according to promise." Emigrant baggage shifting to and fro in the center cabin of this old scow scarcely left room for the passengers. The voyage with its diet of beans, sauerkraut, and hardtack proved a nightmare. Persons who had emptied their pockets of precious dollars in order to obtain transportation of this type wrote long letters to the *Times* to give vent to their disgust at the short rations barely fit to eat, the sleeping accommodations which were virtually nonexistent, and the indescribably nauseating toilet facilities. The paper did its best to appear sympathetic.[18]

The *Times* worried over a confused border policy which made possible the bilking by crooked officials of those who sought permission to emigrate. President Johnson once stated that no passport was necessary to leave Southern ports, but passports or equivalent permission were consistently demanded at embarkation centers. Before the wife of Governor Isham Harris left to join her husband in Mexico, she took the precaution of writing to the President. He again replied that no permit was necessary "for her or anybody else," but, the *Times* reported, when she presented herself to a local provost marshal, he hesitated. After reading the President's letter, the confused official gave her the passport. This latter document, the paper added, she actually did not need.[19] Such were the problems with which the *Times* wrestled.

The success of the *Times* was due in large measure to the efforts of one man, its unusual editor, Governor Allen of Louisiana. Douglas Southall Freeman, writing of his career during the Civil War, has called Allen "the single great administrator produced by

[18]*MT*, March 24, 1866.   [19] *MT*, May 12, 1866.

the Confederacy." By establishing an efficient system of state stores and by trading openly with Mexico, he rescued Louisiana "from the direst straits . . . ."[20] Allen, a very popular leader, had dreaded leaving the South. Before his departure he had addressed a proclamation to the people of Louisiana, urging them to remain strong in the face of an unknown future:

> If my voice could be heard and heeded at Washington, I would say, "Spare this distracted land—oh spare this afflicted people. In the name of bleeding humanity, they have suffered enough!" But, my countrymen, this cannot be. I am one of the proscribed—I must go into exile—I have stood by you, fought for you, and stayed with you, up to the very last moment, and now leave the office of governor with clean hands. . . . Fellow citizens in this darkest hour of my life . . . I have nothing to regret. . . . I go into exile not as did the ancient Roman, to lead back foreign armies against my native land—but rather to avoid persecution, and the crown of martyrdom. I go to seek repose for my shattered limbs.[21]

In addition to having been governor, Allen was a Confederate brigadier general in Louisiana and had suffered a shattered right leg on August 5, 1862, in the Battle of Baton Rouge. Earlier he had been wounded in the face while leading his regiment in the Battle of Shiloh, on April 6, 1862. He was also the author of *Travels of a Sugar Planter* (1851). Several of Allen's estates fell into the possession of carpetbagging Yankees who shamelessly exploited them and carried hundreds of hogsheads of sugar out of his plundered "sugar houses." With his largest plantation "a wide waste of fallow fields grown up with weeds," Allen had reluctantly decided that exile was the only way out. Although he once enjoyed an income of more than $80,000 a year from his plantations, Allen, a most scrupulous governor, had refused to accept the benefactions which various Southerners offered him. At the end of the war Allen still had plenty of Confederate money from selling his wartime crops, but it was now worthless. A friend begged him to take a loan of $5,000 in gold after the penniless

[20] *DAB*, I, 192–93.
[21] Dorsey, *Recollections of Henry Watkins Allen*, 298–99.

Governor initially refused it as a gift. Allen borrowed only two horses, an ambulance, and $500, just enough to start him and his small party toward Mexico.

He made his way through Texas with several companions in his old wooden wagon. Whenever his leg pained him unduly, Allen would stretch out in his ambulance while someone else drove the horses. Everywhere he stopped, people afforded the Governor hospitality. A widower without family, Allen had acquaintances throughout the South. While staying overnight with a woman companion at Crockett, Texas, the despondent Allen broke down and cried. Unashamed of his tears, he openly lamented the need to leave the South. The outburst over, he sewed a few pieces of gold into a cloth belt which he planned to wear under his clothing. As Allen sat among close friends, trying to rationalize his predicament, the conversation turned to philosophy, which Allen had always loved. He spoke of Bolingbroke's "Reflections Upon Exile," which he read aloud in the presence of his lady friend and the small group of persons traveling southward with him. As the next morning dawned, Allen put aside Bolingbroke's apologia and faced up to his future.

Placing a silver goblet in his pocket as a souvenir from his admiring hostess, Allen continued on his way. The Governor traveled light, and she described him as dressed "in a loose suit of checked linen, the coat made like a full hunting shirt." Allen's party usually bivouacked secretly at farmhouses along the Texas roads at night. His aide, a Colonel Denis, wrote a friend: "We left San Antonio on the 17th of June, 1865, literally loaded with presents of all sorts, made by kind friends, to the Governor: boxes of wines, fine liquors, preserves, cigars, coffee, etc."[22]

After his arrival Allen was immediately taken by the charm of Mexico City, which he called the "garden-spot of the Continent." He admired the fine carriages, elegantly furnished houses, and the society of that capital. Staying at the San Carlos Hotel, Allen became a member of that circle of Confederates who were welcomed at Maximilian's court. But social success, he realized, was

[22] *Ibid.*, 326.

not to be confused with financial security. He had little or no money, and despite the favors of the great, he was reduced to teaching English classes in order to earn his keep.

Friends told him that he should seek employment more befitting his station, and Allen one day wrote his lady acquaintance news of importance: "I have made arrangements to publish a newspaper in English in this place. . . . I am out of money, and must do something to live. I am too proud to beg, and too honest, I hope, to steal."[23] Maximilian had asked him to come to Chapultepec Castle to discuss starting an English language newspaper in Mexico. As the paper was to communicate his policies to immigrants, the Emperor provided a subsidy of ten thousand dollars to found the *Mexican Times.*

The Confederates, naturally, were the newspaper's chief patrons, contributors as well as readers. Its editor welcomed stories by subscribers, and he tried to get as much news as possible from the States, particularly wartime reminiscences that included such heroes as Robert E. Lee, Stonewall Jackson, and Jo Shelby.

The editor needed almost all the money he received from the Emperor to buy paper and ink for the journal. He could not afford even to employ an assistant and frequently complained of the ensuing effect on his health, which deteriorated rapidly: "I suffer much from my old wounds, and am sometimes so lame I can hardly walk to my office . . . . I pass hours and hours with no one but my Mexican servant to listen to the impatient ravings of a fevered brain." As Freeman puts it, most of Allen's career in Mexico was "a battle with death."[24]

Despite homesickness and ill health, Allen could not bring himself to return to Louisiana: "I cannot ask for a pardon," he confessed to correspondents. Thanking friends back home for offering to intercede with President Johnson on his behalf, he wrote: "A parole I will gladly accept, but I would not beg for pardon at the hands of any mortal power. I bend the knee only to God. I don't think I have done wrong."[25]

As a newspaperman, Allen was able to go to the opera or to a

[23] *Ibid.*, 333–34.   [24] *DAB*, I, 193.   [25] *Ibid.*, 355.

theater almost any night without paying the admission price. But even such events—which should have distracted his attention from the plight of the South—made him lonely. He confessed that sentimental music produced a strange effect upon him. It took him back "to the scenes of my childhood and my early manhood—to the pleasant days I have spent with the warm hearts from which I am forever parted." Separation from friends, not financial worries, gnawed away most at Allen.

Allen would have suffered greater hardships in Mexico, but he was blessed by an almost forgotten personal investment which was, fortunately, not part of his confiscated Louisiana estate. In Paris before the war he had bought three thousand dollars' worth of assorted jewels. Anticipating the outbreak of hostilities, he had deposited with a friend abroad some diamond cuff links, necklaces, and other pieces. Once he received his valuables in Mexico, he sold them, but foolishly invested part of the money in a vineyard near the capital. Another part he poured into his newspaper. He spent still more precious dollars to relieve the misery of others less fortunate than he.

The Governor was one Southerner who had many close friends in Mexico. He gained a reputation as a humanitarian. Despite the fact that shortly before his death he was saving money to have one of his legs amputated, he continued until the last to help out persons in want, whether they were Confederates or not. Unlike some conceited and self-centered generals who went there, he thought constantly about the welfare of his native hosts. After his death friends learned how generous Allen really was. Upon hearing the news of his death, a dirty, impoverished street beggar, of the type that dotted the streets of Mexico, cried out:

"Oh Lord! Lord!" and fell on her knees in sudden grief, tears streaming down her cheeks, wringing her hands, "then I don't know what to do! My last friend is gone. Unless he prays to God in heaven to send us help, I don't know what to do!" Then she went on to say, "Oh madam, he was the savior of ten of us poor women, in my neighborhood, while our husbands were in the army . . . . mine was brought home a cripple . . . . Governor Allen . . . had supplies sent us all, and gave us some money, and now he is dead—gone to heaven, Oh, Lord! Lord!"[26]

Allen's *Mexican Times,* started on a shoestring, was successful among the Confederates not only because it was published in English, but also because of the relief it afforded its readers from Maximilian's wretched official newspaper. While a few Southerners at his court followed the announcements of the *Diario del Imperio,* its columns illustrated the Emperor's continued remoteness from the Mexican people. Overflowing with trivial news of European monarchy and with the social flutterings of dukes and duchesses, the government paper alienated large numbers of Mexicans and some Confederates. Too often it was filled with items of interest to neither group.

On January 8, 1866, when the *Diario* ran an edition with heavy black borders around the edges of each page, the occasion was not, as might have been expected, a tragedy to be shared in common by Mexicans. Instead the paper mourned the death of Carlotta's father, the king of the Belgians. Such familial veneration, quite dissociated from the interests of the Mexican people, was characteristic of the *Diario.* While Maximilian's paper voiced concern about the teaching of Latin in the public schools or about sanitary conditions in hospitals, it made no real impact upon the public. Everyone knew the *Diario* was not interested in personalities outside the imperial circle. Confederates were mentioned only if they were members of the government or of Maximilian's social retinue.

The *Diario's* routine announcements regarding expropriations of private lands ("for government purposes") greatly irritated Mexican landowners. The Confederates, too, suffered guilty consciences over these expropriations for their benefit. Whenever the government journal announced the meting out of severe sentences for resisting expropriation or the death penalty for desertion from the army, Maximilian's *Diario* became a symbol of legalized exploitation by a hated foreign government. Understandably, few Mexicans read the newspaper.

[26] *Ibid.,* 369.

Editor Allen died of general infirmity on April 22, 1866, at the age of forty-six. He had been the moving spirit behind the *Times*, and it was difficult to replace him.[27] His position was taken by the garrulous Major John N. Edwards who later became editor of the Kansas City *Star*. But Edwards could write only high-flown, verbose editorials which proved difficult to read even in an age that appreciated a flowery style. Given to adulation of General Shelby, on whose staff he had served, Edwards filled the *Times* with praise of his hero.

The new editor reported to his readers that Louisiana's incumbent governor, J. Madison Wells, had requested that the body of former Governor Allen be transported back to Louisiana. This request honored Allen's well-known attachment to his native state; he had once written a close friend: "When it shall please God to consign this mutilated body to its last resting place—be it among strangers in Mexico, or friends in Louisiana—I will want no better epitaph inscribed on my tomb than . . . the closing part of your letter: 'Your friends are proud to know that Louisiana had a Governor who had an opportunity of securing a million of dollars in gold, and yet preferred being honest in a foreign land without a cent.' "[28]

Shortly before his death an abortive movement to make Allen governor had been initiated by old friends in Louisiana. An "Allen Circular," unbeknownst to him, had been widely circulated throughout Louisiana on Allen's behalf. Despite the fact that close friends protested "unauthorized use of his name," pointing out that Allen was "liable to arrest and prosecution as the highest civil officer of Louisiana under Confederate authority," big public meetings were held in the early months of 1866 on Allen's behalf by irreconcilables calling themselves "Young Men's Allen Associations." They posted placards, made speeches, and gen-

[27] See Dorsey, *Recollections of Henry Watkins Allen*, 364, and Alfred J. Hanna, "A Confederate Newspaper in Mexico," *Journal of Southern History*, Vol. XII (February, 1946), 67. A sketch of Allen is in Clayton Rand, *Sons of the South*, 122.

[28] H. W. Allen, to R. C. Cummings, December 25, 1865, in Dorsey, *Recollections of Henry Watkins Allen*, 336.

erally campaigned for the "honor of the old South." Little did these faithful partisans realize they were campaigning to elect a dead man.[29]

Although his people could not have him alive, they wanted him anyhow. Into Henry Watkins Allen's coffin was placed the gray Confederate uniform packed into his luggage when he took leave of his Texas friend for a life of exile. He left behind few worldly goods, taking to his grave the stars of his rank, the silver goblet she had given him, and financial obligations that would never be paid.[30]

The new editor of the *Times* and his fellow Confederates memorialized Allen in an appropriate ceremony and then shipped his remains, draped with a Confederate flag and covered with wreaths of coffee flowers, to Vera Cruz by wagon. As the buckboard rumbled over the dusty roads a dour *peón*, who had been a friend of the Governor, stood guard over him just behind the driver of the train. At Vera Cruz dock workers hoisted Allen's coffin aboard a steamer that regularly ran between that port and New Orleans. The steamship company offered free transportation. After Allen's remains arrived home, Governor Wells informed his friends in Mexico that Louisiana planned to erect a monument where its former governor, the founder of the *Mexican Times*, could "sleep in the bosom of his native land."[31]

The *Times* was never the same after Allen's departure. In November, 1866, Edwards lost Maximilian's subsidy after the imperialist regime had begun to fall apart. Edwards then turned the paper over to a non-Southerner, Ford C. Barksdale, who converted the quasi-daily into a semi-weekly newspaper whose masthead proclaimed a dedication to "Mineralogy, Agriculture, Literature, Commerce, & Politics." Its circulation dropped to only

[29] See accounts in New Orleans *Star*, October 17, 1865, and in New Orleans *Crescent*, October 24, 1865, reprinted in Dorsey, *Recollections of Henry Watkins Allen*, 346–49; Willie Malvin Caskey, *Secession and Restoration of Louisiana*, 176–77.

[30] See E. W. Halsey to J. Bankhead Magruder, May 18, 1866, in Dorsey, *Recollections of Henry Watkins Allen*, 371–72; see also pp. 364–65.

[31] *MT*, April 28, June 2, 1866.

a few hundred copies thereafter; the Confederates had tired of reading it in the two years they had been in Mexico, and, by 1867, the paper was on its way to fast oblivion, its Confederate audience practically gone.

Attempting to pose as a more liberal journal, the *Times* got into trouble with General Marquez, the lively black-haired chieftain whom Maximilian had left in charge at Mexico City. As the capital came under siege by the liberal forces of General Porfirio Díaz, Marquez suppressed five issues of the *Times* and imprisoned its editor for a month.

The last issue of the *Times*, published on June 17, 1867, just two days before the execution of Maximilian, graphically portrays the desperate position of those Confederates who could not escape the capital. Not only were they doomed to share bombardments with the natives but severe censure as well. Crowds of angry people assembled outside the offices of the *Times* shouting "*¡Que Mueran los Yankees!*" and "*¡Mueran los cabrones Americanos!*" Barksdale tried to lecture Mexican demonstrators in his columns, stating it was "bad taste to insult a guest in your own house." The Confederates who remained had been invited there by the still existent government of Mexico, it pleaded. It was not the fault of Americans if Mexicans were now overthrowing that government. "Drive foreigners out of Mexico and leave it a thousand times worse off than it now is," the *Times* warned. It asked whether Mexicans wanted to give notice to the world that they were a people "making all endeavors to exclude learning, civilization and progress."[32] But gratuitous advice was not welcomed.

This final issue of the *Times* also reflected the exiles' new sense of kinship with the besieged citizens of the capital. On Sundays they joined the thousands of persons dressed in their best clothing who tried to forget shortages of meat, vegetables, candles, soap, and other supplies by escaping to the *Alameda*. The *Alameda*, a forest-covered park, with miles of winding walks, located in the middle of the city, was the last place where the shells crashing

[32] *MT*, March 27, April 7, 1867.

into the city's outer limits could be escaped. Perhaps a thousand carriages lined up almost hub to hub in that tree-covered refuge. "There people may go and pass the day in security," the *Times* explained.

The paper feared that the many coaches in the great park posed a danger to children. As nightfall approached and youngsters continued to play, they could easily be run over by careless drivers, the paper warned.[33]

An editorial appearing in this final issue of the *Times* shows how little the exiles comprehended the land to which they had come: "Incomprehensible, unfathomable, intangible and unnatural Mexico. Neither can foreigners nor can yourselves understand the people that populate your lands."[34]

[33] *MT*, April 17, 1867. Whiling away the hours in the sheltered *Alameda* the exiles thought of another war. The cannonading of the city and the crack of rifles from outlying battle lines led the *Times* to recall how Confederates had once tried to leave behind similar killings and injustices of the past. Now the Confederates who had stayed on in Mexico City found themselves virtually hostages.

[34] *MT*, June 17, 1867.

CHAPTER XVII

❦

Uprooted

Men swindled each other, litigated in the courts, sued for trivial sums, and, through spite, quarrelled and loafed, and drank and grew turbulent; ridiculed the Mexican religion, and depreciated the country and the people.

Senate Executive Document No. 15 (1867)

THE CYCLONIC WARFARE in Mexico was the immediate cause of the downfall of the Confederate colonies. However, there were other causes which derived from the colonists' own weaknesses. Surely the first of these was that they could neither select nor control the immigrants with whom they were thrown into association. Any Southerner with sufficient enthusiasm to do so could slip across the border via Galveston or Eagle Pass or take ship from New Orleans or Mobile for Vera Cruz. Maury's Southern agents, operating outside the law from cities as widely separated as Charleston and St. Louis, had screened prospective immigrants only slightly—if at all. These agents were eager to collect commissions from Maximilian's government, and by the time they were forced to cease their operations, they were urging ne'er-do-wells, paupers, and even thieves to go to Mexico. As a consequence, the caliber of the colonists deteriorated, as did mutual trust and harmony among them.

The undiscriminating zeal of Maury's agents was perhaps partly responsible for another difficulty. The Confederate colonies were heavily burdened with chair-bound generals bent upon a life of semiretirement and slug-abed politicians unaccustomed to manual labor. There were too few of the energetic farmers and mechanics needed to establish an agricultural community and to work the stubborn soil. A further difficulty was the chivalric temperament. Many of the exiles were interested more in their lost prestige than in work. These men could not fully realize that the status to which they aspired was rooted in a society that was largely dissolved. Each expected to be treated by the others with a deference in accordance with his past position. Such forms were impossible in a hectic, war-torn country. The exiles clashed often with one another—Shelby with Price, Reynolds with Maury, Magruder with Judge Perkins—and these clashes reflected not so much basic animosities as grievances over past grandeurs. This bickering proved disastrous. Success in Mexico required co-operation and tireless work. The cavalier virtues, the old bearing, and the old mannerisms were clearly inappropriate in this troublesome new land. Memories alone could not till the soil, lay roads, or build houses. The colonists needed to share with one another their plans and labors, their horses and mules, their agricultural implements, seeds, and other possessions. This they never quite learned to do.

Furthermore, the exiles found it virtually impossible to adjust their uprooted lives to a culture derived from Spain, the ancient enemy of their English ancestors. The Hispanic world was a Roman Catholic world, one with social institutions and loyalties basically different from those handed down to North Americans by England.

Other difficulties arose inevitably from the exile situation. One dilemma, for both former generals and former privates, was a pressing lack of money. Few of them had much capital. It was one thing for Maury or Price to draw a picture of the delights of colonization; it proved quite another to build barns, warehouses, homes, and businesses without heavy expenditure of funds and labor.

Unless they were engineers or mechanics, few exiles were able to find the jobs promised them by Maury and his colonization bureau. The trained railroad personnel who had at first found it easy to locate work, building and operating Mexico's new railroads, lost their jobs after fighting between the French Army and the *Juaristas* engulfed the area where Mexico's major railroad was being built. The Imperial Railway Company's construction program, which aimed to build a line from Vera Cruz to Mexico City, had to be completed much later by the Juárez government.[1]

A variety of misfortunes dogged the exiles. Discontent was voiced by those who had been consulted least over the course charted for them. Latecomers grew resentful over pre-emption of the best agricultural lands by Confederates who had arrived earlier. Dysentery and tropical fevers decimated weaker Confederates. Few ate properly, for almost everyone experienced short rations. Food shortages, especially of good red meat, helped cause exhaustion, weakened health, and ultimately brought on death.

One of the newest sources of information about the Confederate colonies in Mexico is the recently published diary of William Marshall Anderson. An adventurous Virginia surveyor and amateur archaeologist, Anderson arrived in Mexico in 1865 and received a commission from Maximilian's government through Commodore Maury to survey lands in the northern province of Coahuila for Confederate colonization.. He spent some months near tropical Carlota before traveling about the arid plateaus of Coahuila as an agent for Maximilian. The land which Anderson was to survey consisted of two million acres offered the government for colonization purposes by Carlos Sánchez Navarro, wealthy grand chamberlain to the Emperor. Anderson arrived at Patos, Coahuila, on January 8, 1866, and, with the aid of Jacobo

[1] Begun in 1857, the Mexican railroad network experienced many delays. In 1864 the Imperial Mexican Railway Company, an English firm with a capital of $30,000,000, made plans to build a through line from Vera Cruz to Mexico City. Construction was for a time undertaken by Smith, Knight and Company, a well-known builder of other Latin-American railways. The *New York Herald*, April 19, 1866, reported that the section from Vera Cruz to Paso del Macho had been opened just a year earlier. The project was also slowed down because of the necessity of bringing thousands of tons of supplies from England. H. D. B. Norris, superintendent, once with the New Orleans and Jackson Railroad Company, lived at Cordova until forced to flee.

Emperor Maximilian and his consort, Carlotta, about 1865.

Courtesy Huntington Library

Chapultepec Castle, the official residence of Maximilian and
Carlotta at the time of the Confederate colonization.

Küchler, a local resident, carried on his surveying work until February.[2]

On his way to Mexico by sea, in April, 1865, Anderson had encountered several wives of Confederate officials ("a strong representation from female rebeldom") aboard the steamer *Barcelona*. Anderson's superior, when he surveyed the lands in the district of Mapimí, was General Magruder. Anderson asked himself a number of questions about the experience of preparing lands in Mexico for American colonization:

> But is this country suitable for American settlement? Can they have the patience to collect water for irrigation? Can they bring the means, or use the patience, necessary to produce such an object? There is no timber at hand for building purposes. There can be no doubt that an immense amount of these lands will be one day profitably worked. What will be the cost of Artesian wells? This question will determine the fate of this country.[3]

He believed that neither Europeans nor Americans would settle in rural and remote Mexican areas unless better housing could be provided. He wrote in his journal: "mud houses and dirt floors will never do for them. I do not believe they would settle in Paradise without them."[4] Caught eventually between the cross fire of the *Juaristas* and the French, Anderson was forced, like other colonists in northern Mexico, to retreat southward. Temporarily arrested by the French and suffering from yellow fever, he decided to return home.

Before embarking at Vera Cruz for Cuba and the United States,

[2] Three letters of authorization for Marshall to engage in surveying are in the William Marshall Anderson Papers, Huntington Library; all are dated the same day: M. F. Maury to W. M. Anderson, November 24, 1865. A MS passport signed by French Marshal Bazaine, December 6, 1865, is among these papers, which are cited in Ramón Eduardo Ruiz (ed.), *An American in Maximilian's Mexico*, xxv, 40, 118 n., which indicates that Luis Robles, Maximilian's minister of *fomento* (interior), was anxious that a land office for Coahuila be established. The Navarros, who had actively supported Maximilian and the French intervention in Mexico, were so wealthy that they ultimately offered the imperial government ten million acres at fifty centavos an acre for colonization.

[3] Anderson, 184.   [4] Anderson, 86.

Anderson traveled through Carlota for the second time. In addition to disorder, he noted something that had not been discussed by any other witness, severe damage from a recent earthquake. This must have greatly added to the confusion at both Carlota and Cordova. After sailing, Anderson speculated in his diary concerning what might happen if Americans had been allowed to remain as rulers of Mexico:

> If the French are despised & feared now, in six months after the invasion the North Americans would be cursed & execrated. "*Carajos y Carambas*" would be rattled out with a fierceness and a fury which nothing but a Spanish mind can conceive or a Spanish tongue express.[5]

As unemployment, amoebic infections, banditry, and warfare combined to wreck the future of Anderson and other exiles in Mexico, they came to look upon Maury and his agents as tricksters who had been unwilling to risk bringing their own wives and children there, yet who had counseled others to do so. Those who had mistakenly transported families below the border now faced the hardship of taking them back.

The hazards surrounding the expatriates who doggedly stayed on produced a mounting edginess. More and more they relieved their uneasiness by abusing fellow exiles. Exiles are frequently psychological malcontents both in the new land and in the old. The misfits in Mexico quarreled over such matters as the ownership of a chicken. After one Confederate insulted another publicly at the top of his voice at high noon in Carlota's town square, a duel was averted only by the intercession of wiser heads. Verbal throat cutting, castigation of colleagues, self-pity, and the use of venomous sarcasm did not help the Confederates to establish an amicable community spirit.

Furthermore, as Maximilian's strength declined, the colonists faced an ever increasing danger of attack from the Mexican people. Large segments of the populace were embittered toward the

[5] Anderson, 116, 117, Correspondence from General Jubal Early concerning a lost purse of Anderson's is in the Anderson MSS.

exiles because they had been aided by Maximilian. His backing had, of course, given some Confederates a false sense of security. The most unthinking among them had usurped cultivated lands from mulish Indians whose tiny plots surrounded tracts assigned the exiles. These natives had spent years developing their gardens with rude implements and could be expected to be impatient to repossess their land and take vengeance on the invader. Haughtiness toward the Indians was out of order in the Mexico of the middle 1860's.

At daybreak on May 15, 1866, the small colony at Omealco, about thirty miles from Cordova, was openly attacked by a band of *liberales,* composed largely of disgruntled Indians under the command of the Juárist General Luis Figueroa. His group, described as "cut-throats and robbers who fought with Juarez mainly for the purpose of stealing," swiftly moved into the settlement, rounded up the local residents, ransacked their houses, rifled such personal belongings as watches, shoes, and clothing, corralled their livestock, and confiscated agricultural implements of any worth. These natives acted without authorization from Juárez, but as guerrillas disgusted with Confederates and other foreigners who squatted on lands formerly the property of Mexicans.

The raid on Omealco was less malicious than punitive. After Figueroa's men announced that they were sequestering the land on which the tiny colony stood, they took custody of a bewildered and helpless band of Americans, whom they led away from Omealco toward the sea. For days the prisoners were fed only an occasional ear of corn or a few dry *tortillas* and spare stalks of sugar cane. They were insulted and spat upon as they staggered toward Vera Cruz, where their captors hoped to see them embark upon ships which would take them forever from Mexican shores. Fortunate not to have been shot, they somehow endured their forced march, arriving penniless and destitute at Bianco Bay, near the seaport of Vera Cruz. Had it not been for the aid given by a generous New Orleans Creole who lived nearby and took pity upon them, they might have starved to death. Some of the

Omealcans were able to book passage at once. Others, finding it impossible to sail soon, went to Carlota seeking safety. Their stay was not to be a long one.[6]

An increasing number of marauding bands of the sort that descended upon Omealco forced other scattered colonists to abandon their farms. With gardens and orchards overrun, some colonists threw in their lot with a defending French garrison in Cordova proper. But this could be only a temporary solution. The natives were arrayed against them, and so was history itself.[7]

The name Carlota was enough to doom the largest of the colonies. Once the French started to move out of Mexico in retreat, the natives were emboldened to attack the Confederate center. The story of the fall of Carlota is similar to that of Omealco. About dusk on June 1, 1866, at almost the very hour the Confederate patron saint Carlotta departed from Mexico forever, over one thousand Mexicans swooped down from out of nowhere upon the colony named after her. A year's work was undone in a night. Houses and shops were set on fire. The streets were soon swarming with fleeing householders carrying their possessions, pushing and pulling one another, trying to find wagons, carriages, anything by means of which to escape to the harbor of Vera Cruz. Mexicans who had collaborated with the Confederates were stoned. A billow of smoke enveloped the town. Stores were looted, houses plundered, and men shot on their doorsteps. About one hundred colonists, all those left in Carlota, were marched into the mountains by brigands. A few were carried off from their sick-beds, half-crazed and screaming. They were kept without food for days and "beaten with sabres and pricked with lances." Some died, but the majority made their way back to the French lines, stripped of everything they owned. Farm imple-

[6] See Hill, "The Confederate Exodus to South America," *Southwestern Historical Quarterly*, Vol. XXXIX (April, 1936), 321. The best account of the Omealco raid is Tom J. Russell, "Adventures of a Cordova Colonist," *Southern Magazine*, Vol. XI (August, 1872), 90–102, 155–66.

[7] *Missouri Statesman*, December 15, 1866; *New York Times*, December 7, 1866.

ments were smashed, stock was slaughtered and driven off, dwellings destroyed, and crops left to wither.[8]

Suitcases, trunks, and other possessions were strewn all over the muddy streets of Carlota. Most people lost their remaining savings, the only funds left to pay for the trip homeward. The half-naked Omealcan refugees, after two weeks in Carlota's hotels (thrown open to them free of charge), had to flee once more. French Marshal Bazaine, himself engaged in a desperate rear-guard action, took pity upon half a dozen or so families and, according to the New Orleans *Crescent* for March 7, 1867, generously furnished them transportation to New Orleans. Although the old soldier did his best to help Americans, he was too much involved in getting his own troops safely back to France to be of further help to them.[9]

When the French withdrew from Carlota, in March, 1867, after their cordon of "contra guerrillas" was soundly defeated, the town could not be recaptured and was abandoned by the Confederates, who streaked toward the coast. The Juárez *liberales* turned back parcels of land at Carlota, Cordova, and Omealco to those *peones* who reclaimed them. Peasants were allowed to return to the huts they formerly occupied without paying rent. Their *milpas*—pieces of land formerly reserved for their exclusive use—were again restored to them.

The number of colonists in the Carlota–Cordova Valley had never been great. The most favorable estimates never surpassed several hundred, with no more than several thousand American exiles in all Mexico.[10] Yet, as late as June, 1866, Carlota had sheltered some five thousand persons (if one counts a regiment of French soldiers detailed to protect surrounding communities). Overnight, after the attack, it became virtually deserted. Shuttered houses, burned buildings, and weed-wild streets were all that was left behind. Half a dozen families eked out a living, trying to get together money enough for the trip home.

[8] *Ibid.,* October 5, 1866.   [9] *MT,* June 6, 1866.
[10] Burger and Bettersworth, *South of Appomattox,* 70.

There was no stopping the Juárez tide. In March, 1867, imperialist General Marquez momentarily succeeded in breaking through the Juárist encampments encircling besieged Querétaro, and for a while the Confederates hoped he might be able to save Mexico City. Accompanied by Santiago Vidaurri, the northern frontier chieftain who had defected from Juárez, Marquez assumed command of the remaining five thousand troops in Maximilian's shattered empire. En route from Querétaro to Mexico City, Marquez raised, almost unbelievably, several thousand other volunteers, among them a few Confederates. But the demoralization of Maximilian's imperialists was too deep. The final siege of Mexico City lasted only a few more weeks. On June 2, the day after the Emperor's execution at Querétaro, republican troops under the young Juárist General Porfirio Díaz broke the siege as cannoneers of the liberal army trained their sights on the symbolic, mossy walls of Chapultepec Castle, Maximilian's former residence.

The Juárists had little trouble capturing Puebla, Orizaba, and Paso del Macho. On July 4, 1867, Vera Cruz fell. At Vera Cruz the Confederate exiles, fearing reprisals, patiently awaited transportation home. After Marshal Bazaine's French legions were on the seas, these Southerners were caught in the death throes of Maximilian's regime. Their greatest danger then was the possibility of being charged with collaboration with the imperialists, a charge which in many cases could be made with validity. Nineteen of the most prominent Mexican prisoners captured with Maximilian at Querétaro had been tried and condemned to death. When Juárez triumphantly entered Mexico City on July 15, he assessed severe fines upon wealthy collaborators. Juárez clearly did not plan a general amnesty for those who had fought him or even a pardon that would benefit anyone in the immediate future. All these factors pressed in upon the Confederates and encouraged even the most sanguine of them to flee from Mexico.

It was no longer a question of whether they ought to return to the United States, or even of when, but of how. For most, it was the bitter moment of truth when they must admit that their venture had failed. Long since forgotten by the government that had invited them, most of the Americans still in Mexico stayed only long enough after the fall of the capital to secure ship passage home.

Back in the States, if the newspapers mentioned the plight of the Confederate exiles at all, it was only rarely in terms of pity. The exiles suffered vigorous abuse from the press, sometimes even from Southern newspapers. The discredited colonists were taken to task for not having sought the new homes they thought they needed in one of the states of the Union. Southern newspapers pointed out that plenty of vacant lands existed in such sparsely populated states as South Carolina, Mississippi, Louisiana, and Tennessee. The journals believed that true service to the South might better have been accomplished by settling these areas rather than by going abroad to serve a foreign emperor.[11]

When returning Confederates needed encouragement most, they did not receive it. A bitingly sarcastic account of the destruction of Carlota was carried in the New York *Tribune* for June 22, 1866:

> The far-famed city of Carlota ... consisting of a house, a barn and a stable, has been destroyed. The fields of coffee, by means of which Judge Perkins, of Louisiana, expected to retrieve his lost fortunes have been ravaged; the pineapple plants, out of which General Price was to distil a most delicious fourth-proof brandy, have been uprooted ... the palm roofed shanties under the shelter of which about one hundred Southern emigrants have sought a refuge have burned to the ground.[12]

Thereafter, the New York *Times* and also the *Tribune* ridiculed them in especially brutal terms.

United States newspapers charged that the Confederates had aroused native violence because they had tried to enslave their laborers. Rumors circulated that they had seized workmen, tying

[11] Harmon, "Confederate Migrations to Mexico," *Hispanic American Historical Review*, Vol. XVII (November, 1937), 476–77.

[12] 39 Cong., 1 sess., *House Exec. Doc. No. 76*, 5–6, 17; see also *New York Times*, January 19, 1866, for a bitter attack on the Confederates.

them with ropes and forcing them to labor in the fields under deplorable conditions of servitude. There is virtually no proof that the exiles in Mexico ever contemplated the extension of a Southern "slaveocracy" into Mexico. Some among them may, however, have wished for the introduction of a labor system that was a disguised form of slavery. Maury had hinted at such a system in his colonization literature. The economic system of Mexico had itself encouraged a form of enslaved peasantry. *Peones,* unable to repay landholding masters, incurred lifelong obligations under labor-contract laws that resembled share-cropping arrangements in the post–Civil War South. Under such a system of peonage even the children of debtors could not be released from the bondage of their parents. Whenever *peones* owed an indebtedness to foreign oppressors like the Confederates, Juárist agitators proclaimed it the duty of loyal Mexicans to escape. If such escape were resisted, the resulting violence was charged to those foreigners who had reintroduced "economic slavery" into Mexico. The Confederates, already renowned for a touch of racial intolerance, could easily be saddled with accusations which, though often untrue, helped spell the doom of Carlota and Cordova.[13]

One of the most complete accounts of these colonies in their last days was written on March 3, 1867, by an anonymous observer who took time to record some contemptuous observations, later reprinted in a United States Senate executive document. Although written in the high-flown language of the times, his remarks are acutely informative. The writer was apparently not a colonist himself, nor a Southerner, and was describing Cordova primarily:

> The Cordova colony is a thing of the past. The last two families bowed themselves out of the village of Carlota a week since. Others went last month, six months ago, and during the interim. There were no sorrowing, nor sighs, nor tears, but rejoicing and gladness as each one shook the Mexican dust from his shoes and turned

[13] An explanation of the prevalent Mexican land system is to be found in George M. McBride, *The Land Systems of Mexico,* 32.

his face gulfward. The streets and plaza look a little deserted and the broad mangoes wave their branches in the winds, and sing, in company with the sad night breeze, sort of a mournful requiem.

The writer continues:

Prices went down in a week, rents and credits went the self same way; and men who came without a dollar, and speculated upon their fellows, with hotel bills unpaid, stole, like thieves, as they were out of their own country, and landed on the other side of the Gulf with tales of robbery and misfortune and native treachery in their mouths.

In time, the writer indicates, such persons came to have reasons for damning their homeland less:

The United States, with free schools and free negroes tacked on, was not so finished a humbug after all. . . . What a breaking up followed in a few months—a swallowing of bitter terms, and savage invective—in vulgar phraseology, "dirt eating," humiliating excuses trumped up for going home again, a pulling down of flaring hotel signs, dropping of newspaper notices and defiant letter writing, a shirking of fair contracts and a general swindling of honest men.

The loudest talkers fell early, fell first; even the genial ex-judge, ex-senator from Louisiana [John Perkins] struck his colors in September, pushed off from Vera Cruz, leaving the friends he was instrumental in bringing hither to rough the trials and revolution alone. General Price, for whom there is some slight palliation, broken down and bent with age, misfortune, and grief, left without even notifying the families and men he had drawn here by promises of health and wealth and peace. . . . It was an open quiet tug between principle and starvation, and the latter won—always won. You have heard, perhaps, of moneyless men footing it all the way along the coast to Texas, and of hollow-eyed want on the streets of Cordova and Carlota. The first was not true; the latter was. Prodigality and pride, American characteristics, traveled all the way to Mexico, and were deeply humiliated. . . . Money was thrown away in amusement and lost at monte. . . .

Employment was to be had nowhere; so men wrangled instead, fought over their battles, fought each other . . . shirked the payment of debts, insulted strangers, insulted citizens, bullied and boasted to the end. . . . A Yankee was spotted and shunned, noticed only when a loan or favor was asked. . . .

In Cordova . . . American character is associated with whiskey, braggadocio, rudeness, dishonesty, and indolence. . . . we are . . . bandits because we are foreigners, and belong to no flag whatever . . . off-scourings of all nations . . . like the *condottierri* . . . hired to the chief who pays best. To this we have come at last . . . Let his majesty's government form us into a legion and put us at the front under General Miramon.[14]

[14] *Message from the President of the United States Regarding Conditions in Mexico*, 40 Cong., 1 sess., *Senate Exec. Doc. No. 15*, 144–50.

❀

CHAPTER XVIII

After Surrender

ONLY A HANDFUL of exiles braved conditions in Mexico under Juárez. Among them was Major George W. Clarke, a native of Arkansas who in 1867 founded a journal in Mexico City which succeeded the old *Mexican Times*. He called his newspaper *The Two Republics*. During the 1870's the journal was a modest success, although it was undistinguished in quality. It gives us a few of the names of those Confederates who did not flee Mexico. These remaining exiles had generally not been the leaders of the Confederate migration. In 1870, Thomas Nelson, American minister to Mexico, wrote that there was not "a single notability remaining out of the many Confederate refugees."[1] Clarke himself was almost unknown during the exodus from the South and only by keeping his record quiet, lest he be charged with past sympathy for Maximilian, did he eke out a living under the Juárez and Díaz regimes.[2]

A number of the exiles who stayed in Mexico died there. Texas Governor Murrah died in 1865, Louisiana Governor Allen in 1866, and General W. H. Stevens in 1867. Many of the Confederate officers who had gone to Mexico with Shelby lie in the United

[1] Rippy, *The United States and Mexico*, 251, quotes *U.S. Doc. For. Rel.* (1870), 205.

[2] Frank A. Knapp, Jr., "A New Source on the Confederate Exodus to Mexico; The New Republics," *Journal of Southern History*, Vol. XIX (August, 1953), 364–73.

States National Cemetery in Mexico City. Among them is also General Slaughter, who lived as long as 1901.

Many Confederates remigrated to other countries. General John G. Walker went from Mexico to England, where he became the agent for a group of Confederates who went to Venezuela. General Danville Leadbetter, an official of the Mexican railways under Maximilian, subsequently migrated to Canada.[3] Former Senator Pierre Soulé of Louisiana, associated with Senator Gwin's abortive colonization scheme in Sonora, went to Havana, Cuba, after his arrest during the war and died in 1870.[4] General Hamilton P. Bee, who had fought a vigorous rear-guard action in Texas before going to Mexico, also went to Cuba. Like General Magruder and Senator Soulé, he engaged in business there for a time, as a ship broker.

Some who remained excluded from United States federal and state amnesty proclamations and who were unable to return without permission went to Europe or Canada when finally forced, because of the defeat of Maximilian, to leave Mexico. A few recalcitrants who felt no genuine remorse found it too demeaning to request special Presidential or Congressional pardons. Particularly odious to them were the activities of pardon brokers—persons who had special access to either the President or Congress and who sold their services to applicants for clemency. Repelled by such aspects of repatriation, Judge Perkins, the fiery rebel from Madison, Louisiana, who had drawn up the state's secession ordinance, decided never to try returning to the South as a prodigal son. He fled from Mexico to Paris and ended his years there.[5]

Other exiles remigrated to the rich agricultural land of Brazil, where they were tendered hospitality by a benevolent emperor,

[3] MT, October 29, 1866; Melvin E. Mitchell, "The Movement of the American Confederates to Mexico," (M.A. thesis).

[4] On Soulé see DAB, XVII, 405–406. Gwin himself died much later, in 1885, but lived in relative obscurity in New York after eight months' imprisonment at Fort Jackson in 1865. See DAB, VIII, 64–65.

[5] Such famous Confederates as Robert Toombs and Judah P. Benjamin, both in Jefferson Davis' cabinet, as well as General P. G. T. Beauregard, drifted abroad for years after the war. In England, Benjamin settled down in a new career and never returned to the United States. See Appendix F below.

Don Pedro II. Like Maximilian before him, this European ruler wanted foreigners to help sustain his American empire. Encouraged by two notable books of the time, Ballard S. Dunn's *Brazil, the Home for Southerners* and Lieutenant William Henry Herndon's *The Exploration of the Valley of the Amazon,* several small shiploads of migrants sailed for Rio de Janeiro and São Paulo, joining others who had migrated directly to Brazil after the war. Some of their descendants still live in Brazil today. Others went on, like General Walker, to cast their lot with the Venezuelan Confederates. Still others migrated to Egypt.

General Early, it will be recalled, migrated from Mexico to Canada. Early started to write his memoirs while still abroad. They were a highly partisan record of what *should* have happened during the Civil War. After a residence of several years in Canada, Early slipped back into the South—to take up a law practice at Lynchburg, Virginia. Actually Early's heart was elsewhere. Still the champion of Jefferson Davis and the Lost Cause, the General, however, *tried* to live in his own country, even if he believed it had changed for the worse.

He practiced law sporadically, and, soon after his return, he, with General Beauregard, found a means to use his talents in a more financially profitable way than any of the former exiles did. In 1868, the Louisiana legislature authorized the incorporation of a Louisiana Lottery Company. It was estimated that this organization would yield the state an annual income of $40,000 a year. To give a measure of respectability to the venture, Generals Beauregard and Early were hired to supervise the operation. The lottery, however, came under serious criticism from church groups and the public press. Repeatedly the legislature was petitioned to suspend the charter of the lottery company. It was charged that persons who could not afford to gamble were squandering their earnings. The New Orleans *Democrat* averred that even if "Methuselah had bought a daily ticket all his life he would have spent about $250,000 to win $2,678.85."

To counter such charges, the syndicate that operated the lottery utilized Beauregard and Early as authenticators of its fairness. In 1877 the revered generals published advertisements intended to quiet public criticism. They explained that if the operators of the lottery had indeed drawn some of the largest prizes, it was because half the tickets had remained unsold. The shortcomings of the lottery were bound to reflect upon the generals themselves. They drew large salaries while in its pay. By 1879 other state lotteries had been declared illegal by their state courts. The Kentucky lottery had ceased to operate in 1878, and thereafter the Georgia and Alabama lotteries folded. This left the Louisiana lottery as the main target of prudes and malcontents, with Early and Beauregard bearing the brunt of the criticism. Repeated attempts were made to do away with it. Postmaster General John Wanamaker denounced the lottery as a fraud. From 1887 to 1890 its stockholders reputedly received profits runing from 110 to 170 per cent. Finally, in 1894, in response to antilottery pressure, federal legislation was passed that made it impossible for such a lottery to be operated. Early was to die soon thereafter.

General Early, as the most vocal champion of Lee, of the Army of Northern Virginia, and of Davis, used the presidency of the Southern Historical Society to promote the Southern cause. He engaged in a futile attempt to discredit General Longstreet and other Confederate leaders who, by accepting Northern political appointments, truckled to Unionists. To the end of his life in 1894, at age seventy-seven, the General remained fretful and unhappy. This guardian of Southern heritage was unrepentant. He never took an oath of allegiance to the United States.[6]

[6] In the war's bitter afterglow Early went on defending the Southernism for which he had fought in the Shenandoah Valley. A man like Early remained a subject of popular interest, and his memoirs, which told of how he and his 28,000-man army came within a hair's breadth of capturing Washington, sold well. Generals Lee, Hood, and Johnston also wrote recollections, and other leaders busily collected source materials. Jefferson Davis and Johnston lamentably collected information, in part at least, to justify their conduct in the war and to feud with each other. Self-justification was one of Early's major purposes in his quarrel with his old enemy Sheridan. See Ezra J. Warner, *Generals in Gray*, 79–80. Regarding the Louisiana lottery consult John S. Ezell, *Fortune's Merry Wheel*, 244–49, 295.

Some of the most recalcitrant exiles, particularly ranking generals like Early, considered themselves spiritual preservers of a Confederate social order. These washed-out patriarchs with the long beards tried vainly to set the tone of Southern life. Dreaming of the past, they sought to justify their wartime conduct and to defend the South. Such Southern shortcomings as awkward race relations they sought to drown out in a reverential appeal to tradition and glory.

Certain wartime commanders continued to receive the reverence of their troops. Special adulation was reserved for Lee and other leading officers. "Old Joe" Johnston, and "Fighting Joe" Wheeler, too, remained especially popular. Among the exiles, Shelby, of course, and Price, as well as Kirby-Smith, remained popular. In 1890, Kirby-Smith happened to be riding in a patriotic parade with Johnston during a great Confederate Memorial Day celebration in Atlanta. Suddenly a group of enthusiastic veterans unhitched the horses from the flower-bedecked carriage and insisted upon pulling it themselves along the parade route. Such outbursts of emotion at public events stemmed, of course, from nostalgic and sentimental memories of wartime associations. They were not unknown in the North, but certainly occurred more frequently in the South.[7]

Some general officers never achieved great postwar popularity. A few were tempted to abandon the South only after they had returned from the battlefield. Among these was General Richard B. Taylor, who had fought in the Trans-Mississippi Department and who had later obtained the release from prison of President Davis. Years after the end of the war, General Taylor decided to leave the South for at least a time: "Dismissing hope of making my small voice heard in the mitigation of the woes of my State, in May 1873, I went to Europe and remained many months." Taylor felt that the South's leading "few survivors" were "distrusted as responsible for past errors."[8]

By mid–1867 most Chivalrics—as both die-hard Southerners

[7] Burger and Bettersworth, *South of Appomattox*, 232–33.
[8] Taylor, *Destruction and Reconstruction*, 329, 331.

and exiles were once termed—had returned to the South. By steamer or on horseback, sometimes even on foot, they threaded their way homeward. We know few of the details. The Northern press criticism that exiles underwent influenced them to re-enter the country as quietly as possible. They were not inclined to publicize further their humiliating Mexican experiences. Some of the penniless wanderers returned to the South clandestinely, almost shamefacedly, under names other than their own. The desire for anonymity helps explain why more has not been written about these refugees of the Civil War and why their story has almost been lost to posterity.

With the exception of Early and other hotheads, most leading exiles were now ready to follow Robert E. Lee's injunction to his soldiers to settle down and devote themselves to rearing their children. They wanted to be good citizens of a re-United States. In the words of Douglas Southall Freeman, in his notable book, *Lee's Lieutenants*, the commander in chief "set an example of hard work, of reconciliation, of silence in partisan disputes, and of patience during the years when nearly all prominent Confederates were disfranchised."

For a few Rebels the return home was routine. Although the story is so matter of fact that it is hard to believe, George Creel actually encountered "one bearded colonel who, walking into his home after an absence of four years, merely threw down his hat and complained, 'Good Lord, Sally. Dinner not ready yet?' "[9]

Others found their return home bitterly disappointing. Past days of glory were over. It is never easy for men of spirit to forget a stirring and eventful past and to learn to live wholly in a present that is quiet and colorless. Furthermore, no Confederate leader was completely safe from ridicule or insult in the remaining days of the Radical Reconstruction era.[10]

Shortly after his return to the United States in 1871, Colonel

[9] Creel, *Rebel at Large*, 34.

[10] Only a week after he was home from the war, General Beauregard was approached by an obstreperous drunk who asked him to prove he was not a "damn nigger." In a stream of abuse the man accused Beauregard of being black. One can only imagine the effect of such an accusation upon an aristocratic, high-

Beverley Tucker, the Confederate who had been robbed so many times in Mexico, was dining at the Metropolitan Hotel in Washington one night when a drunken Northern colonel at the next table asserted several times, in an angry tone of voice, that Southern women's reputation for beauty was greatly overrated. When the Northerner next shouted that there was scarcely a virtuous lady to be found in the entire South, this was too much for Tucker. He sprang to his feet, handed the offender his card, and challenged him to a duel; arrangements were made for the encounter to take place in the woods across the Potomac at Arlington, Virginia. Pistols were the weapons chosen, with shots to be fired at ten paces. On the next day both contestants brought their own seconds and surgeons to the appointed spot. Tucker was anxious to dispatch his man, but the Federal colonel suddenly underwent a change of mind. His second approached Tucker and said that the colonel realized he was "in his cups" when he had uttered his offensive remarks. Would Tucker accept an apology? The Southerner replied that he would, but only on condition that amends be made publicly on that very day in the same dining room and at the same hour in which the offensive statements had been spoken. Tucker, furthermore, stipulated that the apology had to be in as loud a voice as the original insulting remarks. The colonel agreed to do so and carried out his promse.[11]

strung Confederate general. On Beauregard see T. Harry Williams, *P. G. T. Beauregard.*

[11] Tucker complained that he was snubbed by important Northern acquaintances. Secretary of State Hamilton Fish, a personal friend, invited him to a reception at the White House. Tucker accepted, determined to be cordial to anyone who spoke to him, but politicians whom he had once known refused to recognize him. Only through Secretary Fish did the Colonel meet President Grant. The Colonel was later nominated by President Cleveland to become minister to Haiti but was unable to assume his post because of political obstruction. Tucker's appointment was blocked in Congress because of charges that he had once been involved in a conspiracy to assassinate Lincoln. The accusation grew out of those confused days immediately after the President was shot. Federal authorities, grasping at almost any reed in order to explain the tragedy, had also accused Jefferson Davis and members of his entourage of plotting to do away with the President and members of the cabinet. Tucker, though later cleared of the charge, carried the onus of the accusation until the end of his life.

Although the war was over and he was back in a Yankee's Union, the Confederate veteran did not intend to take insults from victorious Northerners. In particular, he resented any inference that he had not fought a manly fight for a worthy cause. His substitute for victory was a strong attachment to such nostalgic symbols of his past as chivalry, the almost venerative respect for ladies, and the mystical sanctification of battlefields and battle flags. His feelings led him to change into monuments old muskets and cannon, to honor the memory of Stonewall Jackson, to preserve the Rebel yell, and to foster the legend of a "good South," the South of Lee and the Stars and Bars, of moonlight and magnolias set against the classical beauty of white marble columns.

The Southern male was prone to irateness and arrogance especially when Northerners saw his battle for principles only as a form of treason. To prideful Rebel hotspurs who had to come back into the Union, the war was a struggle to remain free from Northern domination. Tucker was asked once by his son, "Do you think that a Christian ought to challenge anyone to a duel?" He replied, "Of course, Bev, you are perfectly right, but the trouble is I was born just a little bit too soon."[12]

Most of the exiles had to decide how to support their families on a starkly reduced income. For the former politicians among

[12] Colonel Tucker's son Jim, who had also fled to Mexico and Canada after fighting with Jubal Early's command, worked mightily to avenge his father's name. After the war Jim saw an editorial in a New York newspaper which he considered abusive of his father. It referred, as if true, to Colonel Tucker's implication in the plot to assassinate Lincoln. After the young man read this piece, he went to New York, walked manfully into the newspaper editor's private office, shut the door behind him, and fastened the back of the chair under its knob. From beneath his coat Jim Tucker drew a long cattle whip which he had purchased in Cuba. Brandishing it menacingly, he told the editor "that he would whip him to within an inch of his life" if he did not print another editorial retracting the charges against his father. The editor's apology appeared the next day. See Tucker, *Tales of the Tuckers*, 49–51, 60, 91–92, on which these accounts of Tucker's experiences are based; also Ludwell H. Johnson, "Beverley Tucker's Canadian Mission, 1864, 1865," *Journal of Southern History*, Vol. XXIX (February, 1963), 88–99.

them, still barred from holding office, and the soldiers, poor and with no army to serve, the struggle to defeat poverty by seeking other employment was especially distasteful.

In 1868 former Governor Harris, once mayor of Carlota, returned to Nashville to come to terms with Governor Brownlow's armed Reconstruction regime. Harris had never completely surrendered to Yankee supremacy. He found it difficult to become reassimilated into his own homeland until the 1870's, when he was elected to the United States Senate from Tennessee. However, he reserved his special fire for Mexicans, whom he proclaimed "the most unprincipled, hollow-hearted vagabonds on the face of the earth."[13]

The role of the professional soldier who had fought with the Confederacy was a lean, often dispirited one after the war. At first, Southern generals, untrained as they were for other work, had to accept whatever employment they could turn up. It hurt former soldiers to see a commanding officer, according to one story, reduced to selling his wife's jams, pies, and cakes on the streets of Southern cities.

Although one of the most popular Confederate leaders, General Magruder had to be content with any means of employment after his return from Mexico via Havana. He settled in Texas and, whenever he could, lectured on Mexico in various Southern cities. The handsome "bonny Prince John" of the Confederacy could find no other employment. Magruder was a lonely person after the war. His wife lived in Europe during most of their married life. While she had brought his children to Mexico to visit him in 1866, the General did not enjoy a happy home life. As he possessed no particular talents outside the military field, his lot was especially unfortunate. In 1871 he died a lonely man in Houston.

General Thomas C. Hindman, an able soldier who had fought

[13] Harmon, "Confederate Migrations to Mexico," *Hispanic American Historical Review*, Vol. XVII (November, 1937), 479. See also Blair, Niles, *Passengers to Mexico*, 316.

hard for the Confederacy before departing for Mexico with Shelby, also met serious difficulties when he returned to his native Arkansas in 1867. Described as possessing "a wonderful talent to get into fusses," he openly expressed dissatisfaction with the Radical Reconstruction of the state. In truth, law and order were not yet fully re-established, and carpetbag and scalawag officials remained in control. A strained relationship between die-hards like Hindman and Northern Radical officials in the South inflamed the politics of Arkansas, and the General jumped headlong into this explosive environment.[14]

Hindman failed to realize how much Arkansas had changed while he had been in Mexico. Shortly after stepping on his native soil, Hindman incautiously objected, in a speech, to certain inflammatory remarks made to stir up local Negroes by persons he called "political opportunists" from the North. Hindman called an important Northern orator in the state a liar. This proved to be an error for which he would pay heavily.

One summer evening in 1868, as he was peacefully smoking his pipe in his parlor at Helena, Arkansas, with his wife and children at his side, a shot was suddenly fired through the window by an anti-Confederate Southerner. The assassin's bullet struck the General in the jaw and upper throat, tearing away a large part of the neck, and he began to hemorrhage. When told that he was dying, Hindman asked to be placed in a chair on his front porch. Soon the yard was filled with friends. An observer recorded, "As long as he could talk he reviewed his career in a speech of rare eloquence, and he justified it." Toward the end of this tour de force Hindman could scarcely be heard, as he

---

[14] A "most bitter struggle between the different factions" continued in Arkansas as late as 1879, and discontented factions could "at any time overthrow law, destroy order, and turn towns into camps." One observer wrote that "partisans in a state where the use of arms is so common as it is in Arkansas are, of course, violent and vindictive, and a good many lives are wasted in useless struggling." It was his opinion that the state legislature "should enact a law forbidding the bearing of arms" because "murder is considered altogether too trivial an offense in Arkansas." See Edward King, *The Great South*, 284-85.

breathed heavily and tried to speak through a throat full of gurgling blood. When taken back to his parlor couch, he died instantly.[15]

Hindman's close friend, Thomas Caute Reynolds, returned to Missouri about a year after the General's death. In the postwar era of Grant and the Robber Barons, Governor Reynolds also felt uncomfortable. Amassing money and success in business had never been his major aim. Reynolds was a pensive man, one who sought his consolations in the quietude of his inner thoughts. These thoughts, a concentrated aspic of former times, were most painful to him.

Reynolds could never quite forget past scenes of horror in Mexico: the rawhide whippings of deserters, brutal executions in the name of national loyalty, maimings, and killings. He could not purge his mind of the sight of prisoners made to kneel between their coffins and their graves, blindfolded, before the muzzles of a line of muskets, their backs tied to stakes, or leaning against war-gutted churches whose walls sometimes crumbled under the bullets shot into them. In his later years Reynolds recalled a file of about a dozen executioners who without emotion shot to death a sixteen-year-old boy, their bullets piercing both head and body in half a hundred places. He could still see the stream of blood coursing its way past the crouching dark figure of a priest busily attending fallen corpses. But, above all, he never forgot the Emperor whose death his advice had helped bring about.

For a time the former Governor had hopes of recapturing high public office. In 1872 he wrote Francis Lieber:

> If old friends, who are constantly writing or sending messages to me on the subject, succeed in their (at present secret) plan to send me next spring to Washington to succeed that previous political wea-thercock, Frank Blair, in the U.S. Senate, I shall . . . "pot-luck" dinner with you.[16]

[15] Terrell, *From Texas to Mexico,* 30; Charles Ford Nash, *Biographical Sketches of Gen. Pat Cleburne and Gen. T. C. Hindman,* 150, 217–18.

[16] Thomas C. Reynolds to Francis Lieber, August 12, 1872, Lieber Papers, Huntington Library.

Although elected to the Missouri General Assembly in 1874 and appointed by President Chester A. Arthur to a commission to investigate trade with Latin America, Reynolds did not recapture his prewar leadership. A period of aimless drifting in the business world convinced him that life held little hope for him in a Unionist Missouri now dominated by his old dueling enemy, B. Gratz Brown.

On March 30, 1887, Reynolds entered one of the tallest buildings in St. Louis. He climbed the stairs to the last floor. Facing an open elevator shaft, he turned around, moved three steps backward, and dropped to instant death.

The return of General Price—considered by many the patriarch of all the Mexican exiles—was not as painful as that old peacock, grown hard and heavy-jowled, had anticipated. Very few restrictions were placed upon him when his vessel returned to New Orleans from Vera Cruz. Army headquarters merely asked that he faithfully report his future movements within the United States. When the General, his lady, and their daughter, Stella, and son, Quintus, eventually reached St. Louis and took rooms at the Southern Hotel, they were received warmly. The collection which their friends took up for them, which Shelby excoriated so scathingly when he heard about it in Mexico, enabled the Prices to buy a fine residence on Chouteau Avenue, one of the best boulevards in St. Louis.[17]

In 1868 the controversial Commodore Maury received a warm greeting from family and friends on his return home. He had

[17] *Glimpses of the Past*, 42, tells of Reynolds' end. Regarding Price see *Missouri Statesman*, January 11, 1867. Once they reached the comfort of intimate friends and relatives, many Confederates experienced the amenities and welcome of a Price. It was fairly common for the wartime leaders—North and South—to receive gifts from their admirers. The people of Mobile, for instance, presented Raphael Semmes with a house on Government Street, a residence shaded by magnolia trees, and a respite where he passed the remainder of his life as a venerated public figure. Semmes, an admiral and brigadier general (who had come through Mexico on his way home), was, however, barred from his post as a judge in Alabama and for a time had to accept the teaching chair of moral philosophy and English literature at the state seminary at Alexandria, Louisiana. The seminary which developed into the present Louisiana State University

remained in England a total of two years. Maury had been paid five thousand dollars by Napoleon in May, 1866, for a demonstration in France of his electric torpedoes. In June, 1868, Cambridge University bestowed an honorary LL.D. degree upon the famous oceanographer. Before his departure for the States in July, 1868, English admirers had given the scholar-scientist a silver casket containing fifteen thousand dollars in gold. Recognized globally also for his contributions to the laying of a third transatlantic cable, Maury returned home in at least partial triumph.

He was certainly not a discredited exile, but he nevertheless remained a discouraged one. By the time he returned, his friend Maximilian had been cut down by a *nacionalista* firing squad. Slowly, the tired old man wended his way southward from Washington to Richmond. He settled at Lexington, Virginia, shrine city of the Confederacy. At first he did some statistical studies for the Virginia Military Institute and then became a member of the faculty as professor of meteorology without a full teaching load.[18]

In his native state Maury followed the example of Robert E. Lee and devoted the remainder of his life to college teaching. Indeed, many able Southerners, barred from other professions, turned to teaching. Maury and Lee became neighbors at Lexington, the one a professor at V.M.I., the other becoming the venerated president of Washington College, later renamed Washington and Lee University. Maury was also considered for the vice-chancellorship of the University of the South in Sewanee, Tennessee, and was offered the presidencies of St. John's College in Annapolis, Maryland, and of the University of Alabama. All of these he turned down to remain at V.M.I.

The Commodore continued his active publication activities, receiving regular royalties from his popular *Physical Geography*. He also joined in a textbook publishing venture—the University Publishing Company of New York—owned by three thousand

at Baton Rouge, had as its president before the war none other than Union General Sherman. Semmes was jailed for three months on the charge that he had violated the rules of war in escaping from the *Alabama* after he struck her colors in its last battle with the *Kearsarge* in the English Channel.

[18] Burger and Bettersworth, *South of Appomattox*, 72–73.

Southern stockholders. With Southern scholars Joseph L. Le Conte (science) and Basil L. Gildersleeve (Latin), Maury (geography) put together a highly successful academic venture which made them even better known and which supplemented his teaching income substantially. But, as he put it in a letter to a friend, he had originally come home to die. Maury lived on until February 1, 1873, one of the most successfully reintegrated of the Southern exiles, a great scholar who slipped quietly into oblivion, far less well known than most of the leading generals of the Confederacy.

Like Maury and Lee, General Kirby-Smith, former commander of the Confederate Trans-Mississippi Department, eventually entered the ranks of *academia*. On November 16, 1866, the Yorkville (South Carolina) *Enquirer* had reported: "General Grant has written a letter to General Kirby Smith, granting him permission to return home on parole, to be placed on the same footing as other Confederate officers of his rank. He is at present sojourning in Cuba." Kirby-Smith returned to the South and for a time was president of the Atlantic and Pacific Telegraph Company. In 1870 he became chancellor of the University of Nashville. He remained at that post until 1875, when he became professor of mathematics and eventually president of the University of the South, high on "the hill" at Sewanee, Tennessee. The General was also a botanist of note.[19]

Kirby-Smith kept but little contact with former exile friends or even with his many colleagues from Trans-Mississippi command days. Yet, he was most grateful for honors bestowed upon him late in life. In 1886, when elected a member of the Northwestern Literary and Historical Society of Sioux City, Iowa, the General was so touched that he wrote its officers, "I do very greatly appreciate the honor the society has conferred upon me

[19] Much earlier, from 1854–55, Kirby-Smith had acted as botanist for the Mexican boundary commission. His special interest was in fungi and lichens. See "Edmund Kirby Smith," in *National Cyclopaedia of American Biography,* VIII (New York, 1924), 133.

and recognize in it one of the main evidences that sectional difference are fast disappearing."[20]

In this and other messages, Kirby-Smith showed his para-
mount interest to be in reconcilation between the North and the
South. He was not a die-hard, sword-swallowing, and fire-eating
Southerner. In 1887 in a letter to the editor of *Century* magazine,
the General wrote from Sewanee: "Having lost everything by the
war I have since, through self-denial, yet happily, supported my
large family upon a very modest salary. God has helped me in
a way that he never would have done had I been unfaithful to
my trusts."[21] Kirby-Smith who, incidentally, had eleven children,
was referring to the unfortunate charge that he had absconded
with large sums of money from the treasury of the Trans-Mississippi Department.

Kirby-Smith, his long patriarchal beard hanging like an apron
down the front of him, was to be remembered with affection by
several generations of Sewanee students. Calm and serene, he
lived until 1893, to become the last surviving full general of the
Confederate high command. He was also one of the last to receive a complete pardon for his role in the war.[22]

The central figure of the Confederate exodus to Mexico had,
of course, been General Shelby. In the spring of 1867, Shelby, accompanied by a party of five former Confederates, left Mexico,
oddly enough, on the United States gunboat *Tacony*. The vessel had been sent into the Caribbean by the Navy Department to
protect American citizens after the fall of Maximilian. For a short
while it had appeared that the *Tacony* might have to fight her way
out of the Vera Cruz area, whereupon Shelby, typically, told her

20 E. Kirby-Smith to Ben W. Austin, March 27, 1886, Kirby-Smith Papers,
University of North Carolina Library.

21 E. Kirby-Smith to Robert Underwood Johnson, March 8, 1887, Kirby-Smith
Papers.

22 Regarding Sewanee, see "Edmund Kirby Smith," *National Cyclopaedia of
American Biography*, VIII, 132–33, and Kirby-Smith's obituary in *Confederate
War Journal*, Vol. I (November, 1893), 114. Kirby-Smith died on March 28,
1893.

principal officer, "Well, Lieutenant, if there is going to be a row, just count us in." A diarist aboard recorded that General Shelby's offer "was thankfully accepted, and revolvers were prepared for use." He spoke of Shelby as "the celebrated cavalry leader in the Confederate army, of whom it has been said, that had he remained loyal to his country, he would have been Sheridan's stoutest rival." The diarist found it "a caprice of fate that it should be under the protection of the United States flag that he was finally able to leave the unhappy country that he had tried to adopt in place of his own."[23]

General Shelby quickly re-established himself in the South. His postwar career was markedly different from that of other leading Mexican exiles. In June, 1867, he returned for a time to Lexington, Kentucky, where he was warmly received by old friends. Settling on his hemp farm near Aullville, Missouri, Shelby became the father of a fourth son the following year. In 1869, the year in which the nation's first transcontinental rail line was established, he associated himself with the management of two minor railroad companies, the Lexington and St. Louis, and the St. Louis and Santa Fe. The railroads were about to link the West to the nation, and Shelby aimed to be a part of that endeavor.

In 1872, Shelby also invested heavily in coal mining. Operating a mine at Clarksburg, Missouri, he employed some fifty men and was thereby further able to exercise his managerial talents, as well as to restore his reputation as an important citizen of Missouri. Shelby was also part owner of a store at Lexington and a commission merchant for a St. Louis firm. The national financial debacle of 1873, however, made it difficult for him to recoup his prewar economic prominence.

The General's fifth son was born to him in 1871 and a daughter in 1875. During these years Shelby earned a comfortable livelihood, but the fortunes which such tycoons as Collis P. Huntington, Jay Gould, Mark Hopkins, and Leland Stanford were amassing from their railroad exploits did not come to him.

[23] Seaton Schroeder, *The Fall of Maximilian's Empire as Seen from a United States Gun-Boat.*

In time he interested himself in public affairs and politics. Whereas many of the Mexican exiles grew politically and socially brittle, Shelby became increasingly tolerant and kindly, less quick to take offense, more willing to see the other side of every question. In 1882 his new mellowness was put to a critical test. He was introduced to General Sheridan in Washington. The two went to dinner, and over a cold bottle of Heideseick champagne the now plump little Lieutenant General told Shelby: "I was very anxious to go over into Mexico after you. In fact, if my request had been granted you would not have gone to Mexico. While I was waiting for orders you slipped in. The orders to go after you never came, and it was one of my bitterest disappointments." Shelby's reply was reported to the New York *Herald*. He did not boast about how he had evaded Sheridan's force, fifty times larger than his own. Shelby simply stated that he now wished Sheridan had gotten his pursuit orders, "for we found it mightily lonesome over there for two years."[24]

In the same year Shelby appeared as a defense witness in the trial of Frank James, elder brother of Jesse, at Gallatin, Missouri. James was charged with participating in a train robbery. Shelby helped win an acquittal for him at a time when wartime prejudices threatened to hang the bandit. For this action many puritans denounced him. It took courage to stand up for Frank James, an admitted outlaw and bad man. But Shelby had known Frank during the fiercest border raids of the Civil War. At the Battle of Prairie Grove, when both were in grave danger, Frank had helped save Shelby's life, and the General could not forget such past loyalty. Partly because he felt that the James brothers (Jesse was killed in 1882) had committed their last crime, he helped save one of the most notorious outlaws in the United States. Frank James never again pulled the trigger of a revolver.

Although Shelby steadfastly refused to use his own wartime reputation for political advantage, in 1893 he was appointed United States marshal at Kansas City, Missouri, by President Cleveland. Governor Thomas C. Fletcher of Missouri traveled

24 Quoted in O'Flaherty, *General Jo Shelby*, 355–56.

to Washington to tell the President that naming General Shelby federal marshal of the state's western division would do much to heal the wounds between Confederates and Unionists. He reported that "no man was so widely instrumental in helping us bring order out of chaos when the war was over. His influence with the people of Missouri was inestimable and he worked night and day to restore peace by appealing to them to accept the new order of things in a spirit of resignation."[25]

Appointing a Negro as one of his deputies, Shelby, as a United States marshal, came to be almost a figure of veneration in the Middle West. In these later years when his character underwent such a change, the General grew to regret his role in the Civil War. An acquaintance from his native Kentucky, who often visited him at his Kansas City office to chat about old times, noted that Shelby seemed almost repentant about his border-raiding days when, as a young captain of militia, he pursued the helpless followers of John Brown into Kansas under the fire of his guns. He now thought the state of Virginia should erect a monument to Brown as the one great hero of the Civil War. "I am now ashamed of myself," Shelby told his friend a few weeks before his death. "I had no business there. No Missourian had any business there with arms in his hands. The policy that sent us there was damnable, and the trouble we started on the border bore fruit for ten years. I ought to have been shot there, and John Brown was the only man who knew it and would have done it." Shelby had grown to feel "great respect for Old John Brown" and felt that Brown "did in his country what I should have done in mine under like circumstances. Those were days when slavery was in the balance, and the violence engendered made men irresponsible. I now see I was so myself."

Remembering his association with such border ruffians as Quantrill, the General "denounced Quantrill in the severest terms." His Kentucky friend states that Shelby "had outlived and outgrown the bitterness of border times. He was a very just, earnest, sincere man . . . . He repented his actions and reproached

[25] Quoted in *ibid.*, 383. On Shelby's later years see Creel, *Rebel at Large*, 27–28.

himself that he had ever done these things." He seldom mentioned Mexico in public life during these later years. Shelby's repentance was so thoroughgoing that in his last years he even voted Republican.[26]

The General became especially well known for his hospitality to Confederate and Union veterans alike, and threw open his last home, near Adrian, Missouri, for frequent reunions. Curiosity seekers, old soldiers, both blue and gray, and former officers by the score came to see Shelby. Among these visitors over the years was his old camp companion, the prominent newspaperman John N. Edwards (married at the Shelby farm, March 28, 1871), the bandits Jesse and Frank James, and Cole Younger, one of the notorious Younger brothers. Whenever road agents and bad men whom he had encountered during the war visited Shelby, these guests knew they were safe from the eyes of detectives and newspapermen.[27]

Shelby's parade of visitors, prominent and not so prominent, continued until 1897. That year the old warrior died at the age of sixty-seven, a slight, gray-haired figure of a man mourned by thousands of faithful soldiers.[28] One of these, a pallbearer at the funeral, wrote of Shelby with justified feeling (but daring chronological inaccuracy) that the conflict had truly closed for the General after Appomattox: "Its red fires became ashes by the terms between Grant and Lee, and then Shelby became so loyal to the Government of the United States that from the hour he buried the Confederate flag in the turbid waters of the Rio Grande . . . up to the hour of his death, Jo Shelby would as gladly have laid down his life for the Stars and Stripes as during the four years of war he would have laid it down for the Stars and Bars."[29]

[26] Connelley, *Quantrill and the Border Wars*, 288–89.
[27] "Gallatin Missouri," *Missouri Historical Review*, Vol. XLIX (April, 1955), 251; William P. Borland, "Gen. Jo. O. Shelby," *ibid.*, Vol. VII (October, 1912), 19; "This Missouri Confederate and His 'Iron Brigade' Never Surrendered," *ibid.*, Vol. L (October, 1955), 67–69; William A. Settle, Jr., "The James Boys and Missouri Politics," *ibid.*, Vol. XXXVI (April, 1942), 412–29.
[28] Also see O'Flaherty, *General Jo. Shelby*, 327–78, on Shelby's later years.
[29] McDougal, *Recollections*, 210.

President Grover Cleveland, the first Democratic president after the Civil War, was also the first to entrust substantial numbers of high-ranking former Confederates with positions of responsibility. After demonstrating their new loyalty to the Union, many Confederate generals received appointments and honors commensurate with their past prestige in the South. Cleveland's appointments ignored sectional lines.[30]

When General Terrell first returned to Texas from Mexico in 1867, he retired for a time to his plantation in Robinson County and devoted his attention for several years to agricultural pursuits. In 1871 he went back to Austin, where he had practiced law before the war and had planned to spend the rest of his life. Soon he was reappointed a judge, and from 1875 to 1879 he was a member of the Texas state senate where he sponsored legislation to purge the state of Reconstruction laws and to found the state university. This earned him the title of "Father of the University of Texas." He also wrote the first public school bill in Texas. Many volumes of judicial decisions of the Supreme Court of Texas reflect Terrell's handiwork as a reporter for that court. Like Shelby, Terrell seldom made mention of his Mexican experiences. In a biographical sketch submitted to the *National Cyclopaedia of Biography,* he omitted all reference to the years 1865 to 1867. Terrell capped his public service career when he served as minister to Turkey from 1893 to 1897 during President Cleveland's administration.[31]

Some Confederate leaders at first applied for early amnesty, without success. Exiles, especially, were frightened off by such stories as appeared in the New York *Observer* on September 26, 1865, entitled "Rebels Abroad." Part of it read: "It is said that

[30] After President Cleveland appointed former Confederate General Quintus Cincinnatus Lamar secretary of interior, General Wilcox became chief of the railway division of the General Land Office. On his return from Mexico, Wilcox had been offered commissions in Korea and Egypt.

[31] *National Cyclopaedia,* V, 555; Terrell, *From Texas to Mexico,* i. A few Confederate officers, including General Longstreet, who received federal appointments, were called traitors by die-hards.

Attorney-General Speed will not in future give consideration to applications for pardon from rebels not resident in this country. It is supposed that the effect of this will be perpetual expatriation in the cases of many of the extinguished individuals formerly prominent in Jeff Davis's Confederacy."

In 1869, General Joseph E. Johnston personally called on President Grant to protest still another category of refusal to extend pardons by Federal authorities, who would not honor paroles issued at the time of individual surrenders. These battlefield paroles had usually consisted of forms on which Confederate unit commanders filled in the names of their officers and men and which were signed also by Union commissioners. Supposedly these documents had granted Confederates immunity from molestation in return for a pledge not to take up arms again. Until the validity of these paroles was upheld and a host of impossible loyalty oaths modified, proscribed Southerners could neither acquire nor transfer titles to property or obtain copyrights and patents.[32]

Former exiles continued to find it difficult to secure employment or to engage in certain businesses. Furthermore, the Fourteenth Amendment to the United States Constitution barred former Confederate leaders from holding state or federal offices. By a series of subsequent amnesty proclamations, however, Presidents Lincoln, Johnson, Grant, and Hayes pardoned many exiles, as did the United States Congress. But Congress removed political disabilities slowly, inconsistently, and in what one historian calls "piecemeal fashion."[33]

President Johnson issued four general proclamations of amnesty and pardon. His first, of May 29, 1865, was the most important. Although Lincoln's last proclamation, of March 26, 1864, listed only seven excepted classes of persons, Johnson's mentioned fourteen, automatically making necessary a large number of "special pardons." Even General Lee (indicted for treason by a federal

---

[32] Gilbert E. Govan and James W. Livingood, *A Different Valor: The Story of General Joseph E. Johnston, C.S.A.* (Indianapolis, 1956), 378.
[33] Hesseltine, *Confederate Leaders in the New South*, 6.

grand jury at Norfolk, on June 7, 1865) was required to apply individually for pardon. Even though each general amnesty proclamation reduced the number of persons who were unpardoned, many of the Confederate exiles remained without pardons. Johnson's second general amnesty act, of September 7, 1867, left only about three hundred former Confederates unpardoned. His third general amnesty act, of July 4, 1868, left still fewer, many of whom had gone to Mexico and to other places as exiles. Between April, 1865, and January, 1867, sixty-four Confederate brigadier generals and eight major generals were pardoned. By the latter date eighty-six members of the lower house of the Confederate Congress and a smaller number of upper house members had been pardoned, as had a dozen Southern governors.

Although a Presidential pardon restored individual property rights and granted immunity from prosecution for treason, a pardon did not necessarily guarantee the right to vote in a given state nor did it include the right to hold office. One authority puts it this way: "Where these two rights had been removed by Congressional action, it followed that only Congress could restore them. . . . Thus it was necessary for Congress to have an amnesty policy of its own. By special bills, several thousand ex-Confederates were amnestied between 1868 and 1872."[34] On May 22, 1872, a general amnesty law signed by President Grant re-enfranchised many persons, including Mexican exiles not covered by earlier pardons.

Such legislation was passed, however, only over the vigorous protests of Republican die-hards like the powerful "Plumed Knight" of the Senate, James G. Blaine. He and other Radical Republican orators nursed a continuing hatred for those who refused to ask pardon for having led the South out of the Union. Such Northern politicians had a stake in the perpetuation of "The Southern Question." The careers of Blaine, Roscoe Conkling, and Oliver P. Morton flourished because they kept before the public the legend of the "Bloody Shirt"—the politically powerful notion

[34] Eric L. McKitrick, *Andrew Johnson and Reconstruction*, 144.

that the Republican party had won the Civil War. This brand of vindictive "G. A. R. politics" pleased thousands of Northern veterans in those days when the Grand Army of the Republic, still flushed with the glow of victory, had not yet mellowed enough to encamp, as it later did annually, with "the boys in grey."[35]

In April, 1866, General Kirby-Smith had been named, along with Jefferson Davis and General Simon Bolivar Buckner (formerly Kirby-Smith's chief of staff), on a list of persons indicted for treason by the United States District Attorney at Knoxville, Tennessee.[36] In a letter to Kirby-Smith, Buckner complained: "Like yourself I had to begin the world anew, my capital being exactly fifteen cents, in addition to a few hundred dollars which I borrowed."[37] Buckner earned money by writing for the New Orleans *Crescent*, but his main preoccupation, like that of his old commander, was the matter of restoration of full citizenship. Kirby-Smith wrote Grant that he considered that his surrender at Galveston on June 2, 1865, had provided a parole similar to that granted Lee, Longstreet, and other Confederate generals at Appomattox. Fortunately, early prosecutions commenced against Kirby-Smith and other Confederates by the federal government were ultimately suspended. Kirby-Smith was re-enfranchised, however, only in June, 1878, by special act of Congress. Jefferson

---

[35] Whenever an Early or a Davis defied the North publicly, he goaded Blaine and his ilk in the Senate to oppose bills of amnesty that would crown "murderers" and "traitors" with full citizenship. See Matthew Josephson, *The Politicos, 1865–1896*, 207–209.

[36] In his native Kentucky, Buckner became the subject of controversy. On September 12, 1862, Buckner had issued a proclamation denouncing "betrayers" of the state and calling upon Kentuckians to expel those who held "the assassin dagger which is aimed to pierce our heart." Dismissal of treason and conspiracy indictments against Buckner took until 1957, when a circuit court in Kentucky finally exonerated him posthumously. Buckner had become governor of Kentucky without ever having received a federal pardon. In 1957 other Confederate celebrities, including General Breckinridge and John Hunt Morgan (the swashbuckling cavalry raider), were also posthumously exonerated.

[37] S. B. Buckner to E. Kirby-Smith, June 22, 1866, Kirby-Smith Papers, University of North Carolina Library.

Davis was never brought to trial and, because he refused to ask for pardon, never received it.[38]

In 1896 and again in 1898, on the eve of the Spanish-American War—almost a decade after the death of Jeff Davis—Congress passed two "final amnesty bills" to re-enfranchise most remaining Southerners. A few recalcitrants remained beyond the pale, but their names are unknown. Others were proud to be politically rehabilitated.[39]

Pardoned or not, more than three fourths of the Confederacy's general officers were under fifty when the Civil War ended. Most veterans were, therefore, fortunately young enough to adjust to circumstances or to seek a new life out West if not down South. Many young Southerners did not wish to prejudice their future by referring to a defeated past. As late as 1875 the Southern poet Sidney Lanier could write to newspaperman Bayard Taylor, "Perhaps you know that with us of the younger generation in the South since the war, pretty much the whole of life has been merely not dying." Southerners wanted also to look to the future as well as to the past. The exiles realized full well that their adventures were firmly behind them. Only reluctantly did they speak of the Mexican experience—partly to avoid the sort of ridicule which one person who had followed the exile's hegira to Mexico wrote in his autobiography:

> When I read of or hear anyone say anything good of Mexico, I set him down as a "decoyed duck," the victim of some designing promoter, like the billy goat in the Chicago stock yards that has led

[38] A discussion of amnesty and pardon legislation is to be found in Jonathan T. Dorris, *Pardon and Amnesty Under Lincoln and Johnson*; see also U.S. War Dept., *Memorandum Relative to the General Officers Appointed by the President in the Armies of the Confederate States, 1861–1865.*

[39] President McKinley signed the last Congressional general amnesty bill on June 8, 1898. See McKitrick, *Andrew Johnson and Reconstruction*, 144. One Southern general, "Fighting Joe" Wheeler, embodied reintegration of the Confederacy into the Union. Appointed a major general of volunteers during the Spanish-American War, Wheeler commanded a cavalry division. Asked how he felt about again wearing Union blue, the old soldier stated it was as though he were putting on his true uniform again after having been on furlough.

sheep and lambs by the millions into the slaughter pens . . . through the door where they all go, none to return.[40]

This attitude led many exiles to speak of Mexico only within the privacy of their homes. The "New South" was quite willing to let bitter memories die. Thus, except for oral traditions, few reminiscences have come down to us directly from the exiles or their children. As late as 1912, the year General Terrell died at the age of eighty-four, he thought that "too much sectional spirit" still existed to allow him to publish his recollections in full. To the editor of the Houston *Chronicle,* who wanted to print his memoirs, Terrell wrote: "The accompanying batch of *Recollections* may be of a character that should for the present assign them to oblivion. . . . The fact that *after* all this, I represented the United States as Ambassador for a few years at a foreign court, may cause much criticism from those who have never felt the hard fate of an exile, with neither money or country."[41]

Today few traces of the Mexican exodus exist below the border or above it.[42] Carlota and the other Confederate towns have disappeared. The migration is not significant for the number of Southerners who went to Mexico, for probably less than five thousand did so. Nor was it notable for its impact on the land of Montezuma. Because they did not cling together in tight enclaves, the Confederates made little impression on the country's history or its population pattern. Rather, the exodus was striking for its futility, the depth of delusion of its participants, and the inevitability of its failure. The colonists went to Mexico at the wrong time, with the wrong attitudes, and chose the wrong occupations. It was a spontaneous, informal exodus, without proper organization and with few goals. Yet, even if all this had been otherwise,

[40] Noel, *Autobiography, and Reminiscences,* 321.

[41] A. W. Terrell to C. B. Gillespie, January 1, 1912, in Terrell, *From Texas to Mexico,* xvii.

[42] Jonathan Daniels, American ambassador to Mexico from 1934 to 1942, wrote in his *Shirt Sleeves Diplomat* of visits with the son of General Kirby-Smith in Mexico. Brief mention is made of the fate of some major commanders in Douglas Southall Freeman, *Lee's Lieutenants,* III, 769–79.

and if all of them had been men like Shelby—who was self-reliant, resourceful, a worker, relatively unmindful of personal prestige, and willing to side-step quarrels with fellow exiles and who integrated himself almost magically into the Mexican turmoil—the exodus would still have failed. Colonists could not, indeed would not, in most cases, have stayed abroad permanently.

The behavior of exiles through history is of especial interest today when more Americans than ever before have decided to make their homes in foreign lands. Unlike many other emigrants, the Mexican exiles had all been deeply involved in our national life; although chaos at home sent them to Mexico, their responsibilities at home almost inevitably brought them back into the South again.

The attitude of the Mexican Confederates was a mixture of fear, resentment, and apathy. Retreatist, regressive, and displaced emotions created stress; this led to angry aggressiveness. Under strain, some withdrew into themselves, into a world of fantasy. Others reached a degree of resentment that was subjective and self-punitive. Any element of security perceived by the members of the group caused them to renew their counterattack upon the objects which they believed to be the cause of their anguish.

As time passed, obscurity and regret were the motifs of the Confederate migration to Mexico. The emigrants had found no peace in the wilds. Flight below the border had meant deprivation, loneliness, ignominy, and the bitter experience of being cast in the role of hated intruder—experiences so incredible as to be suitable for a novel.[43] The whole experience had been a lost cause. Although their fortunes were mixed during the later Reconstruction period, most of the exiles felt a sense of relief upon returning home. They had emerged from darkness into daylight.[44]

[43] Such a novel, but not a very good one, was written, Harley Duncan, *West of Appomattox* (1961).

[44] Much later, other Americans sought fortunes in Mexico under the regime of its President Porfirio Díaz. Generals John C. Frémont, W. S. Rosecrans, and even Ulysses S. Grant, as well as Edward L. Doheny, John D. Rockefeller, Sr., and Senator George Hearst, all reaped riches below the border. By building railroads, digging mines, and erecting oil derricks, they prospered as the Confederate exiles never had.

❦

Confederates in New Mexico and Arizona

THE CONFEDERACY's most outstanding commander in New Mexico Territory was Brigadier General Henry H. Sibley. There is evidence that his ultimate goal was the conquest of both California and northern Mexico. To secure the provinces of Chihuahua, Sonora, and Lower California by purchase or strategy was a part of his wartime design. Sibley looked upon his operations in New Mexico as a means to that end. Although his campaigns were basically impractical, Sibley tried to tap manpower and matériel resources which he saw in a potentially disloyal southern California and an apathetic Mexico.

In late 1862, General Sibley sent Colonel James Reily, C.S.A., a staff officer, into northern Mexico. His job was to convince the governors of Sonora and Chihuahua that they should refuse Federal forces the use of the West Coast port of Guaymas and the right to transport troops across northern Mexico. While Reily received a warm welcome in Chihuahua, the governor of Sonora, Don Ignacio Pesquiera, was distinctly less cordial. Sonora was geographically closer to California, a Union stronghold. Colonel Reily, therefore, received only confirmation of the Confederate Army's right to buy supplies in Chihuahua and Sonora.

The Union plan to cross northern Mexico in order to attack western outposts of the Confederacy in Arizona and New Mexico had been abandoned by the time of Reily's mission into Mexico. When General George Wright, commanding Union forces in San

Francisco, learned of Reily's trip, he envisioned a Confederate assault upon California through Mexico and, therefore, wrote the Governor of Sonora, threatening reprisals if Rebel hordes were permitted to take refuge in Mexico. Wright sent a gunboat to the harbor of Guaymas, and it stood offshore as his emissary delivered a note of protest to Governor Pesquiera. The Union thereby impressed upon that Mexican official its determination to keep Confederates out of Mexico. Union officers also planned to supply Juárez with as many supplies as they could spare. If the South ever occupied a Pacific seaport, this could help break the Civil War blockade of its own ports. The Union could not afford to relinquish the harbor of Guaymas, or any other West Coast port. See Hall, *Sibley's New Mexican Campaign*, 50–51; Colton, *The Civil War in the Western Territories*, 98.

❦

General Lew Wallace

WALLACE was a "political general" of great ambition, whose obscure role in trying to get the South to surrender and in negotiating with Juárez is still barely understood. Why Wallace went west toward the end of the war is best explained by a glance at his career. General Wallace had incurred the ill will of his superior, General Henry W. Halleck, after the capture of Fort Donelson, Tennessee, in 1862. Indeed, Halleck twice removed him from command. He was restored to command the first time by Lincoln's fortunate intercession and on a second occasion by Grant. Wallace was defeated by Confederate General Jubal A. Early at the Battle of Monocacy on July 9, 1864, but he managed to save Washington, D.C., from capture by a stout defense of the capital against heavy odds. He thereby earned the gratitude of Grant and the War Department.

In early 1865, Grant sent Wallace on an "inspection tour" of the West which was vaguely inspired and even more sloppily executed. With the lukewarm approval of Secretary of War Stanton, Wallace visited Bagdad and Matamoros, Mexico, secretly making contact with Juárist authorities along the border on behalf of the Union high command. Traveling incognito through miles of tangled underbrush, he found his way eventually to Confederate General James E. Slaughter, commanding the area of Texas through which Wallace surreptitiously traveled. Wallace, possibly acting upon some still unknown secret authority, boldly proposed a cessation of hostilities. He urged the return to the Union of at least Texas, Arkansas, and Louisiana, a proposal which Slaughter and his staff considered repulsive and branded as the "blackest treason of the Confederacy."

Wallace asked Grant to place him in command of Texas, in a letter dated February 22, 1865, with a division of infantry and a brigade of cavalry. He wanted "orders to report directly to yourself." He promised to "completely sever communication between the Rio Grande and middle eastern Texas" with these forces. He also wrote that he would seek to "make accommodations with the rebels" and would seek "a private interview with Kirby Smith. Permit me to hope," he wrote Grant, "that you will not delay creating the department and despatching the troops. In selecting troops please send me Western men." On March 14, 1865, he wrote his wife from Matamoros: "What I aim at now is nothing less than bringing Texas, Arkansas, and Louisiana *voluntarily* back into the Union. . . . I met the Confederate officials at Point Isabel, just across the bay, and spent a couple of days and nights with them very pleasantly. We carried over our tents and cooks, and if our good people could have seen General Slaughter and myself lie down to sleep together . . . I fear my character for loyalty would suffer in the esteem of some we know in old Montgomery." Wallace had met Slaughter under a flag of truce and made certain proposals for surrender to be taken under advisement by Slaughter, General J. G. Walker, commanding in Texas, and Kirby-Smith.

It was General Walker who looked upon Wallace's scheme with disfavor and who refused to discuss it. Walker, in fact, conveyed to Slaughter what Wallace termed "something very like an official reprimand." Although Wallace personally saw Walker in Galveston, the Confederate general refused to take the matter any further; admonishing Wallace as follows in a letter of April 6, 1865: "Whenever you are willing to . . . treat as equals with equal, an officer of your high rank and character, clothed with the proper authority from your government will not be reduced to the necessity of seeking an obscure corner of the Confederacy to inaugurate negotiations." That finished off Wallace.

Washington, like the Confederates, paid little attention to Wallace's plans to obtain a surrender. His suggestions for increasing the volume of supplies to Juárez were also lost in the confusing shuffle of the War Department's mail room. Unsuccessful in interesting the White House in his plans, the General grew tired of his uncertain role and resigned his commission. Toward the end of the war he disappeared from public view and led a small corps of volunteers into Mexico, where he requested, and received, a temporary commission as a major general in the Mexican Army. He stayed there for about two years.

Much later Wallace wrote to President Díaz of Mexico (August 15, 1889) that because "Mr. Seward, secretary of state, had contented himself with protests to Napoleon, and was opposed to any positive step which might serve the emperor as an excuse for recognizing the Confederacy . . . my mission to the Rio Grande was without Mr. Seward's knowledge; in fact, of the persons constituting the administration, they were known only to President Lincoln and Mr. Stanton. In an interview with President Lincoln upon the subject, he admonished me not to mention the business to Mr. Seward. Mr. Lincoln and Mr. Stanton accepted General Grant's view of the failing condition of the Confederacy, and agreed with him that the time was come, in our own interests, as well as those of Mexico, to help President Juarez, at least privately."

Wallace's subsequent negotiations with the Mexican *liberales* under Juárez were, of course, interrupted by the death of President Lincoln, but Wallace did bring back to Washington General José M. J. Carvajal, authorized by Juárez to negotiate loans in the States and to make purchases for the liberal armies in Mexico. Wallace gives details about arms sent to Juárez in his *Autobiography* (pp. 866ff.). See also pp. 816–17, 827, 832–33, 843.

❦

The Kickapoo Indians

THE KICKAPOO TRIBE formerly lived along the Kaw River in Kansas. Their status within the United States was thrown into confusion and doubt by the military skirmishes of the Union and Confederate forces throughout Indian territory during the Civil War. When each of the contestants made an effort to compel these Indians to take sides, they refused. Their reserves, overrun by thousands of strange whites, became veritable islands as the war swept through the Indians like a flood. In 1864, faced with the threat of starvation and disease following a series of cold winters during which their lands were ravaged by outlaws and bandits, about four hundred warriors, accompanied by their women and children, decided to leave United States territory for sanctuary elsewhere.

They fled southward, first to Texas. When pursued by the Confederates, the refugees bolted the boundaries of the former United States and headed into Mexico. From the pen of a French staff officer we have a picture of these migrating Indians as they appeared in Mexico. He wrote that their chief wore a large silver medal bearing the face of France's King Louis XV, a medallion awarded the tribe many years earlier, on the reverse side of which was inscribed, "A sa fidèle et bien-aimée tribu des kinkapoos, Le Roi Louis le quinzième."

Although these Indians did not now find refuge under a French king in Mexico, they did find a regime willing to give them lands on which they might live in peace. They were fortunate to receive a land grant from the government of Maximilian. But the dusty foreign reservation, whose boundaries were sketchy and ill defined, located in the arid Santa Rosa Mountains south of the Río Grande, proved less than hospitable. When it became too difficult for the Indians to wrest a livelihood from the barren lands, they made frequent raids across the river into Texas to attack a series of little green settlements in and around San Antonio. As Texas defenses against such depredations improved, the Kickapoos found these raids increasingly futile and were forced to eke out a living from the dry and wrinkled land by farming. After they finally withdrew into their Santa Rosa Mountain stronghold, little was heard from the Kickapoos. Some of their nomadic descendants have remained until this day. Their untold story illustrates the disruptive threat which the Civil War posed for certain groups of Indians hopelessly divided by the War. But, most of all, the Kickapoo exodus to Mexico illustrates the lengths to which even they would go to escape the threatened loss of personal rights and the muddying of tribal allegiances.

During the Civil War other Indians also rebelled against their masters and undertook migrations similar to those of the Kickapoos. In 1862–63, Cherokees deserted to the Federals because of reluctance to fight their old neighbors, the Creeks. In deciding to leave their homeland for exile in Mexico, such Indians contributed to the general exodus from the South. Swindled by crooked Indian agents and railroad attorneys, these Indians deserted from both Confederate and Union ranks.

Their departure was symptomatic of a determination to combat injustices similar to those which had chafed Shelby's men. After the Confederate western front began to fall apart, a vacuum had been filled by Indians, border *bandidos*, bushwhackers, and other irregulars. Hostile Indians, who for centuries had moved about freely without restraint, found themselves hemmed in by opposing forces of both North and South. Following the sun and their food supplies on the buffalo plains became increasingly difficult for such Indians. Confused by the fighting of the Civil War, they pounced upon the opportunity of a nation divided to strike at the hated white man; arrows were aimed impartially at troopers who wore both blue and gray. In the West, even after the whites had made peace with each other, the Indians kept fighting. Above the border Geronimo and his Apache braves did not finally surrender until 1886, and below the border Shelby ran into half-blood renegades, other than the Kickapoos, who also continued on the warpath toward all whites because of the confusion in Mexico. See Ruth Murray Underhill, *Red-Man's America: A History of Indians in the United States* (Chicago, 1953), 138.

🏵

Deserters and General D. M. Frost

WHILE THE BULK of the former Confederates were classified as bona fide exiles, some had deserted the Confederate Army while the Civil War was in progress. During the last year of the war the Southern armies lost three times as many men by desertion as from combat or sickness. By the spring of 1865 fewer than one-fourth of the total Southern troop strength was actually in the field. Some deserters headed for Mexican communities near the border. From time to time a few even reported for Union duty to the United States consul at Matamoros. Others skulked about the sleepy towns of Sinaloa and Sonora. Living off the land as best they could, all hoped the war would quickly end. By 1863 as many as one hundred or more cavalrymen from General Drayton's command had deserted toward Matamoros in one day alone. Few such deserters were persons of importance within the Confederacy. Only occasionally did an officer of high rank desert his post. But whenever this occurred, it caused scandalous comment—especially in the South.

One such case was the desertion to Mexico of General D. M. Frost of Missouri, one of Kirby-Smith's former brigade commanders—New York born, a West Pointer, and former state senator from Missouri. In 1864, Frost fled from the Confederacy to Matamoros with his family. All efforts to get him to come back were in vain. He tried to explain why he would not return in a letter to the Confederate War Department at Richmond. Having fled to Mexico, he could not leave his wife unprotected "in this place," he reasoned. The only way out of his predicament was to be allowed to resign his military commission. Although aware that deserters were not usually accorded such a courtesy, Frost later explained, "I was in great trouble at being obliged to take this course, for the longer I was absent from the Army the more my heart clung to it." Frost genuinely regretted his defection. Unlike many former Confederate renegades, who were content to disappear into the hills of Mexico, he had a conscience. And this conscience gnawed at him for the rest of his life, as he was most anxious to restore himself in the eyes of fellow officers. Most of his colleagues felt that it was proper enough for him to have gone to Mexico, but not while the war was still in progress. During the time Frost was south of the border and for twenty years thereafter, he devoted much effort to trying to clear his name with the United Confederate Veterans Association.

Frost was not, however, one of those officers who escaped to Mexico with government funds in his possession. And, indeed, such were few in number. While an occasional person did abscond with Confederate monies or supplies, there is no substantial evidence that they numbered any more than a handful of persons. Most of the exiles escaped with perhaps no more than a few hundred dollars in personal funds. See scattered mention of Frost in O'Flaherty, *General Jo Shelby, Undefeated Rebel*, 56, 57, 152, 156, 157, 158; Cunningham, *General Stand Watie's Confederate Indians*, 84; and Adamson, *Rebellion in Missouri, 1861*, 4, 40, 49, 54, 57–58, 60, 69.

❧

Announcement for Forns' Colony

HO FOR MEXICO!

NOTICE TO EMIGRANTS

"THE FORNS' COLONY."

The Imperial Commissioner of Colonization is hereby authorized to dispose of 25 square leagues of land (108.459 acres) of my Hacienda of Limon situated on the Panuco River, in the Department of Tamaulipas, giving *gratis* every allternate [*sic*] section—640 acres to a man with family, 320 to an unmarried man—with preemption right in each case to as much more at $2 per acre.

I will give, also gratis, enough land for a town, as well as for a road 16 yards wide traversing the entire colony from North to South.

J. O. FORNS

Mexico February 9 1866

The offer of Mr. Forns is most princely: the land is situated in the Huasteca country on the mountain borders of the "Tierra Caliente." It is said to be healthy, and is admirably adapted to the cultivation of coffee, cotton, sugar, rice, tobacco, and the whole list of inter-tropical fruits, and productions; it is also a good stock country, with an abundance of timber. The Panuco River is navigable up to it, and boats are running on that stream. Provisions are plenty, but labour is said not to be very abundant, the usual price being 37½ cents a day, and found.

Those who come from any of the Gulf ports may take shipping

direct to Tampico, taking care not to come later than the first or middle of May, on account of the rainy season which commences in June. Emigrants are advised to send out their pioneers first, to make ready for their families to follow.

The best time for planting the first corn crop is in June, after the rains have commenced. This is the surest of the three corn crops. November is the time for planting again; cotton, corn and tobacco may be put in the ground now, and gathered from March onward, till the rains again.

Immigrants shoul [sic] not begin to arrive at Tampico before the last of March. Mr. Forns will then be on his Hacienda to receive them and to show them the lands.

This is a well-wooded country, and immigrants will do well to provide one or two good portable saw mills for each settlement. They should also bring with them seed of all sorts.

The Collector of the Port of Tampico is authorized to pass the effects of immigrants duty free—to issue them the certificates which secure them all their rights under the Decree, and to speed them on their way.

M. F. MAURY
Imperial Commissioner.

APPENDIX F

🏵

Confederate Exiles in Other Countries

GENERAL JOHN MCCAUSLAND, who remained abroad because of bitter feelings against him in a vindictive West Virginia, lived in three countries before returning home: Mexico, France, and Canada. Other exiles, who never got to Mexico, occupied interesting posts abroad. General Henry H. Sibley, Confederate commander in New Mexico, served from 1869 to 1874 as a general of artillery in the Egyptian Army (and also invented the Sibley tent, based on a Sioux lodge construction). His last years were, however, spent in poverty and ill health. Various claims to Congress for relief were repeatedly denied Sibley. Major General Charles W. Field served as inspector general of the Egyptian Army before later becoming doorkeeper of the United States House of Representatives. Major General W. W. Loring, as Loring Pasha, became commander of the Egyptian Army itself. See William B. Hesseltine and Hazel C. Wolf, *The Blue and the Gray on the Nile.*

The *Mexican Times* for February 3, 1866, and in other issues reported at length on the Canadian exiles, Generals Breckinridge, McCausland, Gillmore, and others. Also among the exiles in Canada was James M. Mason. This Confederate diplomatic commissioner had represented the Confederacy in England with Maury. He was also internationally known because of his abduction during the war from the British mail packet *Trent,* in company with fellow agent John Slidell. Mason reached Canada in 1866 and returned to the States only after three years of exile.

Also in Canada was General John Cabell Breckinridge of Kentucky, Buchanan's vice-president at age thirty-five, candidate for the Presidency in 1860, and onetime floor leader of the Senate, as well as Confederate secretary of war. Breckinridge had been an earnest Unionist before the war who had stayed on in the United States Senate through the first five months of Lincoln's administration, after his welcome had worn thin. Despite his hope that secession might be avoided, Breckinridge's Unionism was misunderstood by many Northerners in the Senate, from which he was expelled as a "traitor" in August, 1861. At the end of the war Breckinridge escaped southward through the Carolinas and Georgia with Jefferson Davis. He remained unrepentant and, at age forty-four in 1865, found himself an unemployed politician. A brilliant man, he probably would have been a more balanced and moderate Confederate president than the unyielding Davis.

After the war the unrepentant Breckinridge went first to Cuba, then to England, and finally to Canada. On June 10, 1865, after a two-month trip from Richmond, Breckinridge sailed into the harbor of Cardeñas, near Havana, Cuba, the first Confederate cabinet member to reach safety abroad. An associate of Breckinridge's described his reception in Cuba glowingly:

> We were overwhelmed with attentions, and when the governor-general telegraphed that General Breckinridge was to be treated as one holding his position and rank, the officials became as obsequious as they had been overbearing and suspicious. . . . the transition from a small open boat at sea, naked and starving, to the luxuries and comforts of civilized life was as sudden as it was welcome and thoroughly appreciated.

See John Taylor Wood, "Escape of the Confederate Secretary of War," *Century Magazine*, Vol. LXVII (November, 1893), 123. About his stay in Toronto, the St. Louis *Weekly Missouri Democrat*, on December 26, 1865, stated: "General Breckinridge is keeping house in an humble, retired way. He is much respected by the citizens, and is invited to two or three parties a week at the residences of the first families. A son of John C. Breckinridge is a clerk in a banking house at Augusta, Ga. . . . he manages to send money to his father in Canada." Breckinridge returned to the States in 1869. Although popular in the South, where he embarked upon a postwar career in business, political disabilities kept Breckinridge from ever again holding public office. See also Burger and Bettersworth, *South of Appomattox,* 80–81.

Another Confederate cabinet secretary, Robert Toombs, also fled to Cuba, then to France, but ultimately returned to the South. He never took an amnesty oath or any other oath. When asked by Northerners why he had not sought pardon from Congress for his rebellious acts, he replied: "Pardon for what? I have not pardoned you all yet." Toombs died in 1885 without having political disabilities against him removed.

p. 228
oblivion

Some exiles never again saw the Western Hemisphere. Former Secretary of State Judah P. Benjamin, who went to England from Cuba after the war, became a well-known barrister and "Queen's Counsel," who argued cases in the House of Lords and before the British Privy Council, wearing a full wig with knee breeches, black stockings, and buckled shoes. One of the most famous lawyers in Europe, Benjamin was the only barrister to become a leader of both the American and the British bars. Upon his retirement he was given a testimonial dinner by the bar of England. Benjamin died in Paris in 1884, never having returned to the United States. See Meade, *Judah P. Benjamin,* 350ff.

Not until 1875 did General P. G. T. Beauregard decide to live permanently in the United States. He reputedly received offers to be a general in the Brazilian and the Japanese armies, to command the pope's army in Rome, and to be a military adviser to Louis Napoleon of France. He also considered offers to become commander in chief of both the Argentine and the Roumanian armies—with the title of prince accompanying the latter position. He was likewise invited to join the Egyptian Army at a high salary.

The subject of Confederate exiles in Brazil is too large to treat in this book. Although it has never been written about extensively, see Madeline Dane Ross and Fred Kerner, "Stars and Bars Along the Amazon," *The Reporter*, September 18, 1958, pp. 34–38. Regarding Confederates in Venezuela, see Alfred J. and Katherine A. Hanna, *Confederate Exiles in Venezuela*, and William W. White, *The Confederate Veteran;* both books discuss Confederate exiles elsewhere as well.

Bibliography

THE FOLLOWING BIBLIOGRAPHY is only a partial list of useful sources. It is by no means inclusive. Additional references are included in the footnotes.

Manuscript Materials

William Marshall Anderson Papers, Henry E. Huntington Library, San Marino, California.

James W. Eldridge Manuscripts, Henry E. Huntington Library, San Marino, California.

Colección La Fragua, Biblioteca Nacional, Mexico, D.F.

Graham Papers, Missouri Historical Society, St. Louis.

William Gwin Collection, Bancroft Library, Berkeley, California.

Isham G. Harris Papers, Tennessee State Library and Archives, Nashville.

Edmund Kirby-Smith Papers, University of North Carolina Library, Chapel Hill.

Francis Lieber Papers, Henry E. Huntington Library, San Marino, California.

Matthew Fontaine Maury, "Letter Regarding Colonization Possibilities" (February 7, 1865), Henry E. Huntington Library, San Marino, California.

Papeles del Imperio de Maximiliano, Archivo de la Nación, Mexico, D.F.

Sterling Price Papers, Missouri Historical Society, St. Louis.

Thomas Caute Reynolds, Letter Books, Confederate States of America Papers, Library of Congress, Washington, D.C.
Thomas Caute Reynolds Papers, Missouri Historical Society, St. Louis.
James S. Rollins Papers, Missouri Historical Society, St. Louis.
Thomas Snead Papers, Missouri Historical Society, St. Louis.

Theses and Dissertations

McPherson, Hallie M. "William McKendree Gwin, Expansionist." Unpublished Ph.D. Dissertation, University of California (Berkeley), 1931.
Mitchell, Melvin E. "The Movement of the American Confederates to Mexico." Unpublished M.A. Thesis, Mexico City College, 1956.
Simmons, Lucy. "The Life of Sterling Price." Unpublished M.A. Thesis, University of Chicago, 1922.
Zvenigrad, Abraham. "The Matamoros Trade During the Civil War." Unpublished M.A. Thesis, Stanford University, 1919.

Government Documents (Mexican and United States)

Mexican Government. *Correspondencia entre la Legación de la República Mexicana en Washington, el Departamento de Estado de los Estados Unidos de América, y el gobierno de México.* New York, 1866.
———. *Legislación Mexicana. Colecció completa de las disposiciones legislativas . . . .* Vol. IX. 49 vols. Mexico City, 1878.
———. *Responsabilidades contraidas por el gobierno nacional de México con los Estados Unidos en virtud de los contratos celebrados por sus agentes, 1864–1867.* Mexico, 1867.
United States Congress. *Papers Relative to Mexican Affairs Communicated to the Senate, June 16, 1864, By the President of the United States.* Washington, 1865.
———. 39 Cong., 1 sess., *Congressional Globe.* Washington, 1866–67.
———. 39 Cong., 2 sess., *House Exec. Doc. Nos. 1, 73, and 76.* Washington, 1866–67.
———. *Papers Relating to Foreign Affairs Accompanying the Annual Message of the President to the Second Session, Thirty-Ninth Congress,* Parts II and III. Washington, 1867–1868.
———. 40 Cong., 1 sess., *Senate Exec. Doc. No. 15.* Washington, 1867.
United States Department of State. *The Present Condition of Mexico.*

Bibliography

Message from the President of the United States, in 39 Cong., 1 sess., *Senate Exec. Doc. No. 6,* Washington, 1867.

United States Navy Department. *The War of the Rebellion: Official Records of the Union and Confederate Navies,* Series I, Vols. II, XXVI, XXVII and Series II, Vols. II and III. Washington, 1895–1927.

United States War Department. *The War of the Rebellion: Official Records of the Union and Confederate Armies,* Series I, Vol. XLVIII, Parts I and II. Washington, 1880–1901.

———. *List of Staff Officers of the Confederate States Army.* Washington, 1891.

———. *Memorandum Relative to the General Officers Appointed by the President in the Armies of the Confederate States, 1861–1865.* Washington, 1905.

Newspapers

Missouri Republican, 1860–68.

Missouri Statesman, 1865–67.

Mexican Times, 1865–67. (Original file in Louisiana State University Library, Baton Rouge. Microfilm copies at Library of Congress and Henry E. Huntington Library.)

New Orleans *Times,* 1865.

New York Times, 1865–67.

New York *Observer,* 1865.

New York *World,* 1865–66.

Richmond *Dispatch,* 1865–66.

St. Louis *Weekly Missouri Democrat,* 1865.

Yorkville (South Carolina) *Enquirer,* 1865–66.

Also utilized were the files of *L'Estafette, L'Ère Nouvelle, La Sociedad,* and *El Pájaro Verde,* contemporary newspapers in Mexico, for the period 1865–67; *Diario del Imperio,* 1863–66. (Original file in Biblioteca del Instituto Nacional de Anthropología y Historia, Mexico, D.F.)

Printed Books

Abel, Annie Heloise. *The American Indian Under Reconstruction.* Cleveland, 1925.

Adamson, Hans Christian. *Rebellion in Missouri, 1861.* Philadelphia, 1961.

Anderson, John Q. *A Texas Surgeon in the C.S.A.* Tuscaloosa, 1957.

Andrews, Eliza F. *Wartime Journal of a Georgia Girl.* New York, 1908.

Avary, Myrta Lockett. *Dixie After War.* Boston, 1937.

Barber, A. W., comp. *The Benevolent Raid of General Lew Wallace.* Washington, 1914.

Bemis, Samuel Flagg, ed. *American Secretaries of State and Their Diplomacy.* 10 vols. New York, 1928.

Blaine, James G. *Twenty Years of Congress,* 2 vols. Norwich, 1886.

Blanchot, Charles. *L'intervention française au Mexique.* Paris, 1911.

Blessington, Joseph P. *The Campaigns of Walker's Texas Division.* New York, 1875.

Boykin, Edward. *Ghost Ship of the Confederacy: The Story of the Alabama and Her Captain, Raphael Semmes.* New York, 1958.

Brownlee, Richard S. *Gray Ghosts of the Confederacy: Guerrilla Warfare in the West, 1861–1865.* Baton Rouge, 1958.

Buchanan, A. Russell. *David S. Terry of California, Dueling Judge.* San Marino, 1956.

Buck, Paul H. *The Road to Reunion, 1865–1900.* Boston, 1937.

Burger, Nash K., and John K. Bettersworth. *South of Appomattox.* New York, 1959.

Callahan, James Morton. *American Foreign Policy in Mexican Relations.* Morgantown, 1909.

———. *Evolution of Seward's Mexican Policy.* Morgantown, 1909.

———. *The Diplomatic History of the Southern Confederacy.* Baltimore, 1901.

Carter, Hodding. *The Angry Scar, the Story of Reconstruction.* New York, 1959.

Case, Lynn M. *French Opinion on the United States and Mexico, 1860–1867.* New York, 1936.

Caskey, Willie Malvin. *Secession and Restoration of Louisiana.* Baton Rouge, 1938.

Caskie, Jacqueline. *Life and Letters of Matthew Fontaine Maury.* Richmond, 1928.

Chesnut, Mary Boykin. *A Diary From Dixie.* Boston, 1949.

Chester, Samuel. *Pioneer Days in Arkansas.* Richmond, 1927.

Cochran, Hamilton. *Blockade Runners of the Confederacy.* Indianapolis, 1958.

Colton, Ray C. *The Civil War in the Western Territories: Arizona, Colorado, New Mexico, and Utah.* Norman, 1959.

Connelley, William Elsey. *Quantrill and the Border Wars*. New York, 1956.

Corti, Egon Caesar. *Maximilian and Charlotte of Mexico*. 2 vols. New York, 1928.

Coulter, E. Merton. *The South During Reconstruction, 1865–1877*. Baton Rouge, 1947.

Creel, George. *Rebel at Large: Recollections of Fifty Crowded Years*. New York, 1947.

Cunningham, Frank. *General Stand Watie's Confederate Indians*. San Antonio, 1959.

Daniels, Jonathan. *Shirt Sleeve Diplomat*. New York, 1947.

Davis, Edwin Adams. *Fallen Guidon*. Santa Fe, 1962.

Dictionary of American Biography. 21 vols. New York, 1930.

Dorris, Jonathan T. *Pardon and Amnesty Under Lincoln and Johnson*. Chapel Hill, 1953.

Dorsey, Sarah A. *Recollections of Henry Watkins Allen*. New York, 1866.

Dunbar, Rowland, ed. *Jefferson Davis, Constitutionalist: His Letters, Papers, and Speeches*. 11 vols. Jackson, Mississippi, 1923.

Duncan, Harley. *West of Appomattox*. New York, 1961.

Dunn, Ballard S. *Brazil, the Home for Southerners*. New York, 1866.

Early, Jubal A. *Autobiographical Sketch*. Philadelphia, 1912.

Eaton, Clement. *A History of the Southern Confederacy*. New York, 1954.

Edwards, Jennie, comp. *John N. Edwards*. Kansas City, 1889.

Edwards, John N. *Shelby and His Men, or the War in the West*. Cincinnati, 1867.

———. *Shelby's Expedition to Mexico*. Kansas City, 1872.

Elton, J. F. *With the French in Mexico*. Philadelphia, 1867.

Estrada, Gutiérrez de. *Mexico y el archduque Fernando Maximiliano de Austria*. Mexico City, 1863.

Ettinger, Amos A. *The Mission to Spain of Pierre Soulé, 1853–1855*. New Haven, 1932.

Ezell, John S. *Fortune's Merry Wheel: The Lottery in America*. Cambridge, 1960.

Farber, James. *Texas, C.S.A.: A Spotlight on Disaster*. New York, 1947.

Fay, Edwin H. *This Infernal War: The Confederate Letters of Sgt. Edwin H. Fay*. Ed. by Bell Irvin Wiley. Austin, 1958.

Freeman, Douglas Southall. *Lee's Lieutenants: A Study in Command.* 3 vols. New York, 1944.

Fremantle, Sir Arthur James. *Three Months in the Southern States.* Mobile, 1864.

Frias, Juan de Dios. *Reseña Historica de la Formación y Operaciones del Cuerpo de Ejército del Norte durante la Intervención Francesa.* Mexico City, 1867.

Frost, D. M. *Letter to Gen. Sterling Price, Accompanied by Official Documents.* St. Louis, 1865.

"General Sterling Price," *The United States Biographical Dictionary—Missouri.* New York, 1878.

Gramp, W. E. H. [W. E. Hughes]. *The Journal of a Grandfather.* St. Louis, 1912.

Grant, Ulysses S. *Personal Memoirs of U. S. Grant.* 2 vols. New York, 1886.

Hall, Martin H. *Sibley's New Mexican Campaign.* Austin, 1960.

Hanna, Alfred J. *Flight into Oblivion.* Richmond, 1938.

———, and Kathryn Abbey Hanna. *Confederate Exiles in Venezuela.* Tuscaloosa, 1960.

Harwell, Richard B., ed. *The Confederate Reader.* New York, 1957.

Hawthorne, Hildegarde. *Matthew Fontaine Maury.* New York, 1943.

Heartsill, W. W. *Fourteen Hundred and 91 Days in the Confederate Army.* Ed. by Bell Irvin Wiley. Jackson, Tenn., 1953.

Henry, Robert S. *The Story of the Confederacy.* New York, 1936.

Hesseltine, William B. *Confederate Leaders in the New South.* Baton Rouge, 1950.

———. *Ulysses S. Grant, Politician.* New York, 1935.

———, and Hazel C. Wolf. *The Blue and Gray on the Nile.* Chicago, 1961.

Hinton, Richard J. *Rebel Invasion of Missouri and Kansas and the Campaign of the Army of the Border Against General Sterling Price.* Chicago, 1865.

Horgan, Paul. *Great River: The Río Grande in North American History.* 2 vols. New York, 1954.

Hyman, Harold M. *Era of the Oath: Northern Loyalty Tests During the Civil War and Reconstruction.* Philadelphia, 1954.

Jaffe, Bernard. *Men of Science in America: The Story of American Science Told Through the Lives and Achievements of Twenty Out-*

234

standing Men from Earliest Colonial Times to the Present Days. New York, 1958.

Jahns, Patricia. *Matthew Fontaine Maury and Joseph Henry, Scientists of the Civil War.* New York, 1961.

Johnson, Ludwell H. *Red River Campaign: Politics and Cotton in the Civil War.* Baltimore, 1958.

Johnson, Robert Underwood, ed. *Battles and Leaders of the Civil War.* 4 vols. New York, 1888.

Josephson, Matthew. *The Politicos, 1865–1896.* New York, 1938.

Kerby, Robert Lee. *The Confederate Invasion of New Mexico and Arizona, 1861–1862.* Los Angeles, 1958.

King, Edward. *The Great South.* Hartford, 1875.

Lea, Tom. *The King Ranch.* 2 vols. El Paso, 1957.

"Letters of Thomas Caute Reynolds," *Glimpses of the Past.* Publication No. X, Missouri Historical Society. St. Louis, 1943.

Lewis, Charles Lee. *Matthew Fontaine Maury.* New York, 1943.

Lonn, Ella. *Desertion During the Civil War.* New York, 1928.

Martin, Percy F. *Maximilian in Mexico: The Story of the French Intervention, 1861–1867.* London, 1913.

McBride, George M. *The Land Systems of Mexico.* New York, 1923.

McDougal, Henry C. *Recollections, 1844–1909.* Kansas City, 1910.

McElroy, Robert. *Jefferson Davis, the Real and the Unreal.* 2 vols. New York, 1937.

McKee, Irving. *"Ben Hur" Wallace: The Life of General Lew Wallace.* Berkeley, 1947.

McKitrick, Eric L. *Andrew Johnson and Reconstruction.* Chicago, 1960.

Meade, Robert Douthat. *Judah P. Benjamin, Confederate Statesman.* New York, 1943.

Miers, Earl Schenk. *The Great Rebellion: The Emergence of the American Conscience.* Cleveland, 1958.

Mills, W. W. *Forty Years at El Paso.* El Paso, 1901.

Monaghan, Jay. *Civil War on the Western Border.* Boston, 1955.

Moore, Avery C. *Destiny's Soldier.* San Francisco, 1958.

Moore, Frank, ed. *The Rebellion Record: A Diary of American Events with Documents, Narratives, Illustrative Incidents, Poetry, etc.* New York, 1869.

Moore, John Bassett. *History and Digest of International Arbitrations to Which the United States Has Been a Party.* 6 vols. Washington, 1898.

Mosgrove, George Dallas. *Kentucky Cavaliers in Dixie: Reminiscences of a Confederate Cavalryman.* Ed. by Bell Irvin Wiley. Jackson, Tenn., 1957.

Nash, Charles Ford. *Biographical Sketches of Gen. Pat Cleburne and Gen. T. C. Hindman.* Little Rock, 1898.

National Cyclopaedia of American Biography. 51 vols. New York, 1929.

Niles, Blair. *Passengers to Mexico.* New York, 1943.

Noel, Theophilus. *Autobiography and Reminiscences.* Chicago, 1904.

Noll, Arthur Howard. *A Short History of Mexico.* Chicago, 1890.

Nunn, W. C. *Escape from Reconstruction.* Fort Worth, 1956.

Oates, Stephen B. *Confederate Cavalry West of the River.* Austin, 1961.

O'Connor, Richard. *Sheridan the Inevitable.* Indianapolis, 1953.

O'Flaherty, Daniel. *General Jo Shelby, Undefeated Rebel.* Chapel Hill, 1954.

Owsley, Frank L. *King Cotton Diplomacy: Foreign Relations of the Confederate States of America.* Chicago, 1931.

Parks, Joseph H. *General Edmund Kirby Smith, C.S.A.* Baton Rouge, 1954.

Patrick, Rembert W. *Jefferson Davis and His Cabinet.* Baton Rouge, 1944.

Pratt, Fletcher. *Stanton, Lincoln's Secretary of War.* New York, 1953.

Ramsdell, Charles G. *Reconstruction in Texas.* New York, 1910.

Rand, Clayton. *Sons of the South.* New York, 1961.

Rippy, J. Fred. *The United States and Mexico.* New York, 1931.

Rister, Carl Coke. *Border Command: General Phil Sheridan in the West.* Norman, 1944.

Riva Palacio, Vicente, ed. *México a través de los Siglos.* 5 vols. Mexico, 1889.

Roberts, W. Adolphe. *Semmes of the* Alabama. Indianapolis, 1938.

Ruiz, Ramón Eduardo. *An American in Maximilian's Mexico, 1865–1866: The Diaries of William Marshall Anderson.* San Marino, 1959.

Salm-Salm, Agnes. *Ten Years of My Life.* London, 1876.

Salm-Salm, Felix. *My Diary in Mexico in 1867.* London, 1868.

Santleben, August. *A Texas Pioneer.* New York, 1910.

Schroeder, Seaton. *The Fall of Maximilian's Empire as Seen from a United States Gun-Boat.* New York, 1887.

Semmes, Raphael. *Memoirs of Service Afloat, During the War Between the States.* Baltimore, 1869.

Seward, Frederick W. *Reminiscences of a War-Time Statesman and Diplomat, 1830–1915.* New York, 1916.

Sheridan, P. H. *Personal Memoirs of General Philip Henry Sheridan.* 2 vols. New York, 1886.

Singletary, Otis A. *Negro Militia and Reconstruction.* Austin, 1957.

Soley, James Russell. *The Blockade and the Cruisers.* New York, 1895.

Snead, Thomas L. *The Fight for Missouri.* New York, 1886.

Stickles, Arndt M. *Simon Bolivar Buckner.* Chapel Hill, 1940.

Taylor, Richard. *Destruction and Reconstruction: Personal Experiences of the Late War.* Ed. by Richard B. Harwell. New York, 1955.

Terrell, Alexander Watkins. *From Texas to Mexico and the Court of Maximilian in 1865.* Dallas, 1933.

Thomas, Benjamin P. *Abraham Lincoln: A Biography.* New York, 1952.

Thompson, Samuel B. *Confederate Purchasing Operations Abroad.* Chapel Hill, 1935.

Tilley, Nannie May, ed. *Federals on the Frontier: The Diary of Benjamin F. McIntyre, 1862–1865.* Austin, 1963.

Tucker, Beverley Randolph. *Tales of the Tuckers.* Richmond, 1942.

United Daughters of the Confederacy, Missouri Division. *Reminiscences of the Women of Missouri During the Sixties.* Jefferson City, 1920.

Vandiver, Frank E. *The Confederate Command System.* Baton Rouge, 1956.

Wallace, Edward S. *Destiny and Glory.* New York, 1957.

Warner, Ezra J. *Generals in Gray: Lives of the Confederate Commanders.* Baton Rouge, 1959.

Wayland, John W. *The Pathfinder of the Seas.* Richmond, 1930.

Welles, Gideon. *Diary of Gideon Welles.* 3 vols. Boston, 1911.

Wesley, Charles H. *The Collapse of the Confederacy.* Washington, 1937.

White, William W. *The Confederate Veteran.* Tuscaloosa, 1962.

Williams, Frances Leigh. *Matthew Fontaine Maury: Scientist of the Sea.* New Brunswick, New Jersey, 1962.

Williams, T. Harry. *P. G. T. Beauregard, Napoleon in Gray*. Baton Rouge, 1955.

Willson, Beckles. *John Slidell and the Confederates in Paris, 1862–1865*. New York, 1932.

Wortham, Louis J. *A History of Texas From Wilderness to Commonwealth*. Glendale, 1924.

Young, Bennett H. *Confederate Wizards of the Saddle: Being Reminiscences and Observations of One Who Rode with Morgan*. Boston, 1914; reprinted, Kennesaw, Georgia, 1958.

Printed Periodicals

Borland, William P. "Gen. Jo. O. Shelby," *Missouri Historical Review*, Vol. VII (October, 1912), 10–19.

Box, Sam. "End of the War—Exiles in Mexico," *Confederate Veteran*, Vol. II (March, 1903), 121–23.

Coleman, Evans J. "Senator Gwin's Plan for the Colonization of Sonora," *Overland Monthly*, Vol. XVII (May–June, 1891), 499–519, 593–607.

Cornwall, W. A. "Maximilian and the American Legion," *Overland Monthly*, Vol. II (1871), 445–48.

Dale, Edward Everett. "The Cherokees in the Confederacy," *Journal of Southern History*, Vol. XIII (May, 1947), 159–85.

Delaney, Robert W. "Matamoros, Port for Texas During the Civil War," *Southwestern Historical Quarterly*, Vol. LVIII (April, 1955), 473–87.

Diamond, William. "Imports of the Confederate Government from Europe and Mexico," *Journal of Southern History*, Vol. VI (November, 1940), 470–503.

Donnell, F. S. "The Confederate Territory of Arizona," *New Mexico Historical Review*, Vol. XVII (April, 1942), 148–63.

Ellison, Simon J. "An Anglo-American Plan for the Colonization of Mexico," *Southwestern Social Science Quarterly*, Vol. XVI (September, 1935), 42–52.

"E. Kirby-Smith," *Confederate War Journal*, Vol. I (November, 1893), 114.

"Gallatin, Missouri," *Missouri Historical Review*, Vol. XLIX (April, 1955), 250–52.

Hanna, Alfred J. "A Confederate Newspaper in Mexico," *Journal of Southern History*, Vol. XII (February, 1946), 67–83.

———. "The Role of Matthew Fontaine Maury in the Mexican Empire," *Virginia Magazine of History and Biography*, Vol. LV (April, 1947), 105–125.

———, and Kathryn Abbey Hanna. "The Immigration Movement of the Intervention and Empire as Seen Through a Mexican Press," *Hispanic American Review*, Vol. XXVIII (May, 1947), 220–46.

Hanna, Kathryn Abbey. "Incidents of the Confederate Blockade," *Journal of Southern History*, Vol. XI (May, 1945), 214–29.

———. "The Roles of the South in the French Intervention in Mexico," *Journal of Southern History*, Vol. XX (February, 1944), 3–21.

Harmon, George D. "Confederate Migrations to Mexico," *Hispanic American Historical Review*, Vol. XVII (November, 1937), 458–87.

Hill, Lawrence F. "The Confederate Exodus to South America," *Southwestern Historical Quarterly*, Vol. XXXIX (October, 1935), 100–134; (January, 1936), 161–99; (April, 1936), 309–26.

———. "Confederate Exiles to Brazil," *Hispanic American Historical Review*, Vol. VII (May, 1927), 192–210.

Holladay, Florence E. "The Powers of the Commander of the Confederate Trans-Mississippi Department," *Southwestern Historical Quarterly*, Vol. XXI (1918), 279–98 and 333–59.

Howell, D. S. "Along the Texas Frontier During the Civil War," *West Texas Historical Association Yearbook*, XIII (1937), 89–95.

Hoyt, William D., Jr., ed. "New Light on General Jubal A. Early After Appomattox," *Journal of Southern History*, Vol. IX (February, 1943), 113–17.

Johnson, Ludwell H. "Beverley Tucker's Canadian Mission," *Journal of Southern History*, Vol. XXIX (February, 1963), 88–99.

Knapp, Frank A., Jr. "A New Source on the Confederate Exodus to Mexico: The Two Republics," *Journal of Southern History*, Vol. XIX (August, 1953), 364–73.

McPherson, Hallie M. "The Plan of William McKendree Gwin for a Colony in North Mexico, 1863–1865," *Pacific Historical Review*, Vol. II (December, 1933), 357–86.

Miller, Robert Ryal. "Californians Against the Emperor," *California Historical Society Quarterly*, Vol. XXXVII (September, 1958), 193–214.

239

———. "The American Legion of Honor in Mexico," *Pacific Historical Review*, Vol. XXX (August, 1961), 229–41.

Moore, J. Preston. "Pierre Soulé: Southern Expansionist and Promoter," *Journal of Southern History*, Vol. XXI (May, 1955), 203–23.

Rippy, J. Fred. "Mexican Projects of the Confederates," *Southwestern Historical Quarterly*, Vol. XXII (April, 1919), 291–317.

Rister, Carl Coke. "Carlota, a Confederate Colony in Mexico," *Journal of Southern History*, Vol. XI (February, 1945), 33–50.

Ross, Madeline Dane, and Fred Kerner. "Stars and Bars Along the Amazon," *The Reporter* (September 18, 1958), 34–38.

Russell, Tom J. "Adventures of a Cordova Colonist," *Southern Magazine*, Vol. XI (August, 1872), 90–102, 155–66.

Settle, William A., Jr. "The James Boys and Missouri Politics," *Missouri Historical Review*, Vol. XXXVI (April, 1942), 412–29.

Shoemaker, Floyd C. "Missouri—Heir of Southern Tradition and Individuality," *Missouri Historical Review*, Vol. XXXVI (July, 1942), 435–46.

"This Missouri Confederate and His 'Iron Brigade' Never Surrendered," *Missouri Historical Review*, Vol. L (October, 1955), 67–69.

Waldrip, William I. "New Mexico During the Civil War," *New Mexico Historical Review*, Vol. XXVIII (April, 1953), 168–82; 251–90.

Walker, Charles S. "Causes of the Confederate Invasion of New Mexico," *New Mexico Historical Review*, Vol. VIII (January, 1933), 76–97.

Watford, W. H. "Confederate Western Ambitions," *Southwestern Historical Quarterly*, Vol. XLIV (October, 1940), 161–87.

———. "The Far-Western Wing of the Rebellion, 1861–1865," *California Historical Society Quarterly*, Vol. XXXIV (June, 1955), 125–48.

Wood, John Taylor. "Escape of the Confederate Secretary of War," *Century Magazine*, Vol. LVII (November, 1893), 110–23.

Worley, Ted R., ed. "A Letter By General Thomas C. Hindman in Mexico," *Arkansas Historical Quarterly*, Vol. XV (Winter, 1956), 365–68.

Index

Index

Roberts, Judge Oran M.: 108
Rodríguez, Luis Enrico: 69
Rollins, James S.: 100–101
Roma, Texas: 82
Romero, Matías: 17n., 34, 35n.
Ruffin, Edmund: 10

St. Louis *Missouri Republican*: 146
St. Louis *Missouri Statesman*: 103
Salinas River, Mexico: 65
Saltillo, Mexico: 69, 70, 108
San Antonio, Texas: 18, 19, 32n., 40,
    45, 80, 85, 103
San Luis Potosí, Mexico: 70, 77, 98,
    108, 117, 152
Santa Anna, Gen. Antonio Lopez de:
    96
Santa Rosa Mountains, Mexico: 219
Sauvage, Baron Enrique: 110, 112n.
Scales, Lt. Thomas: 118, 119
Schofield, Gen. J. M.: 16
Semmes, Comdr. Raphael: 30, 31, 129,
    130, 198n., 199n.
Sewanee, Tennessee: 200, 201, 201n.
Seward, William H.: ix, 24, 25, 31,
    34, 55, 56, 139, 218
Shelby, Elizabeth Nancy: 12, 97, 111
Shelby, Gen. Joseph O.: ix, 6, 34, 38,
    76, 79, 80, 100, 124, 150, 167, 196;
    refusal to surrender, 3; enters Mex-
    ico, 4, 19–20; value to the South,
    11; independence, 12; wartime tac-
    tics, 13–15, 17, 161; officers in his
    command, 18; experiences in north-
    ern Mexico, 21–24 ff.; supplied by
    Mexican contrabandists, 27; con-
    templated exile, 36; participant in
    conference, 43; supports officers
    planning Mexican exodus, 44–45;
    Iron Brigade relatively intact, 46;
    Union forces unable to stop exodus,
    56; involvements with Juárists, 57–
    61, 66–67, 76–77; encounter with
    Gwin, 62–64; attacked by Indians,
    65–66, 112n.; opposition by French
    Army, 67–68, 70; truce with French,
    69; involvements with Maximilian,

67, 69, 74–75, 152–53; reaches
Mexico City, 72–74; aids settlement
of Mexican colonies, 88, 108–111,
212; reunited with military cronies,
90; pre-empts house of Gen. Santa
Anna, 96; in freighting business, 97–
98, 109–10; swears to remain
abroad, 99, 129–30; joined by family, 107; unrepentant feelings, 107,
128; role in collapse of Mexican
colonies, 120, 152; joined by Maury,
134; friendship with Reynolds, 147;
praised by Maj. Edwards, 170;
clashes with fellow exiles, 175; remains popular, 191; troubles with
Price, 147, 198; leaves Mexico, 201;
later life in Missouri, 202–206;
reminiscences with Gen. Sheridan,
203; champions James brothers,
203–204; attitude toward Negroes,
204–205, 212
Shelby, Joseph, Jr.: 97
Shelby, Orville: 97
"Shelby's Mule" (a song): 13
Shenandoah (Confederate raider): 46,
    118, 119
Sheridan, Gen. Philip H.: 17n., 25,
    31, 47, 54–56, 55n., 56n., 79, 122,
    124, 138, 141, 157, 163, 190n.,
    202, 203
Sherman, Gen. William Tecumseh: 12,
    38, 39, 48, 101, 124, 158
Shreveport, Louisiana: 29, 50, 51,
    80, 148
Sibley, Gen. Henry H.: 32n., 213,
    225
Sinaloa, Mexico: 62, 221
Slaughter, Gen. James E.: 37, 54,
    94, 188, 215
Slayback, Col. Alonzo: 19, 87
Slidell, John: 226
Smith, Col. Peter: 81
Snead, Col. Thomas L.: 18, 107n.
Sonora, Mexico: 4, 28, 62, 63, 213,
    221
Soulé, Pierre: 129, 130, 188
Southern Historical Society: 190

247